D1338261

EDITED BY LEONARD HOLLIS

The
Rose
Annual
1975

THE ROYAL NATIONAL
ROSE SOCIETY

Copyright © 1975 Leonard Hollis
Published by
THE ROYAL NATIONAL ROSE SOCIETY
Bone Hill, Chiswell Green Lane, St Albans, Hertfordshire
Telephone: St Albans 50461. *Telegrams:* Natiorose, St Albans
Printed and bound in England by
Hazell Watson & Viney Limited
Aylesbury, Buckinghamshire

Contents

Patrons, Officers and Council   6

Presidents and Awards   8

Arrangements for 1975   9

The Society's Gardens   12

Report of the Council   15

Annual Accounts   18

The President's Page   20

Perfume   DR. A. S. THOMAS   22

The Birthday Present   L. A. SLATTER   30

'Peace' and the Modern Hybrid Tea   DR. ROGER WAIGH   32

Rose-crowned into the Darkness   MARGARET STEWARDSON   34

Tea-Scented Roses   L. ARTHUR WYATT   38

On Planting a Garden of Roses   GRAHAM THOMAS   53

The First of the Summer's Roses   SIR PETER MASEFIELD   58

Obituary—Svend Poulsen   64

Colour Development in Floribunda Roses   E. B. LE GRICE   66

Shoot Your Roses   H. WILLIAMSON   70

Roses from Cuttings   J. H. BARTRAM   77

Purely for Pleasure   SUSAN BONE   81

BARB   J. L. HARKNESS   84

Rose Nutrition in a World of Scarcity   E. F. ALLEN   91

A Rose Novice and his First Garden   DR. A. K. BROWN   101

A Breeder's Reply   A. P. C. DICKSON   104

Redouté Redivivus   G. D. ROWLEY   107

Roses as Garden Plants   C. E. LUCAS PHILLIPS   111

The Rosarium of Sangerhausen   HUMPHREY BROOKE   116

'Comte de Chambord'   GRAHAM THOMAS   121

Beautiful Pot Roses by use of Growth Retardants
   S. K. BHATTACHARJEE   122

The Incomparable Rose   ALINE CHAPMAN   124

Observations on Foliar Feeding and Black Spot
   F. C. H. WITCHELL   128

Codswallop E. W. PARNELL   132

Symposium on the Twelve Best Recurrent Climbing Roses
    LEONARD HOLLIS   134

Is it Really True? MARTIN WATTS   145

The International Rose MICHAEL GIBSON   148

Growing Roses in the Cape Peninsula F. H. L. SAWYER   152

Saint George for Merrie England! JOSEPH MARSH   154

The Decorative Classes JULIA CLEMENTS   156

Book Reviews   160

The Summer Rose Show PETER WOOD   169

The Northern Rose Show I. O. MATTHEWS   173

The Autumn Rose Show ROY HAY   176

The Provincial Display Gardens S. MILLAR GAULT   179

The Trial Ground and Display Garden, 1974 L. G. TURNER   183

The Awards to New Roses in 1974   185

International Awards 1974   187

The Rose Analysis L. G. TURNER   190

Why Roses?   200

COLOUR PLATES   *facing page*

'Sugar Sweet'   5

'Mary Sumner'   16

'Meipuma'   17

'Souvenir d'Elise Vardon' (T.) and 'Adam' (T.)   46

'Monsieur Tillier' (T.) and 'Clg. Devoniensis' (Clg. T.)   47

'Archiduc Joseph' (T.) and 'Mme. Bravy' (T.)   54

Shrub roses 'Buff Beauty' and 'Nevada'   55

'Gloire de Dijon' (Clg. T.) and 'Maman Cochet' (T.)   100

'Baronne Henriette Snoy' (T.) and 'Mermaid' (Climber)   101

'Wee Man' (min.) and Humphrey Brooke   120

'Comte de Chambord' (Portland)   121

'Pink Perpêtue' and 'Handel'   140

'Schoolgirl'   141

Class 101. Summer Show. "Conflict and Harmony"   160

'SUGAR SWEET' (floribunda – HT type)
'Wendy Cussons' × *'Prima Ballerina'*
Raised by John Sanday (Roses) Ltd
THE HENRY EDLAND MEMORIAL MEDAL AND TRIAL GROUND CERTIFICATE 1974
See page 185

CONTENTS

                                                              facing page
Class 55. Autumn Show. "Carnival"   161
'Alpine Sunset'   184
'Old Master'   185
'Eye Paint'   196
'Dublin Bay'   197

MONOCHROME PLATES   *facing page*
E. F. Allen, M.A., President 1975–76   20
R. C. Balfour making presentation to Dr. R. C. Allen   40
'Bobbie James', a vigorous, creamy white climber   41
'Canary Bird' and R. hugonis, two of the earliest roses   60
The late Svend Poulsen and 'Else Poulsen'   61
R. filipes 'Kiftsgate' at the Mill House, Sutton Courtenay   70
Shoot your Roses – action shots   70 & 71
'Zéphirine Drouhin' clothing a tripod   71
Roses from Cuttings   80 & 81
Roses growing in a boscage of azaleas   110
Uncrowded, 'Iceberg' stands 5ft 6 in. among herbaceous plants   110
A low hedge of roses 'Natalie Nypels' and 'Red Favourite'   111
The "Hybrid Musk" rose 'Penelope' throws out big swags of
  blossom   111

COMMITTEES FOR 1975

FINANCE AND GENERAL PURPOSES COMMITTEE

*E. F. Allen
*E. J. Baldwin
*R. C. Balfour
F. M. Bowen
H. G. Clacy
*E. V. Elwes
*F. Fairbrother
K. E. Fisk

*D. L. Flexman
S. M. Gault
*F. A. Gibson
A. N. Harding
J. L. Harkness
R. L. Pallett
C. Pawsey
*H. N. Raban

Mrs H. Robinson
D. H. Scott
J. H. Shotter
S. C. Thomson
Dr J. T. Watts
H. Wheatcroft
F. Wiltshire

NEW SEEDLING JUDGING COMMITTEE

*E. F. Allen
*R. C. Balfour
W. K. Bentley
F. M. Bowen
A. M. Cocker
A. P. C. Dickson
Miss J. E. Fulford

S. M. Gault
J. L. Harkness
Leonard Hollis
E. B. Le Grice
J. S. Mattock
C. Pawsey
*H. N. Raban

C. F. Roberts
Mrs H. Robinson
B. W. W. Sampson
J. H. Shotter
W. E. Tysterman
H. Wheatcroft
H. Williamson

EXHIBITIONS COMMITTEE

*E. F. Allen
H. G. Clacy
Dr A. Dick
*E. V. Elwes

Miss J. E. Fulford
S. M. Gault
*H. N. Raban
C. F. Roberts
J. Roscoe

J. H. Shotter
Mrs D. Thorn
Dr J. T. Watts
F. C. H. Witchell

GARDENS MANAGEMENT COMMITTEE

*E. F. Allen
W. K. Bentley
*H. G. Clacy

*E. V. Elwes
F. Fairbrother
*S. M. Gault

J. S. Mattock
*H. N. Raban
Mrs H. Robinson
D. H. Scott

PUBLICATIONS COMMITTEE

*E. F. Allen
*E. V. Elwes
M. D. Gibson

J. L. Harkness
A. G. L. Hellyer
R. L. Pallett

*H. N. Raban
J. H. Shotter

*Denotes *ex-officio* member.

7

PRESIDENTS OF THE
ROYAL NATIONAL ROSE SOCIETY

1877-1904 The Very Rev. DEAN HOLE, V.M.H.

1905-06 CHARLES E. SHEA	1943-44 HERBERT OPPENHEIMER
1907-08 E. B. LINDSELL	1945-46 A. NORMAN ROGERS
1909-10 Rev. F. PAGE-ROBERTS	1947-48 A. E. GRIFFITH
1911-12 Rev. J. H. PEMBERTON	1949-50 E. J. BALDWIN, O.B.E.
1913-14 CHARLES E. SHEA	1951-52 D. L. FLEXMAN
1915-16 EDWARD MAWLEY, V.M.H.	1953-54 WILLIAM E. MOORE
1917-18 Sir EDWARD HOLLAND	1955-56 OLIVER MEE, O.B.E.
1919-20 H. R. DARLINGTON, V.M.H.	1957-58 A. NORMAN
1921-22 Sir EDWARD HOLLAND	1959-60 F. FAIRBROTHER, M.SC., F.R.I.C.
1923-24 SYDNEY F. JACKSON	1961-62 E. ROYALTON KISCH, M.C.
1925-26 C. C. WILLIAMSON	1963-64 Maj.-Gen. R. F. B. NAYLOR, C.B.,
1927-28 H. R. DARLINGTON, V.M.H.	C.B.E., D.S.O., M.C.
1929-30 ARTHUR JOHNSON	1965-66 F. A. GIBSON
1931-32 HERBERT OPPENHEIMER	1967-68 Maj.-Gen. R. F. B. NAYLOR, C.B.,
1933-34 Dr A. H. WILLIAMS	C.B.E., D.S.O., M.C.
1935-36 Major A. D. G. SHELLEY, R.E.	1969-70 JOHN CLARKE
1937-38 HERBERT OPPENHEIMER	1971-72 FRANK M. BOWEN, C.ENG.
1939-40 JOHN N. HART, C.B.E.	1973-74 R. C. BALFOUR, M.B.E.
1941-42 CHARLES H. RIGG	1975 E. F. ALLEN, M.A.

THE QUEEN MARY COMMEMORATION
MEDAL AWARDS

1957 & 1973 ALEX DICKSON & SONS LTD	1964 BERTRAM PARK, O.B.E., V.M.H.
1957 & 1973 SAMUEL McGREDY & SON LTD	1971 C. GREGORY & SON LTD
1957 & 1973 E. B. LE GRICE (HYBRIDISERS) LTD	1973 JAMES COCKER & SONS LTD
1957 HERBERT ROBINSON, M.B.E.	1973 R. HARKNESS & CO. LTD
1957 OLIVER MEE, O.B.E.	1973 JOHN SANDAY (ROSES) LTD
1957 A. NORMAN	

THE DEAN HOLE MEDAL AWARDS

1909 Rev. J. H. PEMBERTON	1950 F. S. HARVEY-CANT, M.B.E.
1910 EDWARD MAWLEY, V.M.H.	1950 E. J. BALDWIN, O.B.E.
1912 GEORGE DICKSON, V.M.H.	1952 D. L. FLEXMAN
1914 CHARLES E. SHEA	1952 BERTRAM PARK, O.B.E., V.M.H.,
1917 E. B. LINDSELL	Mérite Agri.
1918 Sir EDWARD HOLLAND	1952 Dr A. S. THOMAS, O.B.E., V.M.A.
1919 Rev. F. PAGE-ROBERTS	1954 W. E. HARKNESS
1919 GEORGE PAUL	1956 OLIVER MEE, O.B.E.
1920 H. R. DARLINGTON, V.M.H.	1958 A. NORMAN
1921 S. McGREDY	1959 W. J. W. SANDAY
1923 Miss E. WILLMOTT, F.L.S.	1960 F. FAIRBROTHER, M.SC., F.R.I.C.
1924 SYDNEY F. JACKSON	1962 H. G. CLACY
1925 COURTNEY PAGE	1962 E. ROYALTON KISCH, M.C.
1926 C. C. WILLIAMSON	1964 G. D. BURCH
1930 Dr J. CAMPBELL HALL	1964 Maj.-Gen. R. F. B. NAYLOR, C.B., C.B.E.,
1930 WILLIAM E. NICKERSON	D.S.O., M.C.
1931 ARTHUR JOHNSON	1965 H. EDLAND
1933 HERBERT OPPENHEIMER	1965 E. BAINES
1935 Dr A. H. WILLIAMS	1966 EDGAR M. ALLEN, C.M.G.
1935 WALTER EASLEA	1966 F. A. GIBSON
1936 ALISTER CLARK	1967 ALEX DICKSON
1937 Major A. D. G. SHELLEY, R.E.	1967 W. KORDES
1940 JOHN N. HART, C.B.E.	1969 J. W. MATTOCK
1942 CHARLES H. RIGG	1970 JOHN CLARKE
1942 Dr HORACE J. McFARLAND	1971 L. A. ANSTISS
1945 Dr H. V. TAYLOR, C.B.E.	1971 D. BUTCHER
1947 A. NORMAN ROGERS	1972 FRANK M. BOWEN, C.ENG.
1948 Dr G. E. DEACON	1973 LEONARD HOLLIS
1949 W. E. MOORE	1973 HARRY WHEATCROFT, V.M.H.
1949 A. E. GRIFFITH	1974 R. C. BALFOUR, M.B.E.
1950 JOHN RAMSBOTTOM, O.B.E., Dr. SC., M.A.	

8

Arrangements 1975

Shows

Amateur Spring Competition 29 and 30 April.

Summer Show 27 and 28 June.

Autumn Show 12 and 13 September.

The above shows will be held at The Royal Horticultural Society's Halls, Westminster. The Amateur Spring Competition will be staged at the Flower and Rhododendron Show to which, by courtesy of The Royal Horticultural Society, members will be admitted on production of their membership card. *Northern Show* 11 and 12 July at Holker Hall, near Grange-over-Sands, in conjunction with the Lakeland Rose Show.

Terms of Admission

The Certificate of Membership will admit the holder only to all the above shows.
Members also receive two transferable tickets for the Summer Show and two transferable tickets for the Autumn Show.
Prices of admission for the public will be:

Summer Show 27 June 11 a.m. to 5 p.m. 50p, 5 p.m. to 7 p.m. 35p
28 June 10 a.m. to 5 p.m. 35p.
Autumn Show 12 September 11 a.m. to 7 p.m. 35p.
13 September 10 a.m. to 5 p.m. 20p.

Members may purchase additional tickets for the Summer and Autumn Shows at half price. Applications accompanied by remittances must be received at the Society's office not less than three days before the show.

Northern Show 11 July 10.30 a.m. to 7 p.m. 70p, 7 p.m. to 8.30 p.m. 50p.
12 July 9.30 a.m. to 5 p.m. 50p.
Children under 16 free.
Car and coach park free.

RNRS Classes at Provincial Shows and Admission Arrangements

By the courtesy of the organisers of the following Shows, members of The Royal National Rose Society are offered special concessions in respect of exhibiting and free admission which the Council acknowledges with thanks. Unless indicated by an asterisk both concessions will apply. Further details of the Shows offering free admission to RNRS members are given on the Membership Certificate:

Alderley Edge and Wilmslow Horticultural and Rose Society's Show on 12 July.
Ashington Rose Society's Show on 12 July.
Berwick-upon-Tweed and District Rose Society's Show on 20 July.
Bexleyheath and District Rose Society's Show on 21 June.
Bournemouth and District Rose Society's Show on 21 June.
Bramhall, Cheadle Hulme and Woodford Agricultural and Horticultural Society's Show on 9 August.
Bristol and District Group of RNRS Show on 2 July.
Bryndorion (Swansea) and District Rose Society's Show on 5 July.
Clevedon and District Horticultural Society's Show on 22 and 23 August

9

Clontarf Horticultural Society's Show on 12 and 13 July
Colchester Rose and Horticultural Society's Show on 5 and 6 July
Congleton and District Horticultural Society's Show on 19 July.
Coventry and District Carnation, Rose and Sweet Pea Society's Show on 28 June.
Eastleigh and District Rose, Carnation and Sweet Pea Society's Show on 21 June.
Federation of Edinburgh and District Allotments and Gardens Association's Show on 30 Aug.
Formby Horticultural and Agricultural Society's Show on 12 July
Franche (Kidderminster) and District Rose Society's Show on 28 June.
Glamorgan (Vale of) Agricultural Society's Show on 20 August.
Grey Mare Rose Society's Show on 19 July.
Hereford and West of England Rose Society's Show on 5 July.
Hitchin Horticultural Society's Show on 21 June.
Ipswich and East of England Horticultural Society's Show on 12 and 13 July.
Isle of Wight Rose, Carnation and Sweet Pea Association's Show on 21 June.
Lincolnshire Rose Society's Show on 5 and 6 July.
Manx Rose Society's Show on 12 and 13 July.
Northampton and District Rose Society's Show on 30 August.
North of England Rose, Carnation and Sweet Pea Society's Show on 15 and 16 August.
North Western Group of RNRS Show on 6 and 7 September.
Nottingham Rose Society's Show on 12 and 13 July.
Reading Horticultural Federation's Show on 15 and 16 August.
Renfrew Horticultural Society's Show on 20 September.
Rhondda, Pontypridd and District Rose Society's Show on 12 July.
Roundhay (Leeds) Horticultural Society's Show on 15 and 16 July.
★*Royal Caledonian Horticultural Society's Show* at the Corn Exchange, Gorgie, Edinburgh on 20 and 21 September (12 noon to 8 p.m.). (RNRS classes but *not* free admission.)
Scottish National Sweet Pea, Rose and Carnation Society's Show on 2 August.
Southampton (Royal) Horticultural Society's Show on 11, 12 and 13 July.
South of England Group of RNRS Show on 25 August.
★*Southport Flower Show* in Victoria Park, Southport, on 21, 22 and 23 August (10 a.m. to 9 p.m., 9 a.m. to 9 p.m. and 9 a.m. to 5.30 p.m.). (RNRS classes but *not* free admission.)
South-West Counties Rose and Sweet Pea Society's Show on 25 and 26 June.
Teesside Rose Society's Show on 19 and 20 July.
West Cumberland Rose Society's Show on 19 July.
West Midlands Rose Society's Show on 5 July.
Yorkshire Rosarians' Group of RNRS Show on 31 August.

★Please note that the Certificate of Membership does not admit to the Royal Caledonian Horticultural Society's Show, Southport Flower Show or any other Show not listed.

For further details and schedules of the aforementioned Shows application should be made to The Secretary, RNRS.

Display Gardens

Members and their friends are cordially invited to visit the displays of rose varieties that have received awards provided at:

Cardiff—Roath Park	Norwich—Heigham Park
Edinburgh—Saughton Park	Nottingham—The Arboretum
Glasgow—Pollok Park	Southport—Botanic Gardens
†Harrogate—Harlow Car	Taunton—Vivary Park
	Teesside—Borough Park, Redcar

†At Harlow Car, the Gardens of the Northern Horticultural Society, the rose displays occupy a small portion of the ground only and it is hoped that visitors will each be willing to contribute a donation of 20p towards general upkeep.

Rose Bulletin

The Rose Bulletin will be published in October, and all members will receive a copy free of charge. Items of news, topical rose stories and interesting reports from members will be welcomed and should be sent to the Secretary.

Annual General Meeting

Members are requested to take note that the 99th Annual General Meeting will be held at The Royal Horticultural Society's Hall, Westminster, on Tuesday, 9 December, 1975. Formal agenda for the meeting will be dispatched with *The Rose Bulletin.*

Judges Examination

The examination for rose judges will be held at St Albans on Wednesday, 16 July. Applications must be received before 31 May, 1975. Successful candidates will receive a Certificate of Competency.

Lecture Aids

The following equipment is intended for use at lectures and, regretfully, it cannot be loaned for private viewing:

Films

"Focus on the Rose" is a 16-mm. colour film with sound track. Two spools, running time 77 minutes. Every aspect of rose cultivation is covered and also included are beautiful views of the Society's Garden at St. Albans and shots of the Shows. Hire Charge £3.

The Grampian television colour film describing the raising and testing of a new seedling rose is also available for limited circulation. 16-mm. sound, running time approximately 25 minutes. Hire charge £2.

Borrowers are required to indemnify the Society against damage and must undertake to ensure the films will be projected by an experienced operator.

Slides

There are sets of slides available covering:

    General cultivation.
    Varieties with historical connections
    Modern varieties
    The Evolution of the Rose—a set prepared by Gordon Rowley of Reading University.
    Shrub Roses

Full details of all equipment and booking form may be obtained from the Secretary.

Library

The library at St Albans contains a comprehensive collection of books on rose growing and is open to members during office hours (Monday to Friday, 9 a.m. to 5 p.m.). Alternatively, books (not more than two at one time) will be despatched by post, subject to postage being paid by the borrower. A list of books available will be sent on application.

Rose Variety Directory

A directory of rose varieties, compiled from distributors' catalogues, is maintained at the office for the convenience of members wishing to locate a source of supply for particular varieties. It is not possible to give information on varieties no longer in commerce.

Sales

The following items are available from the office:

Publications

Additional copies of the current issues of:

Roses: A Selected List of Varieties	25p	The Rose Annual	75p
Roses: The Cultivation of the Rose	25p	The Rose Bulletin	25p

See also advertisement page 232.

Back editions of The Rose Annual
The Secretary will be pleased to receive any back copies of *The Rose Annual* that may no longer be required. These are often asked for by new members.

Subscriptions and Resignations
Members are reminded that subscriptions are due and payable on 1 January each year and it would assist the office administration if the reminder form, which is enclosed with *The Rose Bulletin*, is returned with the remittance.

Single subscription £1.75 per annum.

Double subscription, for two resident members of the same household, £2.50 per annum. This provides full privileges of membership for both persons but only one copy of any free publications.

Any member wishing to resign must give notice to the Secretary on or before 1 February, after which date the member will be liable for the subscription for the current year.

The Society's Gardens

The Society's Gardens at St Albans are provided for the enjoyment of members and their friends. They are divided into two sections, the Trial Ground and Display Garden.

THE TRIAL GROUND is for new seedlings where some 750 varieties may be seen under-going merit trial. Varieties are submitted before being introduced into commerce and for this reason the majority will be under number. Adjudication is carried out by the New Seedling Judging Committee and varieties are eligible for the Society's Gold Medal, Certificate of Merit and Trial Ground Certificate awards. The President's International Trophy is awarded annually to the best seedling and the Henry Edland Memorial Medal to the most fragrant variety on trial.

Varieties that have received a trial award since 1963 are planted in a bed around the perimeter of the ground.

THE DISPLAY GARDEN occupies approximately seven acres and contains a comprehensive collection of over 900 historical and modern varieties and species.

How to get to the Gardens
The Gardens are situated at Chiswell Green, approximately three miles from St Albans Town Hall and off the main Watford–St Albans Road (A412).

By Road—from North or South take M1 and leave by Exit No. 6, turn towards St Albans on A405 and in one mile take left fork (A412) at "Noke" roundabout. From West, M4 to Slough and A412 via Denham, Rickmansworth and Watford. From East join A1 at Hatfield and then A405 (sign-post Watford) to "Noke" roundabout and A412 as above.

By Train—**British Rail** to St Albans City Station (St Pancras) or Watford Junction Station (Euston) or **Underground** (Bakerloo Line) to Watford Junction, thence by 321 bus.

By bus—No. 321 bus, Uxbridge–Watford–Garston–Chiswell Green–St Albans–Luton.

By Green-Line Coach—No. 712 Luton-London (Victoria)-Dorking. No. 724 Romford-St Albans-High Wycombe. Also routes 713 Dorking-London (Victoria)-Dunstable, 714 Dorking-London (Hyde Park Corner)-Luton and 727 Crawley-Heathrow-Luton to St Albans centre and thence by bus No. 321 or 361. Route 727 also connects with No. 321 bus route at Garston Bus Station.

The fare stage at which to alight from bus or coach is The Three Hammers Inn, Chiswell Green. The Gardens are half a mile along Chiswell Green Lane which is adjacent to the Inn.

Visiting Arrangements for 1975

The Gardens will be open from Saturday, 14 June to Saturday, 27 September, at the following times:

Monday to Saturday	9 a.m. to 5 p.m.
Sunday	2 p.m. to 6 p.m.

Before 14 June and after 27 September the gardens will be open to members only from Monday to Friday (not Saturday and Sunday). The Gardens will be closed on Monday, 25 August.

Terms of Admission

Membership certificates and affiliated society certificates, which must be shown at the turnstile, will admit the holder and one guest free of charge and four additional persons at the reduced price of 11p.

Affiliated Societies may arrange for a party to visit the Gardens during the above hours. Application must be made in writing to the Secretary at least fourteen days beforehand, stating the number in the party and the proposed date and time of the visit. Holders of Certificates and accompanying guests as specified above will be admitted free of charge; all other members of the party will be admitted at the reduced price of 11p.

Price of admission to public, 22p adults, 11 p children under 15. Private parties of 20 or more adults 16p per person.

Refreshments

Tea, coffee, sandwiches and light refreshments may be obtained from the cafeteria at the following times:

Monday to Friday	11.30 a.m. to 1.30 p.m.
	2.30 p.m. to 4.30 p.m.
Saturday	11.30 a.m. to 4.30 p.m.
Sunday	2.00 p.m. to 5.30 p.m.

Picknicking on the lawns is not permitted.

Car Park

A car park is provided but the Council accepts no responsibility for loss or damage to property or vehicles.

Roscent '76

The convention in the Society's centenary year, 1976, will be held at Oxford from Monday, 5 July to Thursday, 8 July, and will be preceded by the National Rose Show at Westminster on Friday and Saturday, 2 and 3 July.

The opening session of the Conference will be held in the historic Sheldonian Theatre and the lectures will be presented in the modern setting of the spacious Zoology Building.

Exhibitions of photography and art, also floral displays by leading floral art societies, are being arranged.

The photographic exhibition will include a section devoted to photographs of many of the most important roses of the past 100 years; the Society has a number of these, but we still wish to locate and borrow high quality colour transparencies or negatives (from which prints will be made for display) of the following:

H.T.s, H.P.s, Pernetianas and Teas:

'La France'
'Lady Mary Fitzwilliam'
'Dean Hole'
'Frau Karl Druschki'
'Ulrich Brunner'
'Maman Cochet'
'George Dickson'
'Soleil d'Or'
'Rayon d'Or'
'Souv. de Claudius Pernet'
'Betty Uprichard'

'Emma Wright'
'Dame Edith Helen'
'Ophelia' (or 'Mme. Butterfly')
'Mrs Henry Bowles'
'Mrs Henry Moorse'
'General MacArthur'
'Golden Emblem'
'Lady Pirrie'
'Mme Edouard Herriot'
'Shot Silk'

Polyanthas, Floribundas and Shrubs:

'Baby Faurax'
'Cécile Brunner'
'Paul Crampel'

'Miss Edith Cavell'
'Else Poulsen'
'Kirsten Poulsen' or 'Karen Poulsen'

Others:

'Mme Alfred Carrière'
'American Pillar'

'Gloire de Dijon'
'Lady Hillingdon' (Clg.)

If you can help please write NOW giving, for each photograph:

    The Name of the Rose
    Whether Colour Transparency or Colour Negative
    Size

Another section of the exhibition will be devoted to rose photography of 100 years ago (or thereabouts). For this, good negatives of roses or rose gardens taken between 1870 and 1900 are required. If you should happen to possess any such historic negatives and would loan them for the purpose of producing prints for the exhibition, please write NOW, stating for each:

    The name of the Rose or Rose Garden
    Size of negative
    The camera used (if known)
    The (approximate) date of the picture.

PLEASE DO NOT SEND ANY PHOTOGRAPHIC MATERIAL UNTIL ASKED

Mementoes of the centenary, including tea towels, glass goblets and china dishes, will be available later this year.

To ensure you receive information regarding the centenary and convention, ask for your name to be added to the Centenary Mailing List.

Report of the Council

For the year 1974

Membership

The number of new members enrolled during the year was 2,877 compared with 5,200 last year. Although the number of resignations has been less than last year, there has been a greater accumulation of unpaid subscriptions, in spite of many reminders, and the paid-up membership of the Society has now fallen to 66,753. A fall was forecast in last year's report and, while it is disappointing, it is not surprising in view of the large number of pensioners among our members and the difficulties so many people must be experiencing in maintaining subscriptions in these inflationary times. Your Council intends to intensify its efforts to increase membership and appeals to all members to publicise the benefits of membership of the Society at every opportunity. Personal recommendation is by far the most effective method of recruitment.

Our efforts to enrol new members are considerably helped by the rose nurserymen who insert the Society's leaflets in their catalogues and the many rosarians who, by talking at meetings and by showing slides and films, encourage rose lovers to join the Society. We also appreciate the help given by writers in the Press and by radio and television commentators with their praise of the Society's publications and the attractions of Bone Hill. Council expresses its thanks to all these and hopes that their efforts will be intensified as we approach the centenary in 1976.

Finance

The excess of income over expenditure results from the increased income from subscriptions, the agreement reached with H. M. Customs and Excise that the Society is only liable to Value Added Tax on part of its subscription income and economies which the Society has made. This excess and the increased allocation to reserves are satisfactory but we must expect costs to increase still more during the year and the scope for further economies is limited if we are to maintain, as we are sure members will wish, the standard of our publications, our garden and our service to members. Council, of course, hopes very much that it will not be necessary to increase the rate of subscription for some years, but this must depend on increasing our membership.

No additions have been made to the Society's long-term investments during the year. In line with the general trend of the stock market, the value at the 30th September showed a fall during the year from £102,810 to £81,937 but the maturities of the gilt-edged portion of these investments are so spread that it should not be necessary to realise any before they reach their par value on their redemption dates. The reason for the increase in investment income is the higher rate of interest earned on short-term investments during the year.

Publications

The Rose Annual was published in the spring and maintained the high standard associated with the Society's publications under the editorship of Leonard Hollis.

The Rose Bulletin appeared in the autumn and the rise in the cost of paper for this publication is an indication that there will be a significant increase for this item in next year's accounts. In view of this and due to the stock of handbooks now on hand, owing to the decline in membership, the next edition of *Roses: A Selected List of Varieties* has been deferred until 1976. It is hoped that members will appreciate the problem and bear with us.

Shows

The Spring Competition in May was well supported and it was encouraging to see several new exhibitors. One or two minor amendments have been made to the schedule for next year which it is hoped will act as an incentive to encourage more exhibitors to find a little space in their greenhouses for a few roses.

The Summer Show was held at Westminster at the end of June. The amateur exhibitors produced blooms of exceptional quality while the rose nurserymen maintained the very high standard of exhibits for which the Society's Shows are well known though their stands were fewer in number. Congratulations are extended to R. Harkness & Co. Ltd., who won the Championship Trophy as Nurserymen for the fortieth time—a wonderful record.

The Northern Show in July returned to the now familiar setting of Roundhay Park Leeds where the Roundhay (Leeds) Horticultural Society were our hosts.

The Autumn Show, also at Westminster, was held during some of the worst weather of the season. The incessant rain and lack of sun before the show took its toll and it was a great credit to all exhibitors, amateur and nurserymen, who managed to stage such a good show. It was undoubtedly the most difficult show for exhibitors during the past decade.

Mr F. E. Owen deservedly retained the Amateur Championship for the fifth year in succession.

Groups

The South of England Group of the Society was formed during the year under the leadership of Mr Ted Plumpton. Several lectures were held and a small show was staged.

Bristol Group, North Western Group and the Yorkshire Rosarians have been very active during the year. Each Group has held a show with varying success as a result of the exceptionally unfavourable weather. The Conference of the North Western Group in June was well attended.

Judges Examination

The examination for competency in rose judging was held at The College of Further Education, Kendal. 23 candidates attended and 14 passed. The success of the examination was made possible by the assistance of Mr Jack Robinson and his helpers in the area who provided excellent quality blooms for the practical test.

The Trial Ground and Display Gardens

Several new beds have been planted in the Display Gardens and the new Sunken Garden, devoted mainly to miniature roses, and constructed by our outdoor staff

'MARY SUMNER' (floribunda)
('Orangeade' × 'Margot Fonteyn') × ['Elizabeth of Glamis' × ('Little Darling' ×
'Goldilocks')]
Raised by Sam McGredy Roses International, New Zealand
CERTIFICATE OF MERIT 1974
See page 186

'MEIPUMA' (trademarked on the Continent as 'Scherzo') (floribunda)
'*Tamango*'×['*Sarabande*'×('*Goldilocks*'×'*Fashion*')]
Raised by Mrs M. L. Paolino, France
TRIAL GROUND CERTIFICATE 1973
See 1974 Rose Annual, page 183

has created a great deal of interest. During this winter the adjoining area will be developed as three small gardens to help members with planning their own gardens. The Society is fortunate in having as Superintendent Mr Donald Maginnis who with his staff maintains the gardens at such a high standard in spite of the shortage of labour.

The trials were affected by the frequent heavy rain in August and September but the "handpainted" 'Matangi' raised by Sam McGredy Roses International well deserved the award of the President's International Trophy and Gold Medal. The Henry Edland Memorial Medal for fragrance was awarded to 'Sugar Sweet', a floribunda bred by John Sanday (Roses) Ltd.

With a view to decreasing the cost of maintenance of the Trial Ground and materials used in it, a system of rationing of new varieties has been introduced. This will restrict the number of varieties a firm, or an individual, may send, but gives previously successful raisers the right to send additional varieties.

Overseas Visits

The President represented the Society at the rose trials in Madrid and Baden-Baden, where he also attended with the Secretary a very useful meeting of the Presidents of most of the European rose societies. In September he, the Deputy President and Mr F. M. Bowen, the immediate past President, attended and spoke at the International Rose Convention in Chicago in which Mr E. B. Le Grice, Mr Mark Mattock and Mrs Balfour also took part. During the Convention, meetings of the World Federation of Rose Societies were held and members will be glad to know that Mr Frank Bowen is now the President of the World Federation and that the President and Deputy President are Chairman of the Committees on Classification and Convention Liaison, respectively. Many overseas members of the Society attended the Convention and their appreciation of the Society and their eagerness to come to England in 1976 for the Centenary Conference were most encouraging. After the Convention, during a holiday visit to British Columbia, the President gave a talk illustrated with slides to members of the Vancouver Rose Society and a television interview about the R.N.R.S. and the Centenary for the Canadian Broadcasting Corporation.

A party from the Rose Society of South Africa visited Bone Hill on their way home from Chicago.

Centenary—1976

A provisional programme has been prepared for the Centenary Conference in Oxford from the 5th to the 8th July, 1976. This will follow the Centenary Summer Show at Westminster on the 2nd and 3rd July and will include meetings, tours, film shows, art and photographic exhibitions and displays of new roses and floral arrangements. Interested members are advised to inform the Secretary. In addition to the Conference, Council is planning other celebrations including a centenary banquet on 7th December in London and regional dinners and special mementoes. There will also be increased coverage in the 1976 and 1977 Rose Annuals.

Nonagenarians

In September two distinguished and active rosarians, Mr Harry Clacy, D.H.M., member of Council since 1943 and the Honorary Architect, and Mr Herbert Robin-

(continued on page 21)

BALANCE SHEET, 30th SEPTEMBER, 1974

1973 £		£	£	£
	SURPLUS			
84,783	Balance 1 October, 1973			84,783
	Value Added Tax recovery attributable to the previous year		234	
	Excess of Income over Expenditure for year ended 30 September, 1974 ..		4,901	89,918
84,783				
	PRIZE FUND			
500	Balance 1 October, 1973 ..		500	
	Add Robert Shipman Memorial Fund ..		200	700
	RESERVE FOR DEVELOPMENT—TRIAL GROUND, DISPLAY GARDEN AND PROPERTIES			
14,000	Balance 1 October 1973		14,000	
	Add Charge against Revenue Account ..		3,000	17,000
	RESERVE FOR NEW EDITIONS OF PUBLICATIONS, FILM AND CONFERENCE			
23,500	Balance 1 October 1973		23,500	
	Add charge against Revenue Account ..		5,000	28,500
12,000	**RESERVE FOR PENSIONS**			12,000
	CURRENT LIABILITIES			
4,258	Sundry Creditors		5,201	
24,592	Subscriptions received in advance and one quarter of 1974 subscriptions (excluding life members) ..		28,312	33,513
163,633				181,631

1973 £		£	£	£
	FIXED ASSETS			
33,950	Freehold Properties			33,950
	Office Equipment, etc.			
800	Balance 1 October 1973 ..	800		
	Less amount written off ..	400	400	
	Motor Vehicles, Mowers and Equipment:			
2,600	Balance 1 October 1973 ..	2,600		
	Additions less allowance during year ..	2,114		
		4,714		
	Less Amount written off ..	1,214	3,500	
1,650	Library at Professional Valuation (1967)		1,650	
39,000				39,500
103,800	**INVESTMENTS** at Cost			103,800
(102,810)	(Market Value 30 September 1974 £81,937)			
	CURRENT ASSETS			
3,714	Stock of Publications, Badges, etc. as valued by Secretary		4,803	
905	Sundry Debtors for Advertisements, etc. ..		872	
15,261	Balance at Bank on Deposit and Current Account and Cash in Hand		24,202	
734	Income Tax recoverable		2,412	
219	Value Added Tax recoverable		6,042	38,331
163,633				181,631

AUDITORS' REPORT

To the Members, The Royal National Rose Society

We have audited the above Balance Sheet dated 30 September 1974 and Revenue Account for the year ended on that date and have obtained all the information and explanations we have required. In our opinion such Balance Sheet and Revenue Account are properly drawn up so as to exhibit a true and correct view of the state of the Society's affairs according to the best of our information and explanations given us and as shown by the books of the Society. We have verified the Securities representing the investments of your Society at 30 September 1974 and have found the same to be in order.

EVERS & CO., Chartered Accountants, Auditors
SHEPHERD'S FIELD, COURTS HILL ROAD, HASLEMERE, SURREY. 4 November 1974

REVENUE ACCOUNT FOR THE YEAR ENDED 30th SEPTEMBER, 1974

Expenditure

1972/73 £					1973/74 £		
				PUBLICATIONS			
29,729				Expenditure			28,918
797				Less Sales	408		
5,853				Advertising Revenue	5,656	6,064	
		23,079					22,854
				SHOWS			
2,669				Prize Money, Medals and Trophies		2,748	
4,733				Expenses		4,571	
7,402						7,319	
530				Less Proceeds		468	
		6,872					6,851
		13,047		**TRIAL GROUND AND DISPLAY GARDEN**			14,126
				ADMINISTRATION			
20,681				Salaries and Assistance, Superannuation Contributions and Supplementary Pensions	21,601		
2,692				Computer	4,030		
1,502				Rates, Lighting, Heating, etc.	2,487		
5,318				Printing and Stationery	5,961		
15,393				Postages	15,070		
				General Expenses, Telephone, Hire of Rooms, etc...	8,309		
5,302				Repairs and Renewals—office and premises	1,012		
477				Auditor's Fee	450		
400				Bank Charges	1,158		
1,210							
52,975							60,078
3,773				ADVERTISING AND PUBLICITY			6,599
499				PROVINCIAL DISPLAY GARDENS			262
967				GRANTS TO UNIVERSITIES FOR RESEARCH			982
1,500				RESERVE FOR NEW EDITIONS OF PUBLICATIONS, FILM AND CONFERENCE			5,000
2,214				RESERVE FOR DEVELOPMENT, TRIAL GROUND, DISPLAY GARDEN AND PROPERTIES			3,000
814				MOTOR VEHICLES, MOWERS AND EQUIPMENT—Amount written off			1,214
400				OFFICE EQUIPMENT—Amount written off			400
106,140							**121,366**
—				BALANCE—Excess of Revenue over Expenditure for the year			4,901
106,140							**126,267**

Income

1972/73 £					1973/74 £	
				SUBSCRIPTIONS AND AFFILIATION FEES		
94,135				Subscriptions		111,159
1,495				Affiliation Fees		2,524
95,630						113,683
				INCOME FROM INVESTMENTS, etc.		
9,989				Gross		12,584
521				BALANCE—Excess of Expenditure over Revenue for the year		—
106,140						**126,267**

The President's Page

It is a great honour to address all members of this Society as your new President. At the same time I am very conscious that it is also a great responsibility, which I intend to take seriously.

First, I should like to place on record my belief that your Society is now administered more efficiently than ever before by Len Turner, our Secretary, and his staff at Bone Hill. This means that you are enabled to receive our four publications and all other privileges of membership for less than it costs to send 39 letters by first-class post.

Secondly, at a time when you can easily pay £2·95 for a new book of fiction, without illustrations, I think that we must all acknowledge how lucky we are to have such a capable and painstaking Editor as Leonard Hollis. Anyone in publishing will realize the measure of his achievement in maintaining such a high standard in our Rose Annuals at such a low cost.

Thirdly, any visitor to Bone Hill must derive the same sort of pleasure as I feel after a walk round the garden. To the east lies the Trial Ground, where the varieties of the future are tested for three years, surrounded by so many other seedlings which are due to be consigned to early oblivion. To the west is the Display Garden, where most of the better modern cultivars are planted in beds of all shapes and sizes. North-west in this Display Garden lies a group of beds which are at their best in mid-summer: these contain Graham Thomas's collection of historic varieties, to which we are constantly adding other roses of former centuries. South of these beds is found my own great interest—the wild rose collection from all countries of the northern hemisphere. Not yet complete, it is true, but we are always trying to fill important gaps and double-check on botanic names. This is our gene pool and in it are contained the germ cells of rose varieties of the twenty first century. Add to all these riches a collection of modern shrubs, hybrid perpetuals, chinas, miniatures and prostrate, ground-covering roses. Have you seen all these treasures? If not, I do entreat you to visit them during the coming season.

It is now two years since we were forced to increase the subscription to a modest £1·75. It is disappointing to note that this has led to a loss of one third of our membership. But "nothing is either good or bad, but thinking makes it so" and I myself derive consolation from knowing that we have retained 67,000 of our keenest members. I know that you are skilled gardeners—as witnessed by the fine displays at our Rose Shows. I also know that you are good citizens in whatever country you live. Rosarians are not impressed by the much over-worked term "Crisis"—especially when tagged on

E. F. Allen, M.A. President 1975–76

to a shortage of a non-essential sweetener in our diet. But a potential shortage of phosphate, as I have indicated elsewhere, would have to be taken much more seriously.

To all of you I have one request: please try to help your friends and neighbours to withstand "The slings and arrows of outrageous fortune" by joining our Society. It is my view that they cannot afford not to become members.

TED ALLEN

REPORT OF THE COUNCIL

(continued from page 17)

son, M.B.E., the successful rose breeder who was awarded the Queen Mary Commemoration Medal in 1957, reached the age of 90. Even among rosarians, who seem to remain active longer than most, they are remarkable.

Conclusion

In conclusion, Council wishes to express its thanks to the Honorary Architect, Honorary Scientific Adviser, Editor and Horticultural Consultant but especially to the Secretary, the Superintendent and the staff at Bone Hill who have done so much for the Society during the year in spite of the shortage of labour. Mr Ray Palmer, who joined the office staff in 1965, has just resigned to take up work for the mentally handicapped: the Council wishes him success in his new career.

By order of Council,

R. C. BALFOUR
President

DEAN HOLE MEDAL

The Council is very pleased to announce that the Dean Hole Medal has been awarded to Mr R. C. Balfour for his distinguished service as President and in furthering the aims of the Society.

Perfume

DR A. S. THOMAS, O.B.E., V.M.A., D.H.M., S.M.A.

Earliest records tell of man's appreciation of perfumes and of his extracting them. Many beautifully made perfume bottles have been discovered by archaeologists during excavations in Egypt, the Middle East, Greece and Rome. Early literature of China, Arabia, Europe, and northern Africa abounds in enthusiastic references to perfumes. The many poets of Persia (now Iran), in particular are notable in this regard. The roses grown in their country, centuries ago, are still in cultivation and are all strongly scented.

The sense of smell was used in earliest times in finding food and in detecting danger, but as civilization has advanced there has ceased to be much need for these uses. Instead we have the delights of fragrant flowers, the bouquet of wines, the spices in food and incense in places of worship.

Perfumes are attractive and alluring, or repellant and alarming. The word "perfume" means "through smoke" and relates to the burning of incense and the giving off of fragrance with the smoke. Incense in religious rites was amongst the early uses of perfume and it is still used, especially in Hinduism and orthodox Christian churches. The Muslims used thousands of gallons of rose-water in each mosque for purification after recapturing it from the crusaders. Saladin needed more than five hundred camels to bring sufficient rose-water from Damascus to Jerusalem in 1187 to purify the Mosque of Omar before he considered it fit for him to enter. Mohamed II washed the walls of an enormous mosque in Constantinople (now Istanbul), known colloquially as the Blue Mosque, with great volumes of rose-water in 1453. This was the Church of St Sophia (Christian) for many years, then a mosque and now a Muslim museum.

Perfumes so bewitched the sense of smell that early man ascribed to them great medicinal values and offered them in sacrifice to his gods. He mixed fragrant substances with ingredients that were believed to have medicinal value and to have the power to expel the demons of disease. He carried or wore scented herbs to repel hostile spirits. He perfumed the bodies and shrouds of his dead to ward off corruption and to preserve them for a hereafter. Thyme, rue and pennyroyal were plugged into ears and nostrils during times of plague in medieval Renaissance Europe. The medical practitioners sniffed aromatic herbs during such times while attending infected patients or while walking in the streets. Biblical holy anointing oil consisted of two aromatic resins still used in perfumery, storax and galbanum of Persian origin.

Egyptian perfumes were mainly in the forms of ointments, oils and powders. They were kept in beautiful containers of glass and precious onyx. The Egyptians and the Greeks used a different scent for each part of the body.

During the Middle Ages in Europe perfumery had reached a high standard in Asia Minor (Arabia) and the art was taken to Europe by the Moors in the course of their overrunning the southern half of the continent in the fourteenth and fifteenth centuries.

Credit for being the first to produce rose-water, the first of all extracted perfumes, by distillation, is given by various writers to Aben-Zohar, a Jewish physician in Seville, Spain, to Rhazes (850–923) a Persian physician, and to Avicenna (980–1037) an Arabian physician, philosopher, scientist, poet and statesman. Avicenna used R. centifolia. Rose water was distilled in Spain for many years before the technique was used in France in the thirteenth century.

However, perfume was used long before any distilling was done. Myrrh has been used for nearly 4,000 years. When Tutankhamen's tomb was opened in 1922, jars and flasks were found from which the liquid had evaporated but the fragrance was still strong after 3,200 years. Alexander, Cleopatra, Nero and other ancient rulers perfumed their bodies and clothes freely. Only royalty and the wealthy could afford perfumes and they exchanged composite gifts of girl slaves, jewels and scents.

In the Middle Ages European rulers used a great lot of perfume. Philip Augustus of France (1165–1223) engaged the first perfumer in Europe. Elizabeth of Hungary (1207–1231) is said to have had made for herself the first perfume with an alcoholic base. This was of rosemary and was called "Hungary Water". Henry VIII of England (1491–1547) chose to blend a formula—six spoonfuls of rose oil and of rose-water, a quarter ounce of sugar, an ounce of ambergris and two grains of musk. These were simmered for six hours, strained and bottled. This indicates a considerable advance in perfumery. By the end of the Tudor dynasty (1603) there were much greater advances.

By the time of Louis XIV (1638–1715), the great Sun King of France, his country had become the centre of perfumery and Louis was said to be "the sweetest smelling monarch in Europe."

These are just a few of many comparable associations of perfumes with monarchy. As in the case of the first distilling of rose-water, there are several accounts of the first obtaining of the essential oil of roses now called Attar of

Roses or Otto of Roses. Geronimo Rossi claimed to have observed, in 1574, that one could separate a strongly perfumed oil from rose petals. There is, however, a much more romantic version of the first noting of rose oil and, as may be expected, it is the most widely known version.

Early in the seventeenth century in northern India, Princess Nur Mahal ordered great quantities of rose petals to be added to a large canal of water when she and the Mogul emperor were to be rowed on it. The heat of the sun drew oil from the petals and this formed a film on the water. The princess had this absorbed by fine cotton and stored in tightly sealed containers.

Nur Mahal arranged the marriage of a niece, Mumtaz Mahal, to the great Mogul emperor Shah Jehan, and she handed on to her this method of making attar of roses. The magnificent Taj Mahal is the tomb of Mumtaz Mahal, "Elect of the Palace".

In more recent times all students of botany, perfumery, pharmacy, medicine and the like have been and are still being taught that perfumes are derived from essential volatile oils. These develop in certain cells of each particular plant. Most of them are insoluble in water but all are soluble in alcohol, ether or a fatty oil. They are very volatile and have a high carbon content. This makes them very inflammable and they burn so completely that they leave no permanent grease mark. They have a strong aromatic odour and a hot burning taste. They can be distilled best in vacuum stills at a low temperature. So-called fractionated vacuum distillation can be and is used to separate strongly scented components or to eliminate impurities and hydrocarbons (terpenes) of very weak scent. Some very expensive essential oils, for example that of jasmine, are extracted from the petals by odourless solvents. They are isolated then from the solvents by vacuum distillation.

Essential oils can be obtained from all types of plant tissue as in leaves (for example mint, thyme, and the like), in bark (for example cinnamon), in rind (for example lemon and orange), in wood (for example sandalwood and camphorwood), in seeds (for example nutmeg, cloves and carraway) in petals, stamens and pollen (most flowers) or in roots and rhizomes (for example orris).

Gum-resins have been used for many centuries as fixatives to give uniformity to the finished blend of oils and to lessen their volatility.

Essential oils are extracted in various ways. One process, known as enfleurage, consists of using purified lard or high quality olive oil with the flowers so that it absorbs the essential oil. This ability of fats to take up perfumes is availed of in another process in which felt soaked in olive oil is placed above the flowers. Rose and orange blossom perfumes are extracted by another process known as maceration. This consists of infusing the flowers for several hours in warm oil or melted fat. This is treated later with absolute alcohol (pure ethyl alcohol). This removes almost all of the essential oil and it is decanted. The essential oil of roses, attar of roses, is never liquid unless it is warmed. Depending on the colour of the petals used, the age of the petals and the method of extraction it varies in colour from its usual green to lemon, deep pink, or brown. It is always very costly and is seldom pure. In very early times it was said to be worth five times its weight in gold. It would be worth very much more than that now. About two tons of petals (about 60,000 blooms) are needed to obtain one pound of attar of roses. This can vary slightly with seasonal conditions.

Where materials are plentiful and inexpensive, and oil is not required in maximum quantity as with citrus rind, citronella, mint and the like, the oil may be pressed out.

The way in which plants create their perfumes in various tissues is not known. In some instances different tissues of the one plant produce different perfumes.

The final addition in the making of a perfume commercially is a "fixative". This is usually a stable animal substance which prevents the volatile oils from diffusing rapidly. Also, it contributes its own special fragrance.

Four perfumes are of animal origin—musk, civet, ambergris and castor. They are all extremely potent. The adult male musk deer produces a greasy secretion in a gland under the skin of his abdomen. This, after drying and dissolving in alcohol, is used in very expensive perfumes to fortify and fix the basic odour.

The cat-like civet produces its perfume in a gland too. Known as "civetone", it is extremely unpleasant in odour. However, when very greatly diluted it becomes attractive and most useful as a perfume fixative.

Ambergris, the most expensive of the four, is a waxy substance from the sperm whale. It is found on the shore, or floating on the sea, or in the digestive system of the whale. It has a pleasant, musk-like fragrance when warmed. Dissolved in alcohol, it makes an excellent fixative in costly perfumes.

Castor comes from glands of the beaver. Its odour is very strong, lasting, penetrating and pleasant especially when well matured. This is in sharp contrast with the oil which was used medicinally in bygone days! There is no relation between the two oils; the main use of the essential oil in perfumery is as a fixative.

Many perfumes come to be associated with clearly defined districts. Possibly the best known of these is eau-de-Cologne. It is believed that this perfume was made first by Johann Maria Farina (1685–1766) who migrated from northern Italy to Cologne in 1709. The exact formula is still secret but it is known to be a blend and to include oils of neroli, orange, rosemary, citron, bergamot and others. The final product in even relatively simple perfumes may consist of thirty or more components, all dissolved, in secret proportions, in ethyl alcohol which, itself, is prepared specially with denaturants that do not lessen the fragrance. It would be rare to find a completely unblended perfume on the retail market, even though it be given the name of one flower.

Digne, in the Bléone Valley and on the Route Napoléon, is only a small town but it is famous as the centre of lavender perfume manufacturing in France. In the surrounding district vast fields of the silver-grey lavender plants are to be seen. Almost every shop in the town sells lavender perfume. Walking down the main street I have experienced a strong burning sensation in my throat from the all-pervading scent.

Grasse, in the Alpes-Maritimes, near Nice and overlooking the Mediterrannean from an altitude of nearly 400 metres, is one of the world's main centres for the making of perfume. It is surrounded by olive and orange groves and beautiful great areas of scented flowers, especially violets, mimosa ("wattle" to Australians) carnations, jasmine and roses. There are many perfume factories in the old town. In the fields one sees gaily dressed men, women and children gathering the flowers in big baskets. Along the roads pass streams of wagons laden with flowers. In this district rose perfume ranks second to that of jasmine.

At one time R. centifolia (known locally as Rose de Mai) was used exclusively in the Grasse district but it is prone to disease and it blooms only in the spring—the month of May. It has been replaced by 'Ulrich Brunner Fils' (H.P.—Levet, 1881), 'Louis van Houtte' (H.P.—Lacharme, 1869), and 'Marie van Houtte' (T.—Ducher, 1871) all of which are less troublesome, are very fragrant, and give recurrent flowering.

Rose perfume is still produced in Turkey, Syria, Kashmir and India, especially in Amritsar, the holy city of the Sikhs, but apparently it does not exceed local demand. The world's greatest producer of oil of roses has been and probably still is Bulgaria. The distilling of the oil was commenced in both Bulgaria and France late in the seventeenth century, the skill having been introduced to both by the Ottoman conquerors. In Bulgaria the distilling has been done principally in the valley of the Toundja, known as the Valley of Roses. The chief centres in the valley for growing the roses and distilling the oil are Kazanlik, Stora, Zagora and Karlow. A particularly strongly scented strain of *Rosa damascena, R. damascena trigintipetala*, is planted in tremendous numbers in the valley. It is a semi-double red rose. The season for gathering the petals lasts only three to four weeks in May and is preceded always by a colourful national gala festival. The blooms are gathered before sunrise and go straight to the distilleries.

For several hundreds of years roses have thrived in northern Africa, especially in Algeria, Morocco and Egypt. The big French influence in these countries may have helped in fostering rose growing there. The Meilland establishment has named several very modern hybrid tea cultivars for northern African towns. These countries are not by any means all desert. In their fertile areas, notably along the coasts and in their many oases, provided always that adequate water is available, conditions are very good for roses.

When Europe became separated politically into the democratic western part and the communist eastern part, trading difficulties arose and these affected the buying of attar of roses from Bulgaria. Thoughts turned then to these countries in northern Africa for the production of the perfume. It was found fairly quickly that, in some areas, *R. damascena trigintipetala* gave the best results—the same rose that is grown in Bulgaria under the name of 'Kazanlik'. Those areas are far inland, especially in the oases, and the rose is known there as 'El Golea'. This name is derived from one of the oases. In other parts a type of *R. centifolia* gives better results.

There are now well-equipped perfumery factories well south of the Atlas Mountains. More and more roses are being planted year by year. Recently I read that over 1,500 tons of rose blooms are being taken to the factories each year in this area. It is stated that the total production of attar of roses from Bulgaria, France, Africa and the various Asian countries still falls far short of commercial demand.

I have read, too, of attar of roses being distilled also from *Pelargonium odoratissimum*. No comparison was made with the oil derived from roses but, as it is done in only a small way, it would appear to be less desirable.

Chemically, attar of roses and all other essential oils, including those from flowers, oil of cloves, almond oil, mustard oil, camphor oil, turpentine and many others are hydrocarbons. The chemistry of the differences between the varied fragrances is unknown even though fairly good imitations of many of them are made for cheaper perfumes. In modern times plant materials for making perfumes are collected from many countries, including those of southern Europe, northern Africa, China, Java, Thibet, Burma, India, Ceylon, Peru, Cyprus, Uganda, Zanzibar and Australia—especially for boronia. The essential oils are all compounds of odourless elements. Not only are the scented members of this group fragrant but they differ widely in their fragrances.

Vacuum distillation and other methods of extracting perfume are fairly modern. It must be remembered that roses were the most highly regarded flowers in ancient Egypt and by the Phoenicians. Flowers were taken great distances by sea and land for elaborate functions. One cannot believe that the flowers were not at least wilted on arrival at their destination. We read only of the scented petals covering floors to a depth of many inches and of their use on beds and in stuffing pillows. Undoubtedly the attraction of these roses was in the perfume of the petals. Cleopatra provided beds of roses for honoured guests. Nero is reputed to have spent the modern equivalent of $100,000.00 on rose flowers for one feast scattered as petals on the floor. At a later date the Romans introduced the Damask Rose and cultivated vast areas of its plants for sale in the Roman market-places.

Later, rose petals, heps and leaves all came to be used in cookery and for flavouring wines, but it was many centuries after Cleopatra and Nero before attar of roses was made first, The senses of smell and taste are related very closely and smell contributes greatly to taste. In the early centuries perfumes of any sort could be had only by royalty and wealthy people, but by the early years of the eighteenth century perfumes were available to a wider range of society. They, like rose flowers themselves at an earlier time, fell into disfavour because of their alleged associations with immoral practices and excesses. In 1770 an Act of Parliament in England invoked the laws against witchcraft to include means by which women seduced men into marriage, and perfume headed the fairly long list of unlawful deceptions.

Long before the first distilling of attar of roses, perfume in the form of rose-water or the petals themselves were used in scented candles, incense, scented oil for lamps, scented tapers for lighting lamps, pot pourri, cosmetics, lozenges, wines, jams, syrups and cakes.

Only once have I known of a rose gaining favour because of its lack of perfume. That was in Paris in 1973 when one of the world's leading perfumiers sought a cultivar of fairly strong colour, good form and adequate size. This could be reproduced well in colour printing on containers of their perfumes. In addition, though, it had to have no fragrance. This avoided any competition with, and any comparing or contrasting with the perfume in the bottle or the powder or any of their other cosmetics.

Theophrastus (about 370-286 B.C.) the Greek philosopher and "father of botany" listed roses, lilies and violets as the most popular scented flowers of his time. Rose-water was the first perfumed "water" to be made, and attar of roses was the first essential oil to be separated. It is still the basis of all rose perfumes. The priority given to rose-water and attar of roses has been due undoubtedly to man's continuing preference for the fragrance of roses.

This fragrance varies considerably in both intensity and type. During all the centuries there has been a significant percentage of roses with little or no perfume and there have been a few with unpleasant perfumes, for example *R. foetida*, as its name must suggest. It gave to the early Pernetiana roses some degree of this unpleasantness and decreased any pleasant odour possessed by a seed or pollen parent. Some writers claim to be able to distinguish and they list a great many types of rose perfumes such as old rose or damask, musk, citron, apricot, apple, tea, violet, spice, beer and fruit salad—itself a rather varied fragrance, I find! I have a reasonably sharp sense of smell but I cannot discern all these differences—possibly my imagination is deficient.

Several workers with the old roses (now referred to often as the "historic" roses) estimate that approximately one third of them were scentless or had extremely little perfume and that less than one third could be regarded as highly perfumed. These same proportions apply to modern roses. The perfumery people still prefer a very small, carefully selected few of the old roses, despite their blooming only in the spring. The small number of these roses must be stressed. The introduction of Pernetiana Roses in 1900 with their *R. foetida* breeding brought a spate of cultivars with little fragrance, poor form and susceptibility to Black Spot. The vivid yellows and the enlivened reds and coral colours seem to have had least perfume. It is only in recent years that the hybridists have given us strongly perfumed bright yellows. Many generations of crossing and recrossing have given us restored vigour and fragrance with the new colours possibly even enhanced. A bowl of mixed modern cultivars can be relied upon to provide strong perfume in any room. And what perfume is or ever has been more delightful?

A rosebud set with little wilful thorns,
And sweet as English air could make her, she.
TENNYSON, *The Princess.*

The Birthday Present

L. A. SLATTER
(*Amateur rose grower*).

Have you heard the story of the 'Pink Lustre' hybrid tea rose that turned into an 'Orangeade' standard? You will have when you've read this!

Several years ago when the hybrid tea rose 'Pink Lustre' first came on the market, I liked its form and decided I would try it to see if it had potential as an exhibition bloom to add to my collection of exhibition varieties. As I am wary of buying new varieties, since these do not always live up to their descriptions in the catalogues, or have flowers like those on trade displays at shows, I decided, until the variety had been proved, that I would purchase just one plant when I sent in my order for several other varieties, and this I did.

The bushes duly arrived, and were planted and firmed according to "the book" and then left to their own resources until the following year. My soil, incidentally, has a pH. reading of 6·5 and roses usually do well there.

In late April of that year, and after pruning, the roses were given a mulch of farmyard manure, quite a scarce commodity in our area. The plants made quite good growth, with the exception of 'Pink Lustre'. This grew only moderately and gave only three blooms, which were quite large and of good shape and colour. I took off the blooms to see if this would help the plant to grow any stronger. It did make a little more growth but was still only growing moderately.

The following spring I pruned it quite hard and, at the appropriate time, gave this (and the other roses) a dressing of Tonks' Rose Manure. It grew as it did the previous year, making very little good growth and gave just a few worthwhile blooms. Two of these I included in a vase at our local show. I foliar fed the plant using Welgro. It improved it a little, but the plant still had no vigour. I had almost made up my mind that it was not a worthwhile variety but decided to give it one more year to make good. I need not have bothered. When it came to pruning time the following year, two of the shoots had died back, leaving only two weakly shoots. This I thought is it, out it goes. I was on the point of digging it up when I noticed a strong sucker springing from the base. From various observations and experiments I had made with stocks it looked like a sucker of the variety Pfander. I thought, if this grows well and straight, it might make a good standard, so I left the plant alone.

The sucker grew in strength, while the poor 'Pink Lustre' barely moved. It looked as if it would be more profitable to keep the sucker at the expense of the 'Pink Lustre' plant. I let the sucker grow until it was almost five feet high, and over half an inch thick. It was, of course, supported by a stout cane and securely tied.

It so happened that, about this time, some friends of ours came to tea and as usual, we went to look round the garden and discuss the merits of certain plants. Our friends were admiring the roses, when one of them said how much he admired the variety 'Orangeade' and said how bright a standard of that variety would be.

So in late July of the year, having pruned away the miserable remains of the original 'Pink Lustre' plant, I set to work budding the standard stem which was upon test, ripe (the thorns broke away easily), healthy and straight. The variety to bud onto it? Of course, 'Orangeade'! I inserted three buds into the main stem at a height of three feet six inches, one on the north side, one on the west side and one on the south side. Upon examination one month later, I found that all the buds had taken. I lightly retied the buds to prevent them being blown out by the wind. The following February the standard was beheaded leaving a snag about six inches long above the bud at the top, and as the shoots developed and grew they were all pinched when they were three inches long to make them branch out. The shoots were carefully tied to the cane as they grew to prevent damage by the wind. They continued to grow as if to order and the standard was developing into a magnificent plant. When the flowers opened they were beautiful.

Our friends came round again and as usual we went to examine the roses. Upon reaching the 'Orangeade' standard, my friend stood as if spellbound and said, "There, what did I tell you. Doesn't 'Orangeade' make a beautiful standard? Where did you get it from, it's just what I want?" I said, "How would you like it for your birthday? I haven't bought you anything yet". He said, "I couldn't think of anything I would like more." So in November of that year, the 'Orangeade' standard was carefully dug up, taken to my friend's garden, and just as carefully planted, staked and tied.

He thinks the world of it, and prunes and feeds it carefully every year. The 'Orangeade' standard continues to thrive in all its glory and gives great joy to the recipient.

The 'Pink Lustre'? It was consigned to the bonfire years ago. The minute quantity of potash from it probably benefited some other plant.

My friend, believe it or not, is affectionately known as "Bud". Alas, he is now not as well or robust as his 'Orangeade' standard—his birthday present— but I hope he will live to enjoy it for many years yet.

'Peace' and the Modern Hybrid Tea

DR ROGER WAIGH

(*University lecturer and amateur rose grower*)

Having joined the RNRS fairly recently, I was inclined to read the handbook *Roses—A Selected List of Varieties* quite carefully, perhaps more closely than if I had been familiar with earlier versions. As familiarity with the list increased, it became abundantly clear that 'Peace', as parent, grandparent or great-grandparent, has had a quite extraordinary influence on modern roses, particularly, for obvious reasons, on the hybrid teas and floribunda/hybrid teas, quite apart from its influence in setting standards in its own right. No doubt this is old news to experienced rosarians, but I wonder if many other rose growers are aware of what appears to be an increasing trend.

At a rough count, there is a total of 184 hybrid teas and floribunda/hybrid teas in *A Selected List*, of which 170 have been introduced since 1942,[1] this being the date given for the introduction of 'Peace' in this country. Bearing in mind the history of this remarkable rose, it could have been used for hybridizing for a few years before this date, but a few years one way or the other make little difference to the figures.

Using only the parentage given in *A Selected List* and no other source, so that there are obvious limitations and omissions, no fewer than 108 of the eligible varieties are traceable to 'Peace'. Of these, 27 are first generation, including such notable garden roses as 'Mischief', 'Sterling Silver', 'Rose Gaujard', 'Stella', 'Prima Ballerina', 'Karl Herbst' and 'Tzigane', of which 'Karl Herbst', 'Prima Ballerina', 'Mischief' and 'Sterling Silver' are renowned parents in their own right. The second generation is somewhat larger, as might be expected (45 varieties) and includes many fine cultivars: 'Super Star', 'Perfecta', 'Piccadilly', 'Fragrant Cloud', 'Blue Moon', 'Paddy McGredy', 'Duke of Windsor' and so on. As great-grandparent 'Peace' is to be found in a further 25 roses on the list, 'Alec's Red', 'Grandpa Dickson', 'Sea Pearl' and 'Summer Holiday' being a few of the best. In some cases 'Peace' is to be found on both sides of the family tree, so that further breeding is increasing rather than diluting her influence; such are 'Grandpa Dickson', 'Brasilia' and 'John Waterer'.

[1] Owing to World War II, 'Peace' was not distributed in the U.K. until 1947, although it had been distributed in 1942 in some other countries. *Ed.*

To round things off, there are two sports—'Chicago Peace' and 'Kronenbourg'.

It may be unwise to attempt to enumerate the reasons for the success of 'Peace' as a parent, since these will be mainly the qualities which have made 'Peace' such an enormously successful garden rose, and I am sure that these have been described in poetic detail by many better qualified to write about her than I am. To be practical, however, the obvious plus marks are for vigour, disease resistance, rain resistance and freedom of flower. If we are to allow that there is an extra "something", it must be the petal quality that gives the flower that faint translucence, making it appear almost to glow softly. The first four qualities might explain a great deal, but I wonder if the last, less definite, might not be the main reason for the appeal of 'Peace' and her great family. Perhaps it was 'Peace' that supplied the "*je ne sais quoi*" to 'Super Star', 'Mischief', 'Alec's Red' and so on, which enabled each of them to win the coveted President's International Trophy.

To introduce a discordant note, 'Peace' is not perfect. It makes rather a coarse plant, its foliage is not particularly attractive, it has little scent, and its colour is rather washy. With the exception of the last, this seems to be the way hybrid teas are going. I wonder if our rose breeders may have allowed 'Peace' to dominate their thoughts to such an extent, subconsciously, that they now think of "hybrid tea" as being synonymous with "Peace-like", to the detriment of some of the qualities which make roses attractive, being habit, foliage and—deny it though they may—scent. A few, like 'Prima Ballerina' and 'Fragrant Cloud' have a strong scent, but many of the others have not.

So you might call this an appeal to the hybridists to try some completely new lines, and never mind if the blooms droop a bit, or open completely flat, or whatever, as long as they look good and smell nice. It will take some courage, for eight out of the top ten hybrid teas in the Rose Analysis, both Northern and Southern Counties, are traceable to 'Peace', and one of the other two is not excluded from the old lady's family on the information given in *Roses—A Selected List of Varieties*.

Rose-Crowned into the Darkness – Some Allusions to the Rose in Greek and Latin Literature

MARGARET STEWARDSON

At no time in history does the rose seem to have been more greatly loved than in ancient Greece and Rome, and this love is reflected in very many allusions to the rose in the literature. It may be of interest to note just a few of these references, since for many people, to know something of the rich tradition which has always surrounded the rose is to increase the delight that they take in their own latter-day roses.

In Homer, standing at the very beginning of Greek literature, there is no mention at all of the rose as such. However, Dawn is frequently described as "rosy-fingered" in the *Odyssey*[1], and also Homer in the *Iliad* tells how Aphrodite anointed the body of Hector with a rose-based unguent to preserve it against the ravages inflicted by Achilles.[2] There is nothing in Homer to indicate that the rose was cultivated at this time—indeed, Homeric horticulture seems to be altogether confined to the orchard and kitchen garden; Homer paints a detailed picture of the garden of King Alcinous, (father of the princess Nausicaa, one of the many comely ladies encountered by Odysseus in his journeyings), with its never-failing four-acre orchard full of pears, apples and figs, its vineyard and its neat vegetable-beds which "continually are green"[3], but there is no suggestion at all of a flower garden.

Another early reference to the rose, again in her wild state, is found in the "Homeric" hymn which describes the rape of Persephone by the god of the underworld, who stole her away while she was in a meadow, gathering flowers: "roses, crocus, violets, iris, hyacinth and narcissus".[4]

Increasingly, mention is made of the rose in the early (i.e. 7th century B.C.) lyric poets: to take just two examples from many, Sappho of Lesbos tells how her lover excels all other women just as, after sunset, the rosy-fingered moon excels all other stars—"it casts its light over the salt sea and over the flower-studded fields, where the lovely dew falls and the roses bloom"[5]. Again, a fragment of Archilochus (mid-7th century) describes a young girl making merry, holding in her hand a branch of myrtle and a rose blossom, her long hair shading her shoulders.[6] As a later instance, here is Euripides in the fifth century during an interlude in his tragedy *Medea*, telling how the city of

34

Athens is "beloved by Aphrodite, who breathes fragrant breezes over the land, wearing on her hair a garland of sweet-smelling roses".[7]

Worth mentioning, too, is the famous passage of the historian Herodotus where he refers to the so-called "gardens of Midas", (that Midas whose touch turned all to gold), where are roses which grow "of their own accord; each bloom has as many as sixty petals and their perfume surpasses that of all other roses".[8] (The identity of this rose is still, of course, not proven.)

The rose has also passed into Greek proverb. To "speak roses" of someone, or "to sprinkle someone with roses",[9] is to shower them with compliments, while "a hog amongst roses" answers to our "bull in a china shop". Also preserved for us is a fragment of a children's singing game, something like our "Nuts and May":

> *"Where are my roses and my violets?*
> *Where is my pretty parsley?*
> *Here are your roses and your violets,*
> *Here is your pretty parsley."*[10]

A rose proverb is found also among the Romans: "inter vepres rosae nascuntur"—"no rose without a thorn".

Roses were in great demand in ancient Rome, so much so that they were recommended by Varro (writing during Octavian's reign) as a profitable crop for market gardeners—the most famous rose-growing centres in Italy being Tibur (Tivoli), Praeneste (Palestrina) and in particular Paestum, near Naples, whose twice-blooming roses, the "biferique rosaria Paesti"[11] have been immortalized by Virgil, and again by Propertius, with a warning not to waste time "for I have seen the sweet-smelling roses of Paestum, which should certainly have lived, laid low and parched by the morning sirocco".[12]

There are many instances in the literature of roses being used for wreaths and garlands on festive occasions and at banquets; for example Martial says "let the stitched rose be bound tenfold round my hair";[13] (roses and other flowers were sometimes stitched to a philyra or band made from the bark of the linden tree). Horace has some advice for those who are trying to come to terms with middle age: "don't worry about the future; much better to laze under a plane or pine tree, drinking wine and making fragrant our greying locks with roses".[14]

The Rosalia or Rosaria, the feast of roses, was a common, though local festival, being a commemoration of the dead, when the family decked with roses the graves of its departed members; Propertius also links the rose with funeral rites. Thinking his last hour to be at hand during a storm at sea, he says that if only he had died in his bed at home, at least his mistress would have mourned him and have "gently placed my bones on a heap of tender rose petals".[15]

Roses figure too in religious festivals. Lucretius describes how during a procession in honour of the Great Mother, her worshippers were accustomed to strew the path of her image with alms, and "to snow rose blooms, casting a shade over the goddess and her retinue".[16] Religion can produce some unlikely results, and there is a reference in Imperial times to the Rosaliae Signorum, which sounds as though those symbols of war, the standards of the Legions, were at times garlanded with roses.

Sometimes the rose appears as a symbol of extravagance. In 72 B.C. Cicero was retained as counsel for the prosecution by the Sicilians against Verres, whose governorship of the island had been disfigured by cruelty and malpractice. Cicero is fulminating with heavy sarcasm: "Iste bonus imperator", "that splendid officer" he says, "spent all his winters in bed". The first he knew of spring was when he noticed that a rose figured in the décor of his dinner table. Even in summer, he never travelled on horseback, but "rode in a litter which contained a cushion made of transparent Maltese embroidery, stuffed with rose petals. He had a garland of roses on his head, another round his neck, and also held a bag of fine linen full of roses."[17]—the epitome of luxury!

I end with a glimpse of two old men in their rose gardens. Pliny the Younger, in a letter to a friend, describes, with endearing pride and delight, his Tuscan estate tucked away in the foothills of the Apennines. It was evidently a sophisticated mixture of formal and informal garden—the former containing examples of topiary, for there were box shrubs cut in the shape of letters forming both of the name of Pliny, and, magnanimously, that of his gardener. There were also many winding alleys and circular spaces enclosed with cypress trees, "whose deep shade makes these spaces gloomy at the sides, but the centres are quite open to the sunshine—indeed, even roses grow there".[18]

The second glimpse, over two centuries later, is of the scholar Ausonius, who had in his day been tutor to the Emperor's son, and had now retired in his old age to his villa at Bordeaux with its formal rose garden, where, rising at dawn one hot day he saw all his "Paestum roses rejoicing, drenched with dew, while Lucifer, the morning star was rising in the east". This whole poem, "On New-blown Roses",[19] is a delight, and its theme one which appears again and again in European literature:

"as long as a single day lasts, so long is the life of a rose:
maiden, gather roses while the flower and your youth is fresh,
so swift is the passing of the days of your life."

"Collige, virgo, rosas"; forerunner of Herrick's "Gather ye rosebuds while ye may."

I hope that these somewhat random allusions may help to show how deeply the rose is embedded in the cultures of Greece and Rome, and that it may not be too fanciful to say that their civilization did indeed go down "rose crowned into the darkness"[20] of the Dark Ages.

References

1. Homer, *Odyssey*, 2:1 *et passim.*

2. Homer, *Iliad*, 23: 185-7.

3. Homer, *Odyssey*, 7: 112-132.

4. Homeric Hymn, 2: 6-8.

5. *Lyrics of Sappho*, ed. Lobel, 5: 5.

6. *Anthologia Lyrica Graeca*, ed. Diehl: I-25.

7. Euripides, *Medea*, 841.

8. Herodotus, 8-138.

9. Aristophanes, *Nubes*, 910, 1330.

10. *Anthologia Lyrica Graeca*, ed. Diehl: II-36.

11. Virgil, *Georgics*, 4-119.

12. Propertius, 4, 5, 61

13. Martial, 9-93

14. Horace's *Odes*, 2, 11, 14.

15. Propertius, 1-17.

16. Lucretius, 2-627 (*De Rerum Natura*).

17. Cicero, Verr: 2, 5, 11, par. 27.

18. Pliny, *Ep*. 5, 6, par. 3, 4.

19. Ausonius, ed. Schenkl, p. 243.

20. Rupert Brooke: *The Hill*

Tea-Scented Roses

A Survey

L. ARTHUR WYATT

(Amateur grower specializing in "Old" roses)

Origins

For the introduction of the original roses which were to have a major influence in the modern development of the genus, western horticulture stands indebted to an English country gentleman, a small and impecunious horticultural society and, linking them both, an employee of the Honourable East India Company based in Canton, China.

Sir Abraham Hume of Wormley Bury, Hertfordshire, was a keen gardener whose wife, Lady Amelia Hume, not only shared his enthusiasm but was an able botanist in her own right. By a happy chance, Sir Abraham's cousin, Alexander Hume, was in charge of the English "factory", or trading post as we should now term it, at Canton. Through Alexander, and more directly, the East India Company's inspector of tea, John Reeves (1778–1856), the Humes had received several consignments of plants during the first decade of the nineteenth century. The consignment of rose plants which Reeves had procured for them from the Fa Tee Nurseries near Canton in 1808 was probably the most important of all.

In those days, when it took almost as many weeks as it now takes in flying hours to reach England from the Far East, it was often the practice to off-load plants in transit from China to England at the Calcutta Botanic Garden as a half-way house for recovery during the long voyage. This practice led the French horticulturists to assume that the plants had actually originated in India and not China. It also confused some English botanists, too, so that to this day, the class of roses which we term the Chinas are referred to in France and Germany as 'Bengales', while the whole botanical Section which includes the Chinas, Tea-scented and Hybrid Teas was given the name INDICAE. It is not known whether the rose plants sent off in 1808 were rested in India, but it is more than a possibility since they did not reach the Humes until 1809, the year in which Lady Amelia died.

Sir Abraham passed plant material to James Colvill, an eminent nurseryman in King's Road, Chelsea, where its first European flowering was recorded in 1810. From its colour and fragrance it was given the name, 'Hume's Blush Tea-scented China'.

The statement by Shepherd, *History of the Rose*, that "it was not received with great enthusiasm" is not supported by contemporary evidence. It was certainly regarded as sufficiently important for Henry C. Andrews, the foremost English floral artist of his day, to make a plant portrait of it in Colvill's nursery in the same year of its first blooming under the botanical name *R. indica odorata*. This specific name was probably suggested by Robert Sweet, a gardener-cum-botanist who was employed by Colvill at that time. In any event, when Sweet came to write his own description a few years later, he must have realized the mistaken place ascription as he called the rose *R. odorata* which has stuck.

Of even greater significance, the following year, at the height of the Napoleonic War, arrangements were made to provide John Kennedy, another famous nurseryman, with a safe-conduct to take 'Hume's Blush' to the Empress Josephine, a fact remarked upon by *The Gentleman's Magazine* for 14 November 1811. At Malmaison, the greatest botanical artist of all time, Pierre-Joseph Redouté, painted it under the name *R. indica fragrans*. The plate, first published in 1817 with an accompanying text by the botanist, Claude-Antoine Thory, is by common consent, one of the most beautiful of all the 117 rose portraits published during Redouté's lifetime. It is so well known, having been reproduced on greetings cards, place mats and as a framed engraving, that any further description is superfluous.

Dr C. C. Hurst, writing in 1941, believed 'Hume's Blush' to be extinct. It had, in fact, been collected along with hundreds of other rose species and sub-species by the botanist, Dr Dieck of Zöschen, South Germany, in the latter part of the nineteenth century. It formed part of the complete collection exhibited at the World Botanical Congress in Paris in 1908 and was then planted in the Rosarium at Sangerhausen where it has remained ever since. Through the generosity of Herr Hans Vonholdt, the Curator, plant material has been made available to me. The plants display when in young growth the lovely purple-red wood and foliage so characteristic of their descendants while the somewhat sprawling habit is found among several of the early hybrids still in cultivation.

In the hands of French nurserymen, some twenty-two hybrids were raised between 1821 and 1825 but only their names and descriptions have survived.

At this same time, Joseph Sabine, Secretary of the Horticultural Society of London, now the Royal Horticultural Society, was busy arousing the interest of the Society's Council in the garden value of chrysanthemums, which had been first introduced to this country in 1790 from France, although they had originated in China and Korea. Sabine's appetite had been whetted by forty or so Chinese paintings sent to the Society by John Reeves. Evidently Sabine's enthusiasm was infectious, for despite a deficit of £1200 (an enormous sum in those days), the Society decided to send out to China a young gardener in their employ, John Damper Parks, with instructions "to collect among other specimens, as many good varieties of Chrysanthemum as possible."

Parks set out in 1823, met Reeves and was full of praise for the kindness and advice the experienced plantsman offered. In 1824 he returned with sixteen new varieties of chrysanthemum, which must have pleased Sabine mightily, the first aspidistra to be seen in Europe, the yellow form of the Banksian Rose, *R. banksiae lutea* and most importantly for the future development of roses, a yellow form of the Tea Rose which was given the name 'Parks' Yellow Tea-scented China'. John Lindley, then the Assistant Secretary of the Society's garden, with a delightful disregard of mixing the two Classical languages, assigned it the botanical name *R. odorata ochroleuca*. There is not much doubt that Lindley was prompted to discard the Latin *flavescens*, meaning "yellow" in favour of the Greek word meaning "yellowish-white" as being closer to the colour of the blooms.

'Parks' Yellow' was sent by Lindley to Eugène Hardy, Keeper of the Luxembourg Gardens in Paris in 1825 and it quickly became a very popular pot plant. Thomas Rivers records seeing hundreds of plants in the Paris markets "gaily wrapped in coloured paper so that the spending of a franc on such a pretty object is hard to resist". According to Hurst, no living material has been available since 1882. Recent searches, alas, confirm his statement. (It may, of course, still exist in China but that possibility has not been explored.)

Development

The earliest surviving Tea traced so far is 'Mme Roussel', sent out by Desprez about 1830, but the one which firmly established the reputation of the new class was 'Adam', sent out three years later by a nurseryman of the same name of Rheims. As far as is known, it was his sole contribution and it remained a firm favourite throughout the nineteenth century, being relatively hardy. Growth is rather short but it is quite vigorous and produces large, cupped blooms opening flat with a multitude of petals in fawn with coppery salmon in the centre. The description in Shepherd (op. cit.) and evidently copied by the compilers of *Modern Roses* 7, the international checklist of roses, does not accord with the cultivar we have under this name. In the American works it is stated to be semi-double. Our plants came from two widely separate sources and fit most of the contemporary descriptions

R. C. Balfour (left) presenting a special copy of *The Rose Annual* to Dr R. C. Allen, retiring President of the World Federation of Rose Societies, 1971–74 and President, American Rose Society. Seated, facing camera: *left*: Fred Edmunds, Vice-President, A.R.S.: *centre*: Mrs Edmunds: *right*: Mrs Allen

'Bobbie James', a vigorous, creamy white climber, with excellent foliage (*see page* 53)

we have been able to find by English, French and German writers. There is also a further clue to their authenticity which will be mentioned later in another context.

If 'Adam' laid the foundations, the next in chronological order took the rose world by storm. 'Safrano' (1839) as its name suggests brought an entirely new colour to roses, for the extra-long buds are a deep saffron shot with red on the guard petals. It is at this stage they are at their most attractive. On opening, they fade to buff and the deep outer cup displays at the centre an irregular arrangement of shorter petals. Some writers claim that 'Safrano' was the result of the first effort at controlled hybridization but there is no supporting evidence. It would seem, however, that it is closely related to both 'Hume's Blush' and 'Parks' Yellow'. With its long, red-brown stems, sparse foliage and thorns and high bloom yield plus a sweet scent, 'Safrano' had all the components of an ideal florists' rose—the nodding bloom head could be forgiven. On the French Riviera it was grown in large plantations expressly for the winter trade, thousands of blooms being sent to Paris and even London prior to the First World War. Here again, we have one of the mysteries of the rose. English rosarians resident on the French Riviera at the turn of the century stated that 'Safrano' grew almost wild. Today, it has proved extremely difficult to find. From the breeder's viewpoint, it is one of the most important roses ever raised, for it was not only responsible for many later Teas but it linked that class to the Hybrid Perpetuals to form the Hybrid Teas. If this was not enough, it was a contributor to the group we now know as repeat-flowering climbers. There has also been the suggestion put forward by more than one authority that it was one of the parents of the famous 'Gloire de Dijon' which in turn was the basis of another group of climbers known as Dijon Teas. Few other roses can lay claim to such versatility. It seems incredible that the world had to be scoured to find it.

In 1841, an Exeter firm of nurserymen introduced a Tea which is distinguished on several counts. It was raised by Mr Foster, an amateur rosarian of Devonport who named it appropriately 'Devoniensis'. It thus became the first recorded Tea of English origin and later, the first Tea to produce a climbing mutation which occurred in 1858. It is best known in this form, the original dwarf having completely disappeared. The fat red buds open to flat, quartered blooms in creamy white with a hint of pink in the centre carrying an extra-sweet, penetrating fragrance akin to that of many Teas, although the foliage is not typical of the class. It requires a warm wall and time to establish; then it will give an excellent account of itself.

By strange coincidence, the next two important Teas are also white.

'Niphětos' (the name means "snow-like") of 1843 is best known in its later climbing form although Mr Derek Herincx has recently found the dwarf cultivar in East Germany. With its long, pointed buds and freedom of flower, 'Niphětos' was widely grown as a florists' cut-flower at a time when only white flowers were carried in bridal bouquets, a tradition which continues on the continent.

Although 'Niphětos' was also used for breeding, of even greater importance was 'Mme Bravy', sent out in 1846. This is an excellent grower, very free with its cupped cream blooms with pink overtones and a fragrance which has been likened to "expensive face-cream". In the days when honesty in the horticultural trade left much to be desired, unscrupulous nurserymen across the Channel found it financially expedient to cash-in on the high reputation of 'Mme Bravy' by re-introducing it at various intervals under no fewer than six names. English growers, caught by this deception, expressed their annoyance in the gardening press in no uncertain terms . . . and the annoying practice persists. To a lesser degree, the same happened to 'Duchesse de Brabant' (1857) which has three synonyms. The medium sized, self pink blooms of this variety form a perfect globe and have earned the soubriquet in Bermuda of "The Shell Rose". There is a strong, penetrating fragrance. Its tendency to sprawl leads to the supposition that it is directly descended from 'Hume's Blush'.

All the cultivars so far under notice fall into three types of flower form, the deep cupped shape with shorter, irregularly disposed centre petals, the flat quartered shape and the more regular imbricated rosette. Indeed, William Paul complained in *The Florist and Horticulturist* that the Teas had shown no improvement in this direction since the originals had arrived twenty-five years previously.

The hopes of Paul and all other rosarians were finally realized in a rose sent out in 1855 by a Parisian nurseryman, Marest, who named it 'Souvenir d'Elise Vardon'. It took the rose world by storm and rosarians, professional and amateur alike, heaped upon it all the superlatives in their vocabularies. Shirley Hibberd, horticultural journalist and first editor of *Amateur Gardening* called it "the finest of all the Teas"; "a most splendid rose" wrote William Paul; "perfect. A most superb variety" was the verdict of fellow-nurseryman John Cranston, while yet another great nurseryman, Thomas Rivers, added his praise: "Incomparable. Worthy of every care."

Forty years after its introduction, the Reverend A. Foster-Melliar, one of the leading amateur exhibitors of the late Victorian era, could still write: "It is getting quite an old rose now, but though new roses are issued every year by the scores, nothing has been raised to surpass or even equal it."

Looking at 'Souvenir d'Elise Vardon' to-day it is easy to understand the enthusiasm it engendered, for it displayed an entirely new basic form which revolutionized all ideas of floral perfection in roses. In it, the broad outer petals in deep cream gently reflex at the edges while the inner petals are held in a high scroll of light salmon and fawn. Coupled with the deep purple foliage and brown wood, it represents the epitome of all the grace and elegance for which the class is famous. It is not so free-flowering as many other Teas and there are longer gaps in its inflorescence. Growth can only be described as moderate and it is clearly at its finest under glass—hence Rivers' remark.

The helix form of bloom which came to us from "Souvenir d'Elise" (as it was often affectionately known) is frequently referred to as the "typical Tea shape", although in point of fact it occurs only in a minority of Teas raised after its introduction. Evidently the responsible gene or genes are highly recessive.

The fallacy of the "typical Tea shape" arose in all probability following the introduction in 1869 of 'Catherine Mermet', a beautiful bland pink with a sweet scent and the same desirable shape but of better habit and higher bloom yield than 'Souvenir d'Elise Vardon'. These combined qualities made 'Catherine Mermet' a favourite commercial forcing variety, especially in the United States where numerous sports occurred, notably 'Bridesmaid' (1893) and 'The Bride' (1883) a pure white. Their names indicate the uses to which they were frequently put. 'Bridesmaid' remains untraced, but the other two are a delightful pair of "no problems" roses which are among the most popular of the Teas so far re-introduced.

Whether the deserved success of 'Catherine Mermet' prompted more nurserymen to try their hand at raising Teas is difficult to say, but the number of new seedlings jumped from 64 in the period 1861–1870 to 158 in the next decade and then to 262 in 1881–1890, reaching a peak of 402 from 1891 to the close of the nineteenth century. This could be said to have been the high water mark of the Teas when practically every hybridist in Europe and America joined in. Especially notable were the efforts of the Nabonnand family of Golfe Juan, on the French Riviera. During their fifty years of activity from 1873 until 1923, they were alone responsible for raising no fewer than 188 Tea Roses, many of them named by purchase for the royalty and nobility of Europe who wintered in the resorts along that coast.

One such habitué, Lord Brougham and Vaux, left an interesting and valuable account of the roses growing in the gardens of his château at Cannes just before the turn of this century. The interest arises not so much from the varieties as for their performance in that delectable climate which has exactly double the annual hours of sunshine as London. He was, for example, particularly proud of 'Marie Van Houtte' (1871) a beautiful lemon yellow with pale carmine edges which grew in seven years to a circumference of seventy feet. An accompanying photograph confirms that its stated size had not been exaggerated. The silky brick red 'Papa Gontier' (1878) grew to similar proportions with its laden branches supported by posts and chains, while the coppery-pink 'Général Schablikine' (1879) received his Lordship's accolade as his "desert island rose". A decade later, at Eversley in Hampshire, Rose Kingsley counted the latter cultivar among her "indispensables". It still ranks as one of the best Teas for all-round reliability.

To those unacquainted with the Teas, it often comes as a surprise to learn that there were any in shades of red. It is true that the number was not large—possibly eighty out of the 1400 recorded—and nearly all of them raised after 1874 when controlled hybridization began to be practised. It will be recalled that the two foundation Teas were pink and yellow. All their true descendants were consequently in these colours, or combinations of them, and in white. In order to obtain red Teas, hybridists had to look to the closely related Chinas. An old cultivar, not at all well known in England named 'Sanguine' (1835) was apparently the main source for most of the coppery tinted and bright reds. Subsequent crossing back of these seedlings to the crimson Chinas produced deep carmine, crimsons and a few maroons. It is of interest to note that the breeding of red was mainly confined to continental hybridists. Few Teas in this colour range were raised in this country or the United States.

Having arrived at a late stage in development of the Teas, there is a fair sprinkling of survivors and judging by the valuable compilation by the Rose Section of the French National Society of Horticulture (1912), we still have the best of them. 'Papa Gontier' and 'Général Schablikine' have already been mentioned. Others of high merit include 'Archiduc Joseph' (1892), a particularly beautiful coloration and perfect rosette form, the richly scented carmine 'Monsieur Tillier' which so entranced Rose Kingsley at the Paris Exhibition of 1900, and 'Freiherr von Marschall' (1903) which comes close to scarlet. Deep crimson is represented by 'Souvenir de Thérèse Levet' (1886) and 'Princesse de Sagan' (1887) which for many years did good service as a bedder at Kew. For depth of colour, pride of place is held by 'Francis Dubreuil' (1894), a deep velvety maroon with good fragrance, the darkest Tea ever raised.

Further crossings of the Teas and Chinas at the latter end of last century and the early years of this produced two final lines of development. Those seedlings showing closer affinity to the Chinas were termed "China-Teas", although the classification was never officially recognized, while the second group were called "decorative Teas", meaning that they were not suitable for exhibition purposes. Less full petalled than the earlier Teas, and with longer, more elegant buds than the Chinas, they were the perfect buttonhole roses at a time when this delightful custom was widespread. Although many of them such as 'Dr Grill' were of French origin, several of the best known came from Alex. Dickson of Newtownards. They include 'Miss Alice de Rothschild' (1911), a pale lemon, and 'Lady Plymouth' (1914) in buff with a yolk-yellow centre, and one of the most popular white Teas of its time, 'Molly Sharman-Crawford' (1908) with a hint of green in its make-up.

Exhibition-type Teas continued to be raised, and for this reason, they tended to remain in commerce after the decorative types had been discarded. Notable among the survivors are the famous 'Maman Cochet' in a colour combination not repeated until the arrival of 'Kordes' Perfekta' more than sixty years later, 'Mme. Jules Gravereaux' sent out as a Climbing Tea but more likely to remain a large bush in our climate, and 'Alexander Hill Gray', sometimes called 'Yellow Cochet', and honouring the Scottish laird who sold up his estates north of the border and moved to Bath for the sole purpose of growing Teas in the milder climate, although Hill Gray himself admitted his favourite was 'Mrs Foley Hobbs', raised in 1910 by a famous amateur hybridist, Dr J. Campbell Hall. 'Mrs Foley Hobbs' has endured in at least one nurseryman's list right down to the present and is an excellent representative of the class.

The days of the Teas were, however, numbered. Whereas in 1900, Teas still ran second to the Hybrid Perpetuals with the Hybrid Teas trailing a long way behind, by the outbreak of the First World War the situation had changed dramatically. By that time, the Hybrid Teas outnumbered the combined total of the two older classes from which they had been derived by more than two-to-one. The last Tea to be awarded a RNRS Gold Medal was Dr Campbell Hall's 'Muriel Wilson' in 1921. When Dr Hall died ten years later, it would have been difficult to buy more than three dozen varieties of Teas in this country. A few continental firms, such as Ketten Brothers of Luxembourg, offered rather more to anyone willing to go to the expense of importing them. Evidently few did so. Support for the Tea and Noisette classes at the RNRS Shows dwindled and it is now exactly forty years since the Tea trophies were last offered for competition.

Downfall

A number of adverse factors contributed to the eclipse and eventual disappearance of the Teas from British gardens. Being derived from roses of semi-tropical origin, they possess no natural dormancy factor to assist their survival in colder climates and are easily excited into growth when temperature rises above 50° F. While this characteristic made them so attractive for winter forcing, in the open a mild winter spell followed by severe frost could have fatal results unless precautions were taken. This usually meant earthing up the crowns or drawing bracken fronds or long straw round the heads of half-standards, a form of cultivation particularly favoured for the Teas. It must also be recalled that winters in Britain tended on average to be much colder in the period 1840–1940 while summers were hotter than we now enjoy.

The Teas also suffered the disadvantage of a weak pedicel causing the blooms to become pendent on opening. This character inherited from the two ancestral species proved so dominant that it occurs in a majority of Teas and was only eliminated by out-crossing to the Hybrid Perpetuals. To-day, the nodding blooms have a certain period charm, enhanced by the delicate pastel shades devoid of any gaudiness. In this context, like so many of the lighter coloured cultivars in other classes, many Teas are susceptible to rain damage. It has, however, been found that there are equally as many which are rain resistant to an unexpectedly high degree.

The rest of the causes for the fall from favour were man-made. Like the Chinas, Tea-scented roses form relatively small, twiggy maiden plants compared with the Hybrid Perpetuals and Hybrid Teas and the uninitiated recipient would assume that the nurseryman had sent second quality plants and complain accordingly. To overcome this situation, Victorian rose nurserymen resorted to the Manetti under-stock, a hybrid of indeterminate parentage but usually classed with the Noisettes, which had occurred in 1824 at the Botanic Garden in Monza, Italy where Signor Manetti was the curator. While this does produce larger first-year plants than those on Canina rootstocks, and these are satisfactory if they remain *in situ*, the scions do not grow steadily when transplanted and there is a strong tendency to die-back. Mr Derek Herincx has recently proved this to be the case experimentally. As a result, the Teas gained an undeserved reputation for being "difficult".

Many of the rose books written in Victorian times were by amateur rosarians who were keen, and in one case, fanatical exhibitors. They taught that the best roses could only be obtained by high feeding and low pruning.

'ADAM' (Tea) (see page 40)

'SOUVENIR D'ELISE VARDON' (Tea) (see page 42)

'MONSIEUR TILLIER' (Tea) *(see page 44)*

'CLIMBING DEVONIENSIS' (clg. Tea) *(see page 41)*

(Other colour plates of Tea-scented roses appear facing pp. 54, 100 and 101)

Only a few voices were raised in dissent. Notable among them was William Robinson (1837–1935) who preached "natural gardening". He proved in his garden at Gravetye, Sussex, as Lord Brougham had done at Cannes, that the Teas and Chinas are better when left alone. By the time ideas had been revised. the Teas had already been consigned to the *limbus patrum* of roses.

Revival

A few Teas, such as 'Lady Hillingdon' (1910) and 'Mrs Foley Hobbs' hung on in one or two nurserymen's lists in the post-1945 period. During the 1950s, Sunningdale Nurseries briefly re-introduced a few more. In the mid-1960s, however, a series of events brought about a change.

In his book, *Climbing Roses Old and New* (1965) Graham Thomas took the opportunity to describe the virtues of the Tea cultivars which had passed through his hands at Sunningdale and urged, as others had previously done, that someone with adequate facilities should collect together all the worth-while Teas that could be found before indifference and neglect rendered the class totally extinct.

About the same time, a number of articles, some in reminiscent vein and others by rosarians overseas who still grew Tea Roses, appeared in *The Rose*. These literary excursions prompted readers to enquire through the maga-zine's tracing service into the possibility of obtaining some of the once-famous varieties that had been mentioned. A few, such as 'Marie Van Houtte' came to light, but before the search could be completed the maga-zine had to cease publication. As its last editor, I was approached to continue the quest in a private capacity. This was to have much wider repercussions than were foreseen.

The search embraced many other commercially obsolete cultivars in addi-tion to Tea Roses, but it was the trail of the Teas that produced the most pleasant surprises. The first to be successfully traced, 'Catherine Mermet', 'Grace Darling' (requested by a descendant of the Northumberland heroine) and 'Général Schablikine' by happy coincidence proved to be three of the best—just as the Victorian writers had said—and appetites were whetted for more. Fortunately, the supply kept up with the demand, and the generosity of rosarians who still grew Teas, or knew where they could be obtained, was unbounded. It is perhaps invidious to single out any who contributed, but a special acknowledgment is due to Mrs Elizabeth Ball, of Bermuda, who not only supplied budwood from the roses she had described so delightfully in her articles but obtained others from fellow members of the Bermuda Rose Society. Herr Vonholdt, curator of the great collection at Sangerhausen in

East Germany, showed equal generosity which I was able to reciprocate. Mr Derek Herincx of Teddington added his enthusiasm to the search and collected many more rarities, some so little known that they are not recorded as ever having been previously introduced in this country.

Almost a revelation was the number of rosarians in this country who had been quietly nurturing Tea Roses over the years. Most of the Sunningdale collection was reassembled through the kindness of two dedicated rosarians, Mrs Judith Ross of Chorleywood and Mrs Helen Josling of Bexleyheath, and the foresight of another enthusiast, the late Mr A. F. Callick of Bexley, in preserving what were probably the last plants of at least three cultivars, deserves to be remembered.

Identification has often posed problems since some cultivars have arrived either un-named or clearly mis-named. One of the characteristics of the Teas is the strong influence of climatic conditions upon bloom colour. Those from under glass invariably come lighter than open ground plants of the same sort, while autumn blooms frequently show tints not observable earlier in the season. Descriptions in old books and catalogues consequently often lack agreement in this respect. Coloured engravings where they exist help in some cases but confuse in others. Even the best of modern colour photographic processes are presented with a very severe test to reproduce the subtleties of colour variation in some cultivars. Occasionally, however, a chance remark by a writer about a peculiarity of habit or bloom formation provides the vital clue to put the identity beyond all reasonable doubt. It is, after all, important in attempting to re-establish a class of roses which has fallen into obscurity to ensure as far as possible that the nomenclature is accurate. Although the number of unknowns is diminishing, there are still a few which cannot be released because of uncertainty of identity. The plodding, patient work of detection will continue until the question marks are removed.

Assessment

It is too early to draw any positive conclusions about the Teas, but a number of cultivars have been grown in sufficient quantity over several seasons in various parts of the country to enable a few general observations to be made.

Constitutionally, the Teas and many of their relatives, the Noisettes, had a reputation for being tender. While there is not much doubt that this was true in many cases, it seems probable on present evidence that the eighty or so cultivars assembled have survived because they were hardier than the rest. The last four winters have been relatively mild, so the Teas have not been put to a severe test. There is, nevertheless, a documentary and circumstantial evidence on which to rest a case.

In the *Rose Annual* for 1918, there appears a symposium by five amateurs and five professionals on the effects of the winter of 1916–1917, described by several of the contributors as one of the most severe in living memory. All reported that their Teas suffered no worse than any of the Hybrid Teas and Hybrid Perpetuals, and were agreeably surprised that this should be so, especially as war-time labour shortages had prevented the normal practice of mounding-up from being carried out. Also significant is the fact that several of the Teas which were located in this country were reportedly very old open-ground plants, mostly on their own roots, which had been established 40 years and more. It follows that they, too, must have survived the severe winters of 1939–1940, 1946–47 and the "deep freeze" of 1962–1963.

One very good reason which may be advanced for their survival is their ability as a class to withstand the debilitating fungal infections, mildew, black spot and rust. While it cannot be said that they are entirely immune, their resistance to these infections as a class is considerably higher than the Hybrid Teas and Floribundas. Only one variety, 'Adam', has shown any real susceptibility to mildew—a factor which helped to confirm its identity! These observations are supported by reports from rosarians now growing Teas in various parts of the country who have been kind enough to keep me posted.

As to their cultivation, it is an axiom of rose-growing that good drainage is essential for success; for the Teas it is vital. Naturally well drained gravelly soils or light loam resting on a gravel sub-soil suits them best. Heavy clay is an unsuitable medium and the texture must be improved as advised in most manuals on rose-growing before venturing into their culture. Since they are such early risers, the most sheltered situation, preferably with a southerly aspect, should be chosen.

They have also shown themselves to be ideal pot subjects for growing under glass, a mode of culture which can be recommended where it is not possible to plant them out in a greenhouse border. Experience had proved that 8-inch or 9-inch clay pots are preferable to plastic ones and alkathene shrub tubs are best avoided, even when the inadequate drainage holes are supplemented. A good 2-inch layer of crocks covered with coarse sedge peat will provide the necessary drainage. John Innes No. 3 or other similar ready-mixed compost is the most convenient medium, but if these are used, it is advisable to add 14 lbs of John Innes Coarse Grit (not sand) and about 4 lbs of granulated peat to each 56 lb bag of compost. It is also a good idea to add two handfuls of granulated charcoal to each pot of compost. Provided the top inch of soil (which tends to become sour) is removed and replaced with fresh compost each spring, the roses will grow quite happily for up to five years before repotting. Artificial heat is not necessary unless really early blooms are required. Liquid feeding with a compound with high potash content is recommended; preparations designed for tomatoes have been found to be better than those for roses.

Propagation

The range of rootstocks available to the rose-grower has widened considerably since Victorian times, when only *R. canina*, commonly known as "briar", and Manetti were employed. The opportunity has, therefore, been taken to compare the performance of the Teas on a number of rootstocks, including Pfander's, Inermis and Pollmeriana, all of which are selected strains of *R. canina*, Laxa (*R. coriifolia froebelii*) and *R. multiflora*, as well as the two original types. Good results have been obtained with Pfander's; *R. multiflora* is very promising. The other understocks have given variable quality plants, with some cultivars doing better than others worked on the same type of stock. Mr Herincx's test with Manetti had already been mentioned.

In nearly all the Tea-scented roses, the axillary leaf buds have a strong tendency to break and form subsidiary shoots even before the first terminal flower bud has opened. While this precocity is to be welcomed by the gardener, it is a nuisance to the propagator seeking good dormant eyes for budding. Indeed, Foster-Melliar remarked that it was sometimes necessary to sacrifice a whole plant in order to procure sufficient budding material. It also means that the reinvigoration of a debilitated cultivar by careful bud-selection is a slow process. Similarly, the building up of sufficient stock of some cultivars in high demand often means a waiting list.

As if to compensate for this precociousness, it has been found that many of the Teas root quite easily from cuttings and one or two of the "finds" were received in this form and have grown on quite satisfactorily. Some Victorian writers recommended that Teas should be grown in this form rather than as budded plants. Whether this was because Tea Roses worked on Manetti proved so disappointing is hard to say, but many of the larger nursery firms used to offer a selection of Teas on their own roots at commensurately higher prices, presumably to meet this demand. It would be quite uneconomic to do so now.

Scent

The name of the class derives from the resemblance of the fragrance of the two foundation members to the aromatic blends of China teas which were drunk by the higher social orders in Regency times and were so expensive that they were kept away from the "lower orders" in locked caddies. While this fragrance is present in many of their derivatives, it is by no means as widely found as might be supposed. Reference has already been made to the scent of 'Mme. Bravy', an early hybrid. 'Duchesse de Brabant', another early origination, carries a strong, spicy fragrance with "peppery" overtones. This may have been the reason why it was the favourite rose of President "Teddy" Roosevelt, for there are others with better claims to form and lasting qualities. Among later introductions, 'Monsieur Tillier' has a deep damask-like fragrance which is also found in some of the other deep reds and 'Mrs Herbert Hawksworth' (1912) is perfumed like verbena. It must also be said that there are Teas with little or no scent, even to those with a highly developed sense of smell. It is more than probable that it was these, rather than the Hybrid Perpetuals as has been so often claimed, which transmitted scentlessness to many of their Hybrid Tea descendants.

The Future

From the innocent beginnings, some eighty or so Tea cultivars have been so far jointly assembled by Mr Herincx and myself. It is possible that some two dozen more may still be in existence, including two which were found, then tragically lost through an error of cultivation.

An old gardener once said that "there is no such thing as a bad rose but some are better than others." Teas are slow to show their true merits and it would be wrong to pass early judgment upon some of the newcomers. Objective assessment indicates that some of the more famous varieties have lived up to their reputations but others have not. At the same time, some which were little known in this country even during the high tide of popularity of the class have shown themselves to be very good indeed in every respect. It remains to be seen whether the Tea Rose enthusiasts can be persuaded to accept the growers' judgment! Whether it will be possible to keep the collection together depends upon time and space, both of which are limited. A wide distribution in good and capable hands should, however, ensure that they will not be lost again.

Acknowledgments. In addition to those mentioned in the text, special thanks are due to Mr G. W. Dendy of Merrist Wood College, Worplesdon, without whose help the project would not have been possible and to Mr John Anton who has provided a complete photographic record of the collection.

References. Some 150 books, periodicals and catalogues have been consulted. The main sources are as follows:

On origins:

Fletcher, Dr H. R., *The Story of the Royal Horticultural Society* (1969)
Hurst, Dr C. C., "The Origin of our Garden Roses" (Journal of the R.H.S., Vol. LXVI, No. 7, 1941)
Paul, William, *The Rose Garden* (1st edn., 1848)
Redouté, P. J., *Les Roses* (1835 edn.)
Rivers, Thomas, *Rose-Amateur's Guide* (3rd edn., 1843)
Robinson, Ed. E., "A Short History of the Tea Rose" (*The Rose*, Vol. 17, No. 3, 1969)
Shepherd, Roy E., *History of the Rose* (1954)
Vonholdt, Hans (Ed.), *Das Rosarium Sangerhausen* (1966)
Willson, E. J., *The Vineyard Nursery Hammersmith* (1961)

On development:

Brougham and Vaux, Lord, *Roses at Château Eléonore, Cannes* (1898)
Cochet, P. C. M. (Pub.), *Journal des Roses* (1877–1914)
Cranston, John, *Cultural directions for the Rose* (1875)
Darlington, Hayward R., "A study of form in the Rose" (*Rose Annual*, 1918)
Easlea, Walter, "Decorative Teas and China-Teas" (*Rose Annual*, 1919)
Ellwanger, H. B. *The Rose* (1892 edn.)
Foster-Melliar, Rev. A., *The Book of the Rose* (1894 edn.)
Girdlestone, T. W., "The Rose Garden" (article in Robinson: *The English Flower Garden* 1899 edn.)
Hariot, Paul, *Le Livre d'Or des Roses* (1903)
Hibberd, Shirley, *The Amateur's Rose Book* (1874)
Kingsley, Rose G., *Roses and Rose Growing* (1908)
Morris, C. H. R., "King of Teas" (*The Rose*, Vol. 14, No. 3, 1966)
Paul, William *The Rose Garden* (7th edn., 1886, 10th edn., 1903)
    Contributions to Horticultural Literature 1843–1892
Paul A. and Son, Paul, Wm. & Son, *Catalogue of Roses 1843–1922*
Piper, Archibald, "Tea Roses" (article in Thompson: *The Gardener's Assistant*, 1904 edn.)
Rivers, Thomas, *Rose-Amateur's Guide* (10th edn., 1872)
Robinson, Ed. E., "A Checklist of Red Tea Roses" (*The Rose*, Vol. 13, No. 1, 1964)

Societé Nationale d' Horticulture de France, *Les Plus Belles Roses* (1912)
Young, Norman, *The Complete Rosarian* (1971)

On downfall:

Gilmour, Duncan, *Rose Growing* (1888)
Robinson, William, *The English Flower Garden* (1926 edn.)

On revival:

Ball, Elizabeth, "Roses in Bermuda" (*The Rose*, Vol. 14, No. 1, 1965)
    "Treasure House of Roses" (*The Rose*, Vol. 15, No. 1, 1966)
Foley Hobbs R. *et al.*, "Symposium on the effects of the Winter of 1916–17
    on Roses" (*Rose Annual* 1918)
Jäger, August, *Rosenlexikon* (1961)
McFarland, J. H., *Modern Roses 7* (1969)
Steen, Nancy, *The Charm of Old Roses* (1967)
Thomas, Graham S., *Climbing Roses Old and New* (1965)
Vonholdt, H. and Täckelburg, Paul, *Rosenverzeichnis des Rosariums
    Sangerhausen* (Auflage 2, 1971)

On Planting a Garden of Roses

GRAHAM THOMAS, O.B.E., V.M.H.
(Authority on the "Old" roses and Gardens Consultant to The National Trust)

The rose 'Bobbie James' casts wafts of fragrance over the garden, from its
multitude of creamy white blooms at midsummer. I never see it but my mind
goes back to a glorious sunny afternoon at St Nicholas, Richmond, Yorkshire, where the Honourable Robert James developed a beautiful garden. "It
is not a rose garden," he told me; "it is at the moment a garden of roses, a few
weeks ago you might have called it a garden of irises, or of daffodils, and a
few weeks hence it will be a garden of fuchsias." This sums up my ideas

perfectly. I like roses best when they are mixed with other things, a continuing feast of varying beauty, and not too much of anything at one time.

We all like plenty of our favourite plants; irises have their devotees, likewise roses, day lilies, dahlias and dwarf conifers, but it is doubtful whether planting them to excess started before Victorian times. During the nineteenth century, nurserymen were busy producing hundreds of new varieties of popular plants and it is this fact that has given us the opportunity of making gardens devoted to one genus. Not satisfied with a few here and there, we mass our favourites together, often into indigestible blocks. This is all very well, in a way, if one has a really large garden, so that one can enjoy the beauty of different genera to the full in separate areas, and avoid those areas when they are not in flower. This is why we have rose gardens. Whether it is a tiny garden containing only 24 rose plants, or a large one with 2,400 plants, the idea has caught on far more with roses than with other genera. But do not roses look better when grown with other plants?

Here we come to a division. There are those keen rosarians who desire roses to the exclusion of other flowers; they want perfection of growth and bloom for shows, and they do not want to be impeded by other plants when tending their roses, nor to feel the ground is being robbed of goodness by plants other than roses. Theirs is a monoculture. They place the wellbeing of their roses before the continuing beauty of their garden; in reality they like the plant as an individual more than the effect it creates in the larger picture.

Let us assess the rose dispassionately. Grown on their own, shrub roses give the most varied range of attractions: flower, fragrance, foliage, sometimes autumn colour and heps, and this is usually coupled with graceful spraying growth, small or large. The modern bedding roses are mostly stiff upright plants providing a wealth of bloom over a long period and most are fragrant; they are mainly providers of flower colour. Whatever type of rose we grow they are in themselves unsatisfactory as a monoculture since they are unattractive for six or more months of the year, and whatever their floral attractions I am convinced that half of their universal popularity is due to their fragrance. It was mainly their fragrance that made them favoured in early civilizations. There is only one other monoculture that rivals them, that of rhododendrons and azaleas; these are far more *satisfying as shrubs*, since they are more shapely and many are evergreen. Each kind has a short flowering season, but together they all but span the year. Hydrangeas are good for late summer and autumn, but unsatisfactory at other times and the same sort of thing may be said of other big genera.

For all these reasons, and others besides, I prefer my roses to be grown with

'ARCHIDUC JOSEPH' (Tea) (see page 44)

'MME BRAVY' (Tea) (see page 42)

Shrub rose 'Buff Beauty' and 'Frensham' (flori.) with Cardoons and Helianthemum
Shrub rose 'Nevada' with *Bergenia cordifolia* 'Purpurea', Golden Tree Ivy and *Berberis thunbergii* 'Atropurpurea Nana'

other plants around them, and for the rest of this article I want to look into the possibilities of complementary planting in order to make up for the rose's deficiencies. I only intend to write about permanent planting; bedding plants and other forms of "in and out" gardening are things that few of us make time for these days.

Let us first of all take the formal rose garden, often a design of beds in lawn or paving. What could be duller in winter? Assuming that all pruning can be completed by 15 January, is there any reason why the beds should not for the ensuing two or three months provide a carpet of colour from spring bulbs? A lovely and long-lasting mixture is the lilac and blue provided by *Crocus tomasinianus* with *Scilla bifolia* and *Chionodoxa lucilleae*. Another bed might have darker colours: *Crocus tomasinianus* 'Taplow Ruby' or 'Whitewell Purple' with *Chionodoxa sardensis*. Another, pink Chionodoxas with white Scillas, and so on. A further variation would be *Anemone apennina* and *blanda* in their various colours, preceded by aconites and snowdrops. *Scilla tubergeniana*, crocuses of all colours and miniature daffodils also come to mind. The range is great and the mixtures of colours are almost endless. Any cultivation for the roses must be done in autumn, which is a good time to provide a mulch, and further fertilizers can be applied to the roses after the bulbs have died down. If roses die and new ones have to be planted, the bulbs do not mind if they get turned over in the act; they will right themselves within a year.

I never can understand why rose beds of this sort are stocked to their edges with the 3–4 ft or even taller plants, which is the height that many modern roses normally achieve. Why should not a short rose be planted around them, such as 'Marlena', 'Little White Pet' or 'Cri-Cri'? And outside these I would have what may be termed large rock plants which will provide spring colour after the bulbs are over. I have in mind such things as aubrietas, *Alyssum saxatile*, alpine phloxes, followed by violas, achilleas, thrift and dianthus. The alyssum is often frowned upon for being "common-or-garden", but apart from its flowers (most appealing to me in its 'Citrinum' form) it contributes nobly, like the pinks, with grey foliage until autumn. I like silvery and grey foliage particularly with red and pink roses; the vivid blue flower spikes and silver foliage of *Veronica incana* assort well with yellow roses. Flame and coppery roses can take some coppery-purple foliage such as *Heuchera americana*, *Sedum maximum* 'Atropurpureum', or *Viola labradorica* and the golden marjoram, *Origanum vulgare* 'Aureum'. Vivid greenery from *Armeria maritima* 'Alba' will give tone to yellow roses. There are a dwarf white lavender, dwarf cotton lavender and dwarf grey hebes which will add a new foil for some of the subdued but rich toned roses that are Mr Le Grice's speciality. Flowers from the complementary planting are not really needed after June; foliage, soft and hummocky, is the requirement.

The above is a method of growing conventional beds of roses with subsidiary planting. I much prefer to see the roses distributed round the garden in the mixed borders, when the same sort of underplanting can be practised. But there is one kind of mixed planting I try to avoid, and that is the use of modern bedding roses and shrub roses in the same area. Taking shrub roses to mean the species, the old-fashioned, and the modern hybrid shrub roses, very few mix well with floribundas and hybrid teas. It is true that most species flower rather before the bedding roses and that some of the newer hybrid shrubs assort reasonably well with them, but there it stops. The colours of the old-fashioned and the Rugosa roses are shouted down by modern colours, while their quality and shape make the moderns look blowzy and coarse. It is true that some modern shrub roses have a second season of flowering, but it does not compare with the floribundas; on the other hand the quantity of bloom in June of a shrub rose will disgrace a hybrid tea. When Mr Mattock gives us at the shows one of those lovely glimpses of autumn, with great sprays of heps behind his floribundas, we must remember that out of doors they are less thickly displayed and the heps assort better with other autumn treats than with the last of summer's flowers. When not in flower, very few shrub roses add much to the display of foliage; there are a few, like R. rubrifolia, which are exceptions. And this brings me to what is, after the bare winter effect, the rose's weakest point. As a general rule its foliage is poor. I know I have in these pages extolled certain roses for their foliage, but only in comparison with other kinds. Apart from these few exceptions—the corrugated greenery of R. rugosa is one, the rich coppery-purple colour of some moderns is another—they simply do not measure up to the quality and variety of foliage which goes to make a beautiful garden.

In those intervals when a bed of modern roses is out of flower, can one be satisfied with the foliage? Like that of the shrub roses it is small and divided; all of them create a fussy effect of small leaves. While the arching beauty of growth of the shrubs is a redeeming feature, their small leaves and often small flowers both create a spotty effect. They all need the quietening effect of massed foliage, preferably broad and overlapping; that is what I tried to stress in an earlier paragraph about the edging to beds.

With shrub roses, so very suitable for grouping with other shrubs and plants, one can indulge considerable complementary planting. Groups of

Hybrid Musk 'Wilhelm' with huge clumps of silvery cardoons for instance; hummocks of lavender over which arches 'Cerise Bouquet'; 'Golden Wings' with *Geranium* 'Johnson's Blue;' or a hot combination of 'Scarlet Fire' with *Cornus alba* 'Spaethii'. Great bushes of 'Iceberg' sprawling over dark green bergenias, or cool glaucous hostas. Old-fashioned roses—the Gallicas, Mosses, Centifolias and Bourbons, and the Rugosas—their colour being on the blue side of pink and carmine, need a special fillip: clumps of silvery plants in the foreground with lots of white behind from *Philadelphus* 'Sybille' and the like. And the background can be green or copper or grey with the choice of shrubs. Here and there a group of ornamental grass will give a light effect. And of course the whole planting can be beautiful in early spring with small bulbs, followed by the foreground planting and augmented by planting clematises of the Viticella section to climb over some of the stronger shrub roses. These will add colour in August and are best cut down to one foot every January and so never get into a tangle. But they are also small-flowered and small-leafed so should only be used sparingly.

A most satisfying combined planting at Tintinhull, Somerset, a property of The National Trust, is achieved by modern red roses, golden cornus and coppery purple leaves of *Cotinus* and *Prunus*. This lasts from June until autumn, and has an underplanting of spring bulbs. The dark green of a clipped yew hedge is one of the best of backgrounds, as will be proved by a visit to Sissinghurst, another National Trust garden in Kent, where the older roses excel themselves.

My remarks for the use of climbing roses would be much the same. What enhances them more than anything are the large, quiet leaves of vines and *Aristolochia macrophylla*, the Dutchman's Pipe. Today's climbers (pillar roses) are comparatively short, but any climbing rose which achieves more than 6 ft in height is doubly valuable if its blooms nod. This note is one for the breeders!

No rose that grows stiffly upright is ideal for use as a climbing plant except when displayed on a wall. Pillars, arches and other supports gain most from a rose when it grows gracefully. But whatever height or size a rose may attain, however good its flowers or foliage may be, its general effect from the other side of the garden remains finicky or spotty. And so I recommend that the plants that are grown with them—the background, the foreground and the general mixture—should be of quiet, broad style in foliage and should preferably not compete with the flowers of the roses unless a particular colour scheme is desired.

The First of the Summer's Roses

SIR PETER MASEFIELD

(*Amateur rose grower*)

Roses in May are doubly welcome—first and of course, in themselves; secondly for the promise which they bring of six months, or more, of blooms ahead.

When roses first bloom, and in what order, has interested me for many years now and, for the past decade, I have kept a detailed record of the dates on which the first roses have come into flower in my somewhat sheltered garden in Surrey, on the southern side of the North Downs.

One of the many delightful features of the rose is its remarkable reliability —and punctuality. Out of some hundreds of varieties I have found that twelve can be relied upon always to flower in May and, for the most part, in the same order. With three exceptions their times of first blooms have varied relatively little with the years, from an earliest in 1974 to the latest in 1969 and 1970. Two years, 1966, and 1971, appear to come out as "average years" half-way between the extremes. In both the earliest and the latest years, the first blooms have appeared respectively six days ahead of, or six days after, the average.

Invariably the earliest roses to bloom belong to the so-called rose "species", all developed from predominantly yellow, single-flowered wild roses with a common China/Burma/Korea origin. For some reason, roses from the Far East tend to bloom earlier than those from the Middle East or the West.

Out of the two dozen earliest roses which I have recorded, yellows hold the field, followed by single pink roses and then crimson-reds.

Three points stand out from the ten-year records. First comes a list of those roses which can be relied upon to flower in May, whatever the year. Naturally it is not an exhaustive list but it is, I believe, fairly representative. Secondly, there is the normal order of first flowering of the early roses. And thirdly, one can sort out the successive dates upon which summer has first been heralded by the rose in this part of Britain.

Reliable May Roses

My list of twelve Reliable May Roses is set out, in order of flowering, at *Table* 1. It is headed by 'Canary Bird'—alleged to be *Rosa xanthina spontanea* but, I understand from Graham S. Thomas's writings, more likely to be *Rosa hugonis* × *Rosa xanthina*.

TABLE I   TWELVE RELIABLE MAY-FLOWERING ROSES

(In order of dates of first blooms. Ten year averages)

Rose variety or species	Ten year Average May	Earliest Bloom	Latest Bloom
		Dates of first bloom	
1. Canary Bird	10	26 April 1974	23 May 1969
2. *Rosa hugonis*	15	10 May 1974	22 May 1969
3. Frühlingsmorgen	17	6 May 1974	31 May 1968
4. *R. sericea pteracantha*	17	11 May 1966	24 May 1973
5. Climbing Golden Dawn	20	6 May 1974	29 May 1970
6. *R. cantabrigiensis*	21	14 May 1972	30 May 1968
7. *R. rugosa rubra*	22	11 May 1972	30 May 1970
8. Lawrence Johnston	23	13 May 1974	31 May 1965
9. Mme Gregoire Staechelin	25	18 May 1974	30 May 1970
10. Climbing Étoile de Hollande	27	20 May 1974	31 May 1965, 69–72
11. Lady Sylvia	27	23 May 1972 & 74	30 May 1965, 69, 70
12. *Rosa sericea omeiensis*	28	21 May 1974	31 May 1969 & 70

Whatever its proper designation this small, single yellow rose, with a delicious scent, flowers with remarkable reliability (except for one year's fall from grace, in 1969) some four or five days ahead of the almost equally reliable runner up, *Rosa hugonis*, "the Golden Rose of China", of the same Far Eastern genesis. Normally 'Canary Bird's' first blooms, in my garden, vary by only a few days on each side of 10 May—though 1974 took it exceptionally by surprise so that it came into bloom before the end of April.

The other ten roses on the RMR ("Reliable May Roses") list all normally came into flower during the next 18 days, although on several "late-year" occasions (especially in 1969 and 1970) the last three on the list have only just made it in May when other promising candidates dropped out into June.

Summer's Arrival

That leads us to the "rose-recorded indicator" of the varying dates of summer's arrival, year-by-year (*Table* 2).

An analysis shows that one can distinguish a sort of "wave cycle", or regular pattern, of early and late years during the past decade.

Starting with a latish year in 1965, when the mean flowering date of the twelve RMR varieties was 22 May, the pendulum swung to an "average year" (20 May) in 1966 and on to an early year (17 May) in 1967. After that it swung back again to three later years in 1968, 1969 and 1970 and then to another "average year" in 1971. The past three years have seen a further "wave" oscillation from an earlyish year (19 May) in 1972 to a late year (23 May) in 1973 and then to a very early year indeed (14 May) in 1974. So early was 1974 that I recorded my first rose ('Canary Bird', of course) on 26 April —my only April flowering on the books.

If statistical trends are anything to go by, then 1975 should be a moderately early year, 1976 about the average and 1977 late. But forecasting is hazardous when weather is an element.

Main Factors

And obviously the dates of the first flowering roses depend, to some extent at least, upon the weather during the first, formative, months of the year. For example, the 1960s loitered out in 1969 with the latest flowerings for a decade when the first roses did not appear in my garden (R. *hugonis* and R. *sericea pteracantha* this time) until 22 May and 'Canary Bird' on the following day; its latest by a week.

(*Continued on page* 61)

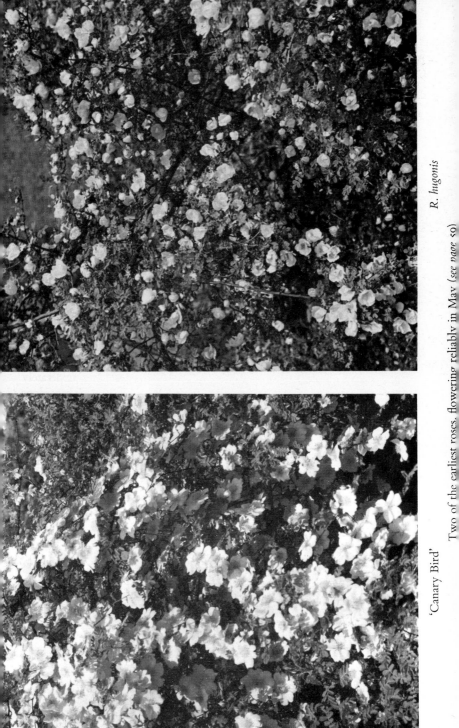

'Canary Bird'

R. hugonis

Two of the earliest roses, flowering reliably in May (see page 50)

'Else Poulsen' was a pioneer of a new race of roses (*see page* 66)

The late Svend Poulsen (*see page* 64)

TABLE 2 THE YEARS 1965-1974

Year by year measurements of average dates of first rose blooms
(Mean flowering dates of the twelve Reliable May Roses)

| | Year | Average date in May of first bloom | Measurement of year | | Earliest bloom | Latest bloom |
			Early, late or average	Days plus or minus		
1.	1965	22		+2	11	31
2.	1966	20	Average year	0	10	29
3.	1967	17	Early year	−3	9	29
4.	1968	24		+2	12	31
5.	1969	26	Latest year	+6	22	31
6.	1970	26	Latest year	+6	16	31
7.	1971	20	Average year	0	8	31
8.	1972	19		−1	5	31
9.	1973	23		+3	14	29
10.	1974	14	Earliest year	−6	26 April	23
	Ten year Average	21	Average year	0	10	29

YEARS IN ORDER OF FIRST FLOWERINGS

		Year	Average date in May of first bloom	
1.	Early	1974	14	Earliest year
2.		1967	17	
3.		1972	19	
4.	Average	1966	20	Average year
5.		1971	20	Average year
6.	Late	1965	22	
7.		1973	23	
8.		1968	24	
9.		1970	26	
10.		1969	26	Latest year

Such a laggard performance was presumably because of the cold north-east winds which continued to blow right through April and May, and through my roses as well—accompanied by a dreary dearth of sunshine. In fact, 18 May 1969 was the coldest May day for 24 years, and apart from one odd day, 10 May (when I recorded 26° C (78° F) at noon), the weather in 1969 did not begin to warm up in Surrey until 20 May. Hence the late year for first blooms.

By contrast, May 1967 was the wettest May for 194 years. But there were bursts of warm sunshine in between showers, and few cold winds. As a result 1967 was the second earliest year for roses in this part of the country—beaten only (and handsomely) by the warm, sunny, April and May of 1974 with just sufficient rain to help growth after the mildest winter for many years. The roses shot out, under the impression that summer had arrived about two weeks early.

Clearly there are also a number of other factors which influence the date of first flowerings. One of them is the time, and the severity, of pruning.

Gordon Edwards, in his delightful *Roses for Enjoyment* comments upon "the nearly constant pattern of 13 weeks" between date of pruning and first blooms. He adds that "of course that figure really relates to the growing season".

I normally aim to complete my pruning by mid-January so that this factor will not influence first flowerings. As an experiment, however, in 1967 I pruned 'Climbing Guinée' on 4 March—much later than usual. Its first blooms came on 3 June—precisely 13 weeks later.

There are other factors too. In my experience a rose on a south wall will flower earlier than a similar rose on a north wall, provided that both are equally watered. Assessment of the annual records seems to show also that the earliest roses require a combination of:

Not less than 13 light hours daily;
A period in which temperatures do not fall below 9° C (48° F);
Adequate sunshine; and
Sufficient water.

In Surrey, south of the Downs, all these add up to an average date of 10 May for the earliest rose and a mean date of 21 May for the dozen "RMRs".

What would be interesting to know is how such parameters compare in, say, the North of England and the North of Scotland?

But why do some roses flower so much earlier, or later than others? I don't know. For instance, the earliest flowering of the magnificent hybrid tea 'Super Star' has been 22 June in my garden—and that in 1974. In general it seems to be a July rose in the south.

A Second XI

Though I have listed just the twelve "Reliable May Roses" from my ten year records, I have come to expect some dozen other varieties also to flower normally in May except in the "late" years—such as 1969, 1970 and 1973. If 'Canary Bird' and *R. hugonis* are not in flower by 16 May then all these other "Second XI" roses will miss May and not flower until early June.

The dozen additional, and less reliable, May Roses, which sometimes lag into June, are as follows—with a record of the average dates of their first blooms during the past ten years. For them the spread of first flowerings is about four days on each side of the average, according to the year.

		Average date of first bloom
1.	'Old Blush China'	21 May
2.	'Frühlingsgold'	24 May
3.	'Ena Harkness'	26 May
4.	'Ramona'	27 May
5.	'Nevada'	27 May
6.	'Hunter'	28 May
7.	'Betty Uprichard'	28 May
8.	'Coralin'	29 May
9.	'Boule de Neige'	30 May
10.	'Conrad F. Meyer'	31 May
11.	'Roseraie de l'Haÿ'	31 May
12.	'Maigold'	31 May

Others which flower in May—but only in "early" years—include 'Albéric Barbier', 'Allen Chandler', the Cherokee Rose, 'Danse du Feu', 'Crimson Glory', 'Elegance', 'Gloire de Dijon', 'Madame Butterfly', 'Madame Edouard Herriot', 'Mischief' ,'Perle d'Or', 'Scharlachglut' ('Scarlet Fire') and 'Soldier Boy'. They started off in the RMR list—and gradually fell by the wayside.

As one can see, few of these "early flowerers" are modern hybrid teas and none of them is a floribunda. They come later.

By the end of May 'Canary Bird' is, usually, in its last flowering stages and looking a bit bedraggled. *R. hugonis* goes on, as a rule, until the end of the first week in June. Both 'Frühlingsmorgen' and 'Frühlingsgold' are, normally, in full bloom and a magnificent sight at the end of the month—together with the great, cousinly, bushes of *R. sericea pteracantha* and *R. sericea omeiensis*.

On a south-facing bank the deliciously scented 'Old Blush China' (perhaps, 'Parson's Pink China' before 1759) continues to flower from about 21 May right on into October. Most sweetly scented of all the early roses in my garden is 'Climbing Étoile de Hollande', in bloom in an average year from about 27 May until late June—and again (but then less scented) in August.

Of others, the glorious climbing 'Madame Gregoire Staechelin' and the debonair 'Lawrence Johnston' (together on a west wall) fade by the middle of June and are gone until next year.

By then the June roses have come in all their glory. The big break-through of opulent blooms comes in my garden usually during the first week in June, after which it is almost a full time job to record them.

But that is another story.

Welcome and delightful as are all the roses in June, none is more warmly welcomed than the first of each summer's roses; the roses in May.

Obituary

SVEND POULSEN

Svend Poulsen was described by the late "Nick" Nicholas of Jackson & Perkins as a dreamer. That he was. A rose breeder can consider himself lucky if one of his dreams comes true. "Uncle Svend", as he was known to the rose-breeding fraternity, lived to see his dream of a whole new race of roses become a fact.

In the harsh climate of Denmark few roses survived the winter in his young days. The H.T. rose, subject to wind and rain damage, was particularly unsuited to the region. So it was that he first of all married the hybrid wichuraiana to the dwarf polyantha to obtain 'Ellen Poulsen', in the style of the roses created at that time by Levavasseur and Turbat. She was the first of the Poulsen ladies whose names are part of rose lore. Uncle Svend would have claimed 'Else Poulsen' in 1924 as his greatest achievement. But who could forget 'Anne-Mette Poulsen' in her full glory, and 'Kirsten Poulsen', 'Karen Poulsen', 'Mrs. Inge Poulsen' and 'Poulsen's Yellow', to name but a few? They revolutionized the rose in their day, standing the worst of the weather, and were the forerunners of the floribunda race developed by Gene Boerner.

Svend Poulsen lived for his family. He delighted in his children and grandchildren. He and his wife Petra always had young people around them, and he remained young at heart to the very end.

Even when he handed over the rose breeding to his son, Niels, he continued to breed cherries and raspberries for his orchard surrounding the family home. On one of my last visits to him he was breeding lilies—still dreaming.

That is the picture I will always carry of him.

SAM McGREDY

(See photograph facing page 61)

THE FIRST OF THE SUMMER'S ROSES

TABLE 3   1965–1974: DATES OF FIRST BLOOMS OF TWELVE RELIABLE MAY ROSES

Rose variety	1965 1	1966 2	1967 3	1968 4	1969 5	1970 6	1971 7	1972 8	1973 9	1974 10	Ten year average May
1. Canary Bird	11	10	9	12	23	16	8	5	14	26 April	10
2. *Rosa hugonis*	14	11	10	17	22	20	11	16	16	10	15
3. Frühlingsmorgen	15	11	11	31	23	25	14	10	24	6	17
4. *R. sericea pteracantha*	16	11	12	16	22	20	13	20	24	18	17
5. Climbing Golden Dawn	17	11	11	26	27	29	28	23	24	6	20
6. *R. cantabrigiensis*	24	22	18	30	23	21	18	14	25	18	21
7. *R. rugosa rubra*	22	19	19	19	28	30	26	11	26	17	22
8. Lawrence Johnston	31	29	20	29	30	26	13	20	21	13	23
9. Mme Gregoire Staechelin	25	27	23	24	25	30	25	24	25	18	25
10. Climbing Étoile de Hollande	31	25	21	28	31	31	31	31	25	20	27
11. Lady Sylvia	30	29	27	26	30	30	25	23	28	23	27
12. *Rosa sericea omeiensis*	29	29	29	29	31	31	26	30	29	21	28
		average year			latest year	latest year	average year			earliest year	Average
Average date of first bloom	22	20	17	24	26	26	20	19	23	14	21 May
	1965	1966	1967	1968	1969	1970	1971	1972	1973	1974	

Colour Development in Floribunda Roses

E. B. LE GRICE
(*Rose nurseryman and breeder*)

It is hard to think of a time when the term "floribunda" as describing cluster roses for bedding purposes was not in common use. Yet this is not long in time and, to get to the beginning, one must include certain "polyantha" roses, such as 'Rödhätte', or hybrid polyanthas, such as 'Dainty Maid'. The name "floribunda" may be indefensible botanically, but it maintains its descriptive position because of its time honoured usefulness.

Like most roses of the nineteenth century the first of this class, in fact if not in name, followed the usual colours of red, pink and white and the later polyanthas from 1900 to 1925 followed the same course, although a number of fiery orange scarlet sports appeared after this from 'Orléans Rose' (Levavasseur, 1909), itself the most prolific provider of sports. As far as I know this fiery colour was never transmitted to any progeny.

When Dines Poulsen began breeding the beginning of a new line he used 'Mme Norbert Levavasseur', polyantha. I think we should remember the importance of Levavasseur & Sons in their contribution to the advance of the rose. It is just another emphasis on the fact that hybridizing is a joint effort. Poulsen chose this variety for its winter hardiness and length of flowering. He crossed 'Mme Norbert Levavasseur' with either red hybrid teas or 'Dorothy Perkins' rambler. Red and pink factors were equally distributed in the seedlings, and often a red parent gave good pink seedlings and the pink parents gave red. In 1912 he produced 'Rödhätte' ('Mme Norbert Levavasseur'×'Richmond') and with this seedling he had raised the first of the typical floribunda type. This cross, to be followed by very many of this type, was to give rise to the problem of near sterility, for these had chromosome counts of 21. Here we must leave Dines Poulsen and turn to Svend Poulsen who carried on the work and made the name of Poulsen famous and almost synonymous with "floribunda". It was 'Else Poulsen' (1924, 'Orléans Rose'× 'Red Star') and 'Kirsten Poulsen', both the same cross and introduced the same year, which first compelled universal attention. Here was the secret of the success of the floribunda rose—colour in the mass—which is our subject.

To avoid confusion I propose to take the colours in groups and follow these through. At first the pink shades were a slightly mauve pink, such as 'Else Poulsen', but clarity and depth of colour soon came. Of these, 'Betty Prior' (1935), 'Cheerio' (Archer) and 'Dainty Maid' (Le Grice) were typical flowers of a clear but varied pink. From then on the emphasis was on double flowers. Kordes produced the double-flowered 'Fortschritt' (1933) and 'Pinocchio' (1940). The latter had a profound influence on the work of Boerner, the hybridist for Jackson & Perkins in U.S.A., who then took over with 'Fashion' 'Vogue' and 'Spartan', as well as 'Jiminy Cricket'. We were now entering the smaller hybrid tea type and colours were varying from pink with gold to salmon pink. 'Sweet Repose' (De Ruiter) was the first clear pink which changed to white and crimson with age. Probably 'Dearest' (Dickson, 1960) was the typical hybrid tea type floribunda in scented, salmon pink, although with its good qualities the double flower had often poor rain resistance. Where the large flowers weathered well they began to drift away from the primary requirement of bedding—the production of many flowers all the time, for big flowers take longer to mature. Probably the rose to hold the premier position would be 'Elizabeth of Glamis', with perfection of growth, colour and perfume, but sadly lacking in hardiness under some conditions. More than enough has been said to emphasize the great diversity in colour, shape and growth in this one colour group.

The red roses show even more variation, from the deep blood red of 'Tonnerre' (Mallerin, 1953) to the vivid orange red of 'City of Belfast'. Svend Poulsen held the field at first with the cerise red of 'Anne Poulsen' (1935), but this rose illustrated the danger of the over-large flower where freedom was sacrificed for size. 'Dusky Maiden' (Le Grice, 1947) was very popular; its single flower of dark red with golden anthers was also sweetly scented. The most widely grown for the longest period was undoubtedly 'Frensham' (Norman, 1946), a vigorous, free-flowering crimson whose enemy, mildew, slowly secured a stranglehold. Among many good red roses is 'Evelyn Fison' (McGredy, 1962), while 'Europeana' (De Ruiter, 1963), despite its mildew and sprawling habit, was notable for its deep glowing red flowers and wonderful purple-red young foliage. Here we have an important factor outside the scope of this article, for the foliage as a foil may mar or enhance the value of the flower colour. Finally, one should mention among the hosts of competitors the brilliant orange-red double 'City of Belfast' (McGredy, 1968). Meanwhile Kordes had produced the dwarf 'Marlena' (1964), a worthy seedling from his brilliant red 'Gertrud Westphal' (1951) and deep glowing red 'Lilli Marlene' (1959). Again, red may embrace so many variants of colour, so many types of growth and height, from the dwarf 'Marlena' to the tall 'Scarlet Queen Elizabeth' (Dickson) that one can only use discretion in choice and marvel at the variety displayed.

It was not to be expected that red and pink would satisfy public demand. I believe that 'Gwyneth', polyantha (Woosnam, int. Easlea, 1923) was the first attempt at a yellow. I feel its parentage is suspect, but its weakness of fading from pale yellow to ivory precluded it from becoming popular, but at least it was an attempt. Then came 'Sunshine' (Robichon, int. Cutbush, 1927), again registered as a polyantha, with delightful small double golden buff flowers. These were both of 14 chromosomes, so perhaps they should not be included, as I believe that all true floribundas should be of 28 chromosomes, or in the earlier form as hybrid polyanthas, 21. It remained for Svend Poulsen to raise the first yellow in 'Poulsen's Yellow' (1939). Unfortunately this faded, as did 'Yellowhammer' (McGredy, 1956). 'Goldilocks' (Boerner, 1945) although a paler yellow, was of good colour consistency. Numerous seedlings were raised until 'Allgold' (Le Grice, 1958), which still remains the best all-round yellow floribunda. Many other attempts have been made. Of these 'Faust' (Kordes, 1957) makes an excellent, vigorous and colourful bush, although, as with all this type, the red staining on the outer petals turns to salmon staining throughout the flower in old age, a common failing with many modern types. In raising 'Arthur Bell' (1965) McGredy contributed a vigorous plant bearing clear, soft yellow, sweetly perfumed flowers which, unfortunately, bleached badly in the sun.

The copper shades also presented a challenge and D. T. Poulsen produced 'Poulsen's Copper' in 1940 (distributed here in 1946). 'Copper Delight' (E. B. Le Grice) followed in 1956 and 'Copper Pot' (Dickson) in 1968. Unfortunately all three fade. It is interesting to find a true polyantha in 1899 in 'Léonie Lamesch' (P. Lambert) with this type of mixed colouring.

One should, at this stage, deal with a new and brilliant colouring, possibly due to the new pelargonidin which Kordes attributes to his 'Baby Château' (1936). Certainly since that time the cinnabar colouring has appeared in many floribundas as well as hybrid teas. A number of vivid orange scarlet cultivars were produced, among which were 'Orange Triumph' (Kordes, 1937), more red than orange although its sport, 'Mary', was perhaps closer to orange; 'Meteor', short and scarlet-red (Kordes, 1958), 'Dickson's Flame' (1958), 'Orangeade' (McGredy, 1959), and 'Orange Sensation' (De Ruiter, 1961).

There were many excellent white floribunda roses, but all were eclipsed by 'Iceberg' (Kordes, 1958), although there is an undoubted need for a short and sturdy plant in that colour.

Finally we come to the group of mixed colours where three main colours predominate in each group. The first began when Boerner experimented with the hybrid tea, 'Grey Pearl' to produce 'Lavender Pinocchio' in 1948.

The difficulty in assessing these colours is indicated in the description—light chocolate-olive-brown. This was the beginning of the lavender shades. The first clear colour was 'Lilac Charm' (Le Grice, 1962). Unfortunately most of these and also their progeny faded; unfading types like 'Ripples' show a tendency to mildew. 'Seven Seas' (Harkness, 1973), clear lilac, is a valuable contribution. The deepest in this shade is probably 'Overture' (Le Grice, 1960).

From time to time derivatives of the same multicolours have produced shades in which the brown predominated, although lilac and pink were visible. The most distinct of these were 'Café' (Kordes, 1956), 'Brownie' (Boerner, 1959), 'Amberlight' (1961), clear buff; 'Tom Brown' (1964), 'Vesper' (1966) and 'Jocelyn' (1971), deep mahogany. All these were raised by Le Grice. 'News' (Le Grice, 1968), claret, deepening to purple, has now given other purple forms although 'Great News', deep purple, should be classed as a hybrid tea; its habit takes after a grandparent floribunda.

It is regrettable that this article must close without mentioning the many border-line colours, especially what I call the mother-of-pearl shades which, while less flamboyant, bring rest to the eye and contrast to the colour scheme.

Sufficient has been written to point to the remarkable diversity of colouring. Much more could be said of the differences of height and habit and, most intriguing of all, the new perfumes associated with the new colours. There is a world of pleasure to be enjoyed through the labours and vision of fifty years of steady purpose behind these roses. Who knows what new treasures await us?

The Men behind the New Roses

In the article headed "Andries Verschuren" on pages 78–80 of the 1974 *Rose Annual*, the varieties 'Charles Gregory', 'Lady Belper', 'Verschuren's Pink', 'Spek's Yellow' and 'Souv. de Jacques Verschuren' were incorrectly attributed to the firm headed by Andries Verschuren, of Haps, Holland. It has been brought to our notice that these varieties were raised by H. A. Verschuren & Sons, also of Haps, Holland, the original firm from which Andries Verschuren branched out to establish his own nursery. *Modern Roses* 7 does not distinguish between the respective Verschuren firms in Haps and this has contributed to the confusion. We tender our apologies to H. A. Verschuren & Sons for this error.

Shoot Your Roses

H. WILLIAMSON, J.P.

(Nurseryman and rose grower)

It sounds a bit drastic, perhaps, put like that, but the result is to prolong the enjoyment of your roses almost indefinitely—if the shooting is done with a ciné camera. Capturing the loveliness of the rose with a still camera and showing it through the medium of coloured slides is a well-established practice, and I should be the last person to say that the "movie" is better—only that it is different, with a different impact and requiring a different technique. The "still" photograph allows for better composition, more perfect detail and controlled time for viewing. The "movie" has the supreme advantage of capturing motion—the flower blowing in the breeze, the coming and going of birds and insects, the action and movement of people tending or just enjoying the flowers—in other words, of bringing the whole picture into living, moving action. An additional advantage is that you can build up a theme or story, instead of just showing a series of pictures. And if you are prepared to go a step further and add sound, with background music, sound effects and commentary, then you have all the ingredients for a fascinating and absorbing, albeit time-consuming hobby, which can add an entirely new dimension to the joy of growing roses.

As to the mechanics of such a proposition, the first essential obviously is a camera. But before we can talk about cameras, we must first decide what size of film is going to be used. Although 16 mm. film is used for most semi-professional documentary films, the size most favoured by amateurs is 8 mm. The reasons for this are two-fold and obvious. The film costs approximately half of the larger size—and the equipment is also lighter and easier to handle and carry. So we shall be thinking in terms of 8 mm. here, and as Super-8 is the size I use, and is the film which is growing rapidly in popularity, it is Super-8 I shall be describing.

The films for Super-8 are always in very convenient cartridge form, and can be loaded into the camera in a matter of seconds. 50 feet in length, and costing about £2.00 each, they usually run at 18 frames per second, though when sound is to be added, many prefer to run them at 24 frames per second. Whatever speed the pictures are taken at, they should be projected at the same speed, and I usually find I can get good enough results at 18 frames per second. As regards the type of film to use, I have always found Kodachrome II very satisfactory for general use.

R. filipes 'Kiftsgate' at the Mill House, Sutton Courtenay (*see page* 115)

Above: You will need a camera . . . and a tripod

Top right: Be prepared to lie on your tummy sometimes to shoot . . .

Centre right: You will need an editor . . . and a splicer

Bottom right: A thrush singing . . . brings a note of reality

Below: You will need a projector . . . and a screen

Bourbon Climber 'Zéphirine Drouhin' clothing a tripod (*see page* 136)

As to cameras, their name is legion and it is a question to be discussed with a photographic dealer, or knowledgeable friend who can be relied upon for good advice. The price of a movie camera can be anything from about £35·00 to £500·00. The highly priced sophisticated cameras can be left for the film enthusiast who has time and money to spare—excellent results can be obtained with cameras which cost less than £50·00. There is, however, one thing which adds greatly to the appeal of a film—the inclusion of good "close-ups". These are most easily taken by a camera with a good "zoom", and preferably with the macro-zoom facility which, by the simple turn of a knob, enables one to move close up to the subject and yet keep it in focus, but this does rule out the very cheapest cameras. Alternatively, you can get a 2 or 3 diopter close-up lens for use with a cheaper camera, which has either a fixed lens or one with only a limited amount of zoom.

You will need a tripod. This should not cost more than about £12·00 and is essential for best results. The temptation to rely upon handhold is always with us, and can be accepted up to a point, if you have a steady hand and are using the camera at a fairly wide-angle setting. But in telephoto and close-up effects, every tiny movement of the camera becomes so magnified when the picture is projected that an otherwise good film can be quite spoilt. It is good practice to use a tripod whenever practicable, unless you can get support for the camera or your wrist from some firm object—not least from the ground itself if you are getting a low shot.

And obviously, you will need a projector, so that you can see the film you have taken so much trouble to shoot. These again vary enormously in price. If you are not intending to use sound, quite a fair projector can be bought for about £30·00. With sound facilities added, it will cost about £100·00 and upwards. With the projector you will need a screen—unless you intend to show it only in your own house and have a white wall. It will cost only £10·00 or so. All prices mentioned are normal shop prices—there are, of course, discount shops who offer many things at lower prices, and some-times one can pick up good secondhand bargains.

The question of whether to add sound to a film is one which is bound to arise sooner or later. Sound is not essential, but it is an enormous asset. It brings the whole thing to life in a quite remarkable way. I remember showing a travel film of mine (of which I was rather proud!) to one of my daughters. She watched it through and "damned it with faint praise"; I added music and commentary, and she watched it through a second time (my family are very long-suffering!) this time with obvious enthusiasm. "What lovely *photography*" she said.

If you decide to add sound, you will need a projector which will record and play back the sound. You will also need to get your film "striped"—i.e. to have the sound track, on which music, commentary, etc. can be recorded, added on the side of the film after it has been edited. I now do this myself, but it is more usual to have it done professionally, and costs about 1p per foot.

Those are the mechanics—now for the technique. Let me say straight away that I am no expert. What I know I have picked up here and there, and mostly by trial and error. And both trials and errors have been plentiful—and expensive!

I said at the beginning that the technique is different from that required in still photography. Yet some things are similar. Roses cannot run away from you like animals—or at you, like children—so you should have time to "compose" most of your pictures with care. And this, of course, should always be done if possible. But at other times you may be getting a shot which will disappear if you are not quick—and then you may have to focus and shoot immediately with little time for composition. Then you just hope for the best. In such cases, composition is not so critical as in still photography. Exposure is usually taken care of by automatic metering and control. As in still photography, light is all-important. Because exposure time is fixed and limited, there is not so wide a range of lights which are acceptable as with stills, where extra exposure time can be given to compensate for low light value. Very brilliant sunlight can give too strong contrasts, dazzle from reflections on leaves etc., whilst dull weather robs the pictures of brightness. What is commonly known as "cloudy bright" conditions are usually the ideal, and if you cannot get the ideal in our uncertain climate, get as near to it as possible.

The first essential in making a film is to decide on a theme, or story, and then on how to deal with it. It can be quite simple, based, say, on the seasons and following the developments and changes of the roses during spring, summer and autumn—or you may think up a quite complicated plot and bully your family, friends and neighbours into taking leading roles. In any case, a little humour helps a lot, used judiciously. In this connection, I have known a close-up of a caterpillar to be quite hilarious. With a suitable comment added it never fails to get a good laugh from the audience!

Having decided on your theme, you will always be on the alert to collect the material. It does not, of course, need to be shot in the order in which it will finally be projected Obviously, if you can get a number of scenes to follow in natural sequence, this is all to the good, but a great deal will, of necessity, have to be put in its correct position in the final editing.

One should avoid too short or over-long shots. Anything less than 4 seconds in duration is usually too short—anything more than 10 is often too long. Shots of static subjects should normally be kept short; if action is taking place, it can be longer. In the case of a static subject, if you want to keep it on the screen for more than 5 or 6 seconds, perhaps to say something about it, then take it from two different angles. 5 seconds taken straight on, and 5 from a completely different angle, one taken close-up, with the other farther away, will give a far better effect than having 10 seconds from one position.

Variation of angle and distance is most important. Avoid taking everything from normal eye-level. Be prepared to lie on your back or your tummy sometimes to get a shot upwards or sideways at your subject. Close-ups of flowers are particularly telling, often revealing details which pass unnoticed by normal eye viewing. For example, a really close close-up of the centre of 'Lilac Charm', with its lovely cluster of red stamens and golden anthers, can be a revelation in beauty.

The "cutaway" shot, in which one leaves the main subject of, say, a girl arranging a bowl of roses, for a quick close-up of the girl's face, intent on her task, and then returns to the main picture, is a recognized and valuable way of adding interest, and preventing a longish sequence from becoming tedious. It can also be used with advantage sometimes to bridge over what might otherwise be an awkward jump in the sequence.

The start and finish of a film should always receive special thought. The opening scenes should be designed to catch the attention and interest of the viewer at the start, whilst the closing one should leave a good and lasting impression. At all costs, a weak finish must be avoided as this could spoil what otherwise might be a good film. Good titling is also important—all too often amateur films are badly let down by crude and ill-conceived titling. I will return to this under the subject of editing.

If your camera does have the advantage of a good "zoom", the greatest care should be exercised in its use. It is invaluable as a quick means of moving from a wide-angle shot to a telephoto one or to a close-up, but most of the better cameras with zoom facilities also have a power-drive attachment, whereby slight pressure on a button will cause the lens to move smoothly from wide-angle to telephoto and *vice versa*. This provides the photographer with perhaps his greatest temptation—to do this whilst filming and so "zoom" into or out of the subject as it is being taken. This can, of course, be done occasionally with great effect, especially if it is a "restricted" zoom, but done frequently it can be quite exasperating. I have watched films on T.V. which would have been greatly improved if 90 per cent of the zooming and panning had been eliminated. Panning is another thing which needs doing with care and restraint. Where the subject to be taken is too large to be embraced by the camera in one position—a large rose-garden, for example— it can be brought into the picture by moving the camera in a slow sweeping motion across the scene to be taken. This can be fine and very effective—but should not be done *too* often or it will have as devastating an effect as the too-frequent zooming. It needs to be done with great care too; the movement of the camera must be slow and very steady, preferably on a firm tripod. One should always film for a few seconds with the camera stationary before commencing the pan and the same again at the end.

When the film has all been taken there comes the editing, and this is where the fun really starts. It makes an admirable game for winter evenings, just as the filming has done during the summer days. For this you will need just two more bits of equipment, which together will cost less than £30·00—namely, an editor, in which you can watch your film on a tiny "screen" as you pass it through, and then cut it where needed, and a splicer to join the pieces together again in the order required. There are two ways of joining film—either by lapping the two ends together and cementing them with a special film cement, or by butting one end against the other and joining them with a transparent adhesive tape. For Super-8 film the former method is generally regarded as preferable. It takes from 60 to 90 seconds to make a good splice once you have got into the way of it. It is very important to do it carefully, and make a strong but smooth joint, or it will give continual trouble later.

As to the method of actually editing the film, no doubt people have all sorts of different ways. I can only tell you how I do it, which is, I am sure, very unprofessional indeed—but it seems to work. When the film comes back from the processing laboratory, I project it in the normal way, having a large sheet of paper by me. After each shot or sequence of shots, I stop the film and give the shot a number and sufficient description to be able to identify it later. I also place a tick or a cross against it to indicate whether it is good enough to include in the final edited film. When the next film comes back, this is treated in the same way, the numbers following in sequence from the first, Supposing ten films in all have been taken, processed and treated in this way I then have, say, 100 shots, numbered from 1–100, each one with a brief description.

With the sheets in front of me I can then plan the order in which the various shots will appear in the final version. Thus, No. 6 may be required as the opening scene and so becomes No. 1, to be followed perhaps by No. 29, which then becomes No. 2 and so on, the new numbers being entered in a column parallel to the original ones. It is now just a matter of cutting the film up and getting the pieces into their right order. This is where the editor is generally used, with which each piece of film can be identified by its description and the numbered order in which it comes. Before cutting up the film, however, it is essential to have somewhere to keep the pieces in their proper order. The simplest and best way of doing this which I know is to have a light wooden lath fixed about 5 ft or 6 ft above floor level, with small headless panel pins driven in at half-inch intervals and numbered from one upwards. The pins must be small enough to allow the sprocket holes in the side of the film to slip easily over them—then the pieces of film dangle neatly from the pins. By having all the pins up and numbered beforehand, each piece of film can be suspended in its new order as it is cut off. The pieces which got a X against them in the projection viewing are thrown out. When finished, everything should be in order and it is then merely a matter of taking down the film one piece at a time, from No. 1 onwards, joining them together, and, hey presto! the film is made.

But it is not yet finished. It will need projecting several times, watching it throughout with a critical eye and jotting down things which need altering. This bit needs shortening—these two scenes would be better if put in reverse order—that bit is slightly out of focus and should be deleted, and so on. Better to have a shorter film of consistently high standard, than a longer one with doubtful bits in it.

Finally there is the titling. If you are going to have a sound track with music and commentary, probably all you will need is an opening title, possibly some "credits" and THE END. If you have no commentary, you may well need a few sub-titles or headings in the course of the film to make it more informative. There are all sorts of titling methods, and whichever is chosen, it should be done carefully and well. Perhaps the simplest way of all is by using Dymotape, sticking it on a suitable background and filming this. It is neat and clear but unimaginative. Better, though more time-consuming, is to use white rub-on lettering on a sheet of non-reflecting glass, find an appropriate picture—a coloured photo, picture postcard, enlarged print of a coloured slide or something similar—lay the glass with its white lettering on the picture and film this. The words will then appear superimposed on the picture, the glass being invisible. There are lots of other methods, of course, including the superimposing of titles on a moving background, which is very effective but needs considerable know-how and special apparatus.

Having included your titles, your film will now be finished so far as the visual effect is concerned, and if you are content to retain it as a "Golden

Silent", the job is completed. If, however, you decide to add sound, you still have quite a lot to do. I find this the most difficult and yet the most fascinating part of the whole proceeding.

The first thing to do is to get the film "striped". This simply means having the sound track fixed on the side of the film with adhesive. When this is done the film is ready for sound to be added. Projectors which play back sound also have recording facilities. The most usual method is to run the film through adding the music and sound effects—fading the music out when the special effects come in, and fading it back in afterwards—then running the film through a second time, superimposing the commentary on the musical background through the use of a microphone. As the voice makes itself heard, the volume of music is suppressed, so that a proper balance between voice and music is maintained. The choice of music is important; it can go a long way towards making or marring a film. It should always be chosen to match the mood of the film, and should be of a generally even-flowing nature, avoiding big crescendos and climaxes, which would fight the voice giving the commentary. Very well-known popular tunes are best avoided, as these may distract attention from the film. The music should enhance the film, and should never compete with it for attention. Sound effects—a thrush singing in a nearby tree, or children playing in the garden, for example—bring a note of reality and add interest to it all.

As for the commentary, this is always very much an individual matter. Usually it should be kept as brief as possible without losing any of its meaning I always take my films through a bit at a time with a watch in my hand, and time every sequence where commentary is to be added. Timing must be very precise, for you should remember that 18 frames go through in a second and if you overstep the mark, you will find yourself talking away about something which is right off the screen. Then I rehearse the commentary in the time recorded, and if it is too long to fit in or even involves hurrying the words, it should be pruned back until it does fit. If conversation is going to be included, be careful not to film the speaker's mouth, unless you are prepared to go further and get complete lip-synchronization. But that is a subject which I do not propose to delve into here. There are, of course, many variations possible in the use of sound. You can add commentary without music, or music without commentary, or music in part and commentary in part, or commentary and sound effects, and so on. It is all very flexible, with infinite opportunities for variation to suit your subject and your wishes.

Roses from Cuttings

J. H. BARTRAM, M.Sc.

In 1971 I was reading in the *Rose Annual* about efforts of various members of the RNRS to get rose cuttings to root. It occurred to me that since the advent of mist propagation many formerly difficult subjects such as camellias had become dead easy to propagate. And what is a rose but a rather specialized shrub? So I went to see my friend Cecil Wyatt of Bovey Tracey, who has a fair sized mist propagation unit. He agreed to do the rooting if I provided the cuttings, and we could discuss our results, if any.

So in mid-September 1971 I selected 36 stems which had just flowered from my rose bushes, 2 each of 18 sorts, both hybrid teas and floribundas. I cut off the stems about 3–4 in. below the dead blooms, and then allowed 4 leaves and cut the stem below the fourth leaf. Cecil put them in a 50/50 coarse sand/peat mixture at 60° F. After one week all the leaves fell off, which caused us some consternation. But the buds in the leaf axils had begun to shoot and examination of two cuttings showed that callusing had taken place. So we removed the dead leaves and left them. In a further 16 days all were rooted, so the mist was turned off and after a further week they were put into a cold house and potted into 3½ in. black polythene pots in John Innes Potting Compost No. 1. We decided to leave them in the cold house to eliminate any winter damage which might confuse the results.

The rooted cuttings produced 2–3 shoots each and grew slowly and then in mid-February, 1972, a black blotch appeared half-way up the stems of one of the plants, spread rapidly *downwards* to the soil and the plant died. Despite using every type of fungicide, a further 29 plants followed suit one by one in the next five weeks. In the last week of March the plants were put outside and 10 days later I planted them in my garden and one more promptly died. Let me now say that we have never encountered this trouble again in all the dozens of experiments we have done, and have no idea even now what caused it.

The 5 plants grew away outside and produced blooms on every shoot in early June; when the blooms died I nipped them off and waited to see what would happen. These 2 or 3 initial shoots did not grow any more at all but 2 or 3 very strong shoots came up from each plant from below ground, presumably from the buried bud which had also produced the roots. This I have since found always happens, and once these new strong shoots are

3 feet high I cut off the old original stem and its branches at ground level, and am left with a strong, well shaped bush, and this can be as little as $3\frac{1}{2}$ months from the taking of the cutting.

While all this was going on I began to take a further selection of cuttings with various ends in view. In late May I went over my bushes for blind new shoots, of which there are always some at this time of the year. There was no bloom to cut off and again I used cuttings four leaves long, the lowest leaf being removed, of course. Once again all the leaves fell off after one week, and the cuttings were fully rooted a week after that. The trays were taken to a cold house for a week and then the cuttings potted on as before. They were hardened off and planted out in the garden seven weeks after taking the cuttings. Three weeks later the first blooms were open. Ten weeks from cuttings to bloom was, we thought, pretty good going and we had 29 plants from 30 cuttings.

The next try was with very soft young shoots 3–4 in. long to see if they would root like chrysanthemum cuttings. No dice! They just rotted in 5–6 days without a vestige of callus, let alone root.

Next was the problem of those leaves. Not only did they restrict the density of the cuttings in the rooting trays, but they were a painful nuisance to clear when they fell off. So a set of "normal" four leaf cuttings from recently flowered shoots was prepared and the leaves trimmed off. These were put in the mist propagation under the usual conditions with another set of leafed cuttings. These latter rooted in 14 days, but the deleafed ones were very slow. After four weeks only half had rooted, and in fact half never did root. Those which did root took much longer than usual after leaving the mist to reach a state where we judged it safe to pot on. So obviously the leaves exert a very important influence on the rooting of the cutting, even if they do fall off after seven days.

Next we tried cutting off half of each leaf before inserting the cutting, but these took only a little less time than the leafless ones, so obviously it is necessary to have as large an initial leaf area as possible to get quick and almost 100 per cent rooting, with the young plants growing away rapidly.

Next we experimented with the size of the cutting, because we were using four buds to produce a new bush, whereas a rose grower uses only one when budding for a new bush. We cut the next batch down to three leaves, two above the soil, and these rooted just as easily as four and in due course when planted out produced just as good bushes and just as quickly as the four leaf cuttings. Next we tried a batch of two leaved cuttings, only one above soil level. These were slow to root, had around 50 per cent failures and grew away very slowly. Obviously the leaf effect was showing again. We were, in effect, cutting off leaves from four leaf cuttings.

We took our last cuttings in mid-September 1972 and, as in September 1971, they took a week longer than the summer ones to root. We intended to go on a bit longer, but things happened which prevented us from doing so. In 1972 we rooted some hundreds of rose cuttings from an assorted collection of 39 varieties of hybrid teas and floribundas and as far as we could see all varieties were just as easy to root and the resultant plants all grew away with no trouble at all.

We started off at the end of February in 1973. I was pruning my roses then and although most of the leaves had gone, the leaf axil buds were beginning to shoot, and as this is the first sign of rooting under mist, I selected some suitable shoots and they were trimmed and put under mist. They were a total failure. Obviously actively growing leaves at the time the cutting is taken are essential for rooting.

So as in 1972 the first lot of 1973 cuttings were blind shoots taken in May, and as before they rooted the quickest of all. From then on we began to see what limitations there were on cutting material. Young soft wood is useless; the best is what is usually called "half-ripened" wood, the middle of a stem that has just flowered. But the lower half of this stem can be used, although it takes rather longer to root.

The thickness of the stem appears to be quite immaterial; everything from a knitting-needle thickness up to half an inch diameter works perfectly well. I was able to get wood from still more varieties in 1973, raising the number to 57, and still no differences showed. I was able to take cuttings from bushes which had been cuttings themselves in 1972, and the time from cuttings to cuttings was just 11 months.

Taking of cuttings continued until mid-October, with rooting time steadily lengthening until the last lot took 6 weeks. Beyond that rooting would not take place. So that gives a cutting season of 6 months from May to October, as against the two months in which budding can be carried out.

In 1973 I tried some cuttings 3 and 4 leaves long from a few perpetual flowering climbers in August. These rooted 100 per cent in 14 days and were potted on as usual. Even before the plants were put out, shoots began to come from below soil level and it will be interesting to see if they grow as vigorously as the original budded plants. All the hybrid tea and floribunda plants from cuttings are every bit as vigorous as the original budded plants.

This area is notorious for fungoid diseases of roses; in fact, a lot of people still say you cannot grow roses in Devon and Cornwall, which makes me wonder what those large thorny bushes around my garden are. But joking apart, regular spraying for fungoid disease is essential, with Black Spot being the real headache, rust next, and mildew only a mild nuisance. I keep the first two at bay with a mixture of urea and maneb, but the air in this area must be full of spores. So we were somewhat apprehensive about what would happen when the cuttings arrived in the mist propagator, an absolutely ideal climate to breed fungoid disease. No outbreak has ever occurred, and this may well be because the leaves fall off after seven days. Spraying is started after the plants have been potted and are moved outside.

This would seem to be a very easy and cheap way of propagating rose bushes, and would certainly use far less ground than the usual method; also the bushes could be planted up at any time, and much less digging is needed—quite an advantage for older people. But could the customers be persuaded to take small rose plants in pots, even though they develop so fast? Doubtless it would be a slow job until a few people had tried and found the method to work.

Among the hybrid teas used were 'Crimson Glory', 'Ena Harkness', 'Fragrant Cloud', 'Pink Favourite', 'Colour Wonder', 'Gold Crown', 'Colorama', 'McGredy's Sunset', 'Peace', 'Super Star', 'Perfecta', 'Rose Gaujard', 'Westminster', 'Mojave', 'Ernest H. Morse', 'Bettina', 'Belle Blonde', 'Montezuma', 'Piccadilly', 'Sutter's Gold', 'Uncle Walter', 'Tzigane', 'Wendy Cussons', 'Mischief', 'Gail Borden', 'King's Ransom', 'Beauté'.

The floribundas included 'Queen Elizabeth', 'Gold Marie', 'Lilli Marlene', 'Honeymoon', 'Dickson's Flame', 'Jiminy Cricket', 'Frensham', 'Korona', 'Orangeade', 'Evelyn Fison', 'Miracle', 'Fashion', 'Elizabeth of Glamis', 'Masquerade'.

The perpetual flowering climbers were 'Maigold', 'Golden Showers', 'Danse du Feu', 'Pink Perpêtue', 'Joseph's Coat', 'Casino' and 'Schoolgirl'.

All the above was written in January 1974 and since then we have learned a little more. The last batch of cuttings taken in October, 1973 started to show Black Spot in May 1974, but we realized this was probably due to the fact that there is an awful lot of Black Spot about by October, and some spores managed to overwinter. We shall be on our guard this year.

The cuttings of the perpetual flowering climbers are growing away nicely and look as though they will be quite successful.

The first successful cuttings are now, of course, large bushes as in fact are the 1973 cuttings, and they appear in no way any less healthy or vigorous than the budded parents—in fact, some are stronger. They all, however, have one rather odd characteristic. After pruning they grow quite a bit faster

Above: Cutting of 'Rose Gaujard' taken in September, 1972 and planted out in February, 1973. The photograph was taken in June, 1973

Below: Cutting taken mid-May, 1973. The photograph, taken in November, 1973, plainly shows in the centre of the plant the thin growth from the original cutting above the ground, with very stout growth appearing all round from below the ground

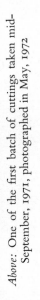

Above: One of the first batch of cuttings taken mid-September, 1971, photographed in May, 1972

Top right: Cutting about 8 weeks after potting. The plant is lying on its side away from the camera to show the excellent root development

Bottom right: Rooted cutting potted on and showing its first flower bud.

than the budded plants, but in May they slow down and both budded and cutting plants bloom together. This happened in 1972, 1973 and 1974

Since writing the above we have rooted successfully *R. rugosa* 'Scabrosa', 'Lord Penzance', Yellow Banksia (*R. banksiae lutea*) and *R. bracteata*.

I should like to thank Cecil Wyatt for all the trouble he has taken to root hundreds of cuttings and pot them on for me. His help was invaluable.

Purely for Pleasure

SUSAN BONE

(*Amateur rose grower*)

It was in the summer of 1966 that I succumbed to a curious phenomenon I can only describe as rose fever. I remember it well. Until then my indifference to the Queen of Flowers was equalled only by my ignorance.[1] Of a placid, indolent disposition, I abruptly and uncharacteristically displayed all the symptoms of an obsessive infatuation—for roses. I simply had to grow them. This conviction I pursued with a single mindedness that brooked no opposition. My husband humoured my whim—he approved in principle of the outdoor exercise—though he vigorously protested at the expenditure involved on what after all was a mere flight of fancy. The novelty would pall, he asserted, in direct ratio to the mounting task of maintenance.

The path of true love never runs smooth, and the first season was memorable for its disasters, culminating in an epidemic of Rust. Alas, I had taken no preventive measures when planting the trees, through ignorance more than negligence, and my grief and indignation were exacerbated by my helplessness as I watched the entire collection, my pride and joy, being defoliated. All survived, and that winter I could have contended for the title of most diligent sprayer of Bordeaux Mixture in rose-growing.

Next season the plants were not plagued by Rust or Black Spot. They were

[1] 1969 *Rose Annual*—"A Shower of Roses."

instead "overwhelmed by the original sin of Mildew". The *Rose Annual* has been a valuable source of instruction as well as entertainment to me, and I read somewhere that Rust bequeathes incipient Mildew to survivors.

A vigilant watch had to be maintained and a programme of intensive spraying instituted, first with one preparation then another in my frantic efforts to control, if not obliterate, this pernicious blight. From May until October on most evenings once the meal was out of the way I disappeared into the garden until darkness drove me in again. "I thought," my husband remarked, "that one of the main advantages of growing roses is that they require so little attention." Then, thanks to the *Rose Annual*, I read of Milfaron. This has proved the most effective treatment in my garden, eradicating the dread fungus from all but the chronically susceptible, such as some of the old shrub roses.

Our garden which is small, boxed in and faces due east offers optimum conditions for Mildew if not for roses. At best it resembled an experimental rose station, at worst an infirmary for the sick, the halt, the lame. The pattern of growth has been inexplicably capricious; even the mighty 'Peace' couldn't manage more than 2 ft 6 in. in height. The notable exceptions were the climbers and ramblers, which flourish and grow apace. There are patches in the beds wherein the rose trees remain in a state of suspended animation, neither growing nor dying. Whilst I have actually lost half a dozen trees out of a total of 300 planted, the overall result has fallen dismally short of the glowing pictures painted in my mind's eye.

The following sums up my experience of rose growing over the past seven years:

1. No amount of spraying in the growing season is as effective as the winter wash treatment.
2. Top dressing with 3 in. of stable manure has shown no appreciable improvement in performance, and has only delayed, not stemmed, the tidal waves of Mildew and Black Spot.
3. The addition of fen topsoil to the native Breckland sand and chalk mixture appears to have been detrimental, and the bed which incorporates fen topsoil to a depth of 12 in. has been spectacularly unsuccessful.
4. Best results have been gained from transplanting the puniest specimens to a nursery bed. They were popped in, over a handful of chopped up rotted turves, with no supplementary feeding, no spraying. Desperate situations demand desperate remedies. These trees were easily lifted out of the beds I had so carefully prepared five years previously with additional topsoil, bonemeal and peat, and mulched with generous helpings of stable manure.

They had been subsequently coaxed with a varied menu of fertilizers to tempt jaded palates.

Once transplanted, these selfsame trees (including 'Peace') ran wild. So much so that the following winter the rugosas had to be spaced out. My husband had to dig them out, for the growth above ground was nothing to the growth below.

It would appear that the assiduous attention lavished on nurturing the trees had only one obvious benefit—it made me feel a lot better.

5. This has led me to the conclusion that whatever I put into my garden will not change its basic nature: it is still closed in, facing east, of poor soil. The anomaly between it and the nursery bed arises because the latter is outside, in the open. The soil there is sandy but of more depth and in better heart. Over-feeding does not redress the balance, it forces a pace of growth which the root system cannot maintain, at the expense of the whole plant.

The amateur such as myself who grows roses in adverse conditions would do well to heed the advice of Jack Harkness on growing roses in his book of that name.

6. Last year I sprayed against Mildew only, with Milfaron, and provided a modest supplementary diet of proprietary fertiliser, but no mulch of stable manure. Results, if anything, were an improvement on previous years because the Milfaron held the Mildew in check. Near drought conditions didn't help, but at least the trees appear to be sturdier.

Ironically, it is my family who reap the greatest benefit from my occupation ("hobby" somehow doesn't do justice to growing roses). They are converts if not disciples, and twice daily in the growing season they make a pilgrimage around the rose beds, to savour their many splendours.

Worth special mention are 'Canary Bird', whose unfurling yellow flags herald the rose summer and send my spirits soaring; the south-facing climbers which follow soon after—'Mme Gregoire Staechelin', 'Étoile de Hollande' and 'Mrs Sam McGredy', though "Mrs Sam's" blooms do suffer from the pitiless daylong exposure to the fierce sun of midsummer. Then 'Nevada', an entrancing sight, all wreathed in creamy smiles, flushing demurely in the warmth of the May sun.

The rose trees in my care are rather like children, each with a personality. I am learning to let them grow at their own pace in their own time; to encourage, not force them. That miracle of creation, the perfect bloom, is an added bonus. The first fine, careless rapture has been replaced by deeper, more substantial pleasures. As my husband has now ruefully conceded, "To fall in love with the Rose is the beginning of a lifelong romance."

BARB

J. L. HARKNESS

(Rose nurseryman and breeder)

Not often, I suppose, has anyone been asked to write an account of a rose trade organization before it is two years old. Such is my present task, for BARB was born on 6 April 1973, and perhaps through its extreme youth, rarely receives the full dignity of its title—the British Association of Rose Breeders.

The objects of the Association are to encourage, improve and extend the introduction and growing of new roses under Plant Breeders' Rights, by the best means that justly and conjointly advance the well-being of breeders, growers, users and the rose itself. BARB came into being because these objects were not being attained previously.

The members are nurserymen of any country, for it is the Association that is British, not the breeders. Their qualification is to hold or operate British Plant Breeders' Rights. The three classes of membership are Breeder Members (like Dickson's introducing 'Grandpa Dickson'); Guest Members (like Kordes authorizing McGredy to introduce 'Peer Gynt'); and Representative Members (like McGredy introducing 'Peer Gynt' on behalf of Kordes). The Guest Members pay no subscription and have no vote. The greater part of the Association comprises the Registered Growers, that is the nurserymen who accept and grow the varieties of the Members.

A Code of Conduct was agreed by the Members. It obliges them to adhere to the Standard Conditions under which the roses are offered to nurserymen; not difficult, because those Conditions allow for considerable variation. The Code forbids Members to offer preferential terms to one particular Grower, while discriminating against the others. It asks Members to take part in various exercises in co-operation as fully as they can, and demands they refrain from introducing roses known to be gravely unhealthy, of poor quality, or plainly inferior to existing sorts. Members are to obtain and maintain Plant Breeders' Rights on all their introductions, unless with good reasons; they are to avoid publicity which excites envy and false hopes by exaggerating the amount of money made by breeding roses. Finally, they must acknowledge with pleasure the good points in another member's rose, and avoid over-estimating them in their own.

The Standard Conditions are the terms under which Members offer their roses to other nurserymen, who become the Registered Growers of the

Association. These Conditions have replaced the assortment of agreements and contracts which formerly each nurseryman had with each breeder. Now a nurseryman who wishes to become a Registered Grower requires only to sign a form accepting the Standard Conditions, and he is at once in business with all the Members of BARB, or as many of them as he wishes. This simple idea has proved attractive to nurserymen, for BARB has now welcomed 183 Registered Growers.

The Standard Conditions provide for the initial supply of budwood to be free of any cost except royalty; and for the Registered Grower to report annually on his propagation and to pay for it. Careful and fair regulations cover charges for subsequent supplies of the same variety; the maintenance of fair practice; the removal of a Grower from the Register; and arbitration. In the last case, The Royal National Rose Society kindly agreed to assist in certain circumstances.

In operation, this scheme has turned out to work as easily as ABC. The Registered Growers, instead of dealing with the assorted (and sometimes cryptic) forms of many Breeders, now fill in one, and write one cheque. BARB distributes the information (and the money) to those Members to whom it belongs. The degree of friendship and trust between the Members is well demonstrated by this arrangement.

The royalty rates are not set by BARB, nor even discussed. They are set by individual members, who are in competition with each other. It is the responsibility of each to assess the market value of his varieties. Each year the Secretary asks them for a list of varieties and prices; he circulates this to the Registered Growers, and no member except the Secretary sees this list before it is published.

Without doubt the influence of BARB has been to reduce royalty rates; the same document includes the varieties of one's competitors, therefore swift comparisons can be made. The rates in the last list varied by a multiple of six from the lowest to the highest. Our Continental friends can be heard complaining that British royalty rates are so low as to constitute unfair competition.

BARB has been at pains to make clear to Registered Growers how the royalty relates to the eventual selling price.

Much information becomes available, as a result of our knowing, for example, the exact number of 'Peer Gynt' budded in the country. This we pass on to the Registered Growers, who all know how many nurseries grow 'Peer Gynt', what the total in the country is, and the names of the 12 nurseries with the most. Two advantages arise from this: suppliers are easily located, and budding programmes can be planned upon intelligent interpretation of concrete information.

The Association's costs are paid for by an annual subscription and levy from the Breeders. The levy is so much per 20,000 stocks budded of each member's varieties, the amount being fixed according to our budget.

In 1973, the first BARB Trials were started on eleven nurseries; the winners will be introduced in 1976. The objects of the trials are to assist Members by seeing one another's varieties, to assist Growers by making them free of our joint opinion of the new introductions, to assist users by increasing their interest and pleasure in the best varieties, and to improve the standard of new roses.

The system is simple, because the trials are judged as maidens. Therefore each Member sent budwood to the others in 1973; judging took place in 1974; the Registered Growers can bud the trial winners in 1975; and the gardeners can buy them in 1976. The 1977 trials have begun similarly with budding in 1974.

We are aware that it is dangerous to judge maidens, although every breeder has great experience of doing so. In order to offset that danger, we require entries to be well tested, and cut-backs to be available for inspection. It is also a condition of the BARB Trials that the varieties must be entered in the RNRS Trials in advance. Before beginning the BARB Trials, we consulted the RNRS President, Deputy President and Secretary, to ensure we did nothing to vitiate the RNRS Trials. The reasons for judging maidens are first a practical one, that few nurseries accommodate cutbacks with the same efficiency as they grow maidens; and, secondly, that the nearer the trials begin to the time of introduction, the more thorough and advanced is the breeder's own testing. By 1973, he has probably reduced his 1976 prospects to about a dozen, but for 1977 he may still have fifty under review. We would rather have a selection of his dozen than of his fifty.

Our judging points differ from those of the RNRS, because we have to consider whether a variety will sell, and whether it will yield an economic proportion of first grade plants. The points are: Habit and Growth 20; Health 20; Beauty of Flowers 15; Freedom of Flower 10; Scent 10; Sales Value 15; Yield of Saleable Plants 10. In the case of Beauty of Flowers, at least 5 points are to be withheld if the blooms weather or age badly. It may seem that Colour is an obvious omission, but this is likely to be a major factor in Sales Value, and an influence in Beauty of Flowers.

At the final meeting, before accepting the top three (from the judging forms submitted by each participant, and added up), we demand certain assurances. These are the disclosure of any adverse factor known to the breeder, but which may not have been obvious to the judges; the state of Breeders' Rights, the time of introduction and availability of enough stock; and the conviction that the rose will do the Trials credit, and is sufficiently distinct from winners in the same or the previous year.

Then we select one, two or three roses to be the BARB Winners. It is specifically forbidden to select them on any basis but that laid down; and any kind of business such as "It's your turn this year, Jack", is prohibited in the rules.

To all these arrangements we have not only unanimous agreement, but also co-operation in the spirit of the thing. It has been common to hear a BARB Member say "Your XYZ looks great, I reckon it could win." And to be answered by the breeder, "It got some mildew last autumn," or "It might fade in the South, so keep an eye open for that." Or some other helpful comment designed to ensure the chosen varieties are a credit to the trials, rather than a catch-all-you-can to the breeder.

BARB is in the habit of sending information to its Registered Growers. They receive each year details of all the BARB varieties on offer, under Name, Colour Group, Class, Commission Rate and Breeder. These are also present-ed in colour groups, so that someone short of yellow hybrid teas, for example, can quickly see what we have. The information sheets have also been used to supply suggested Catalogue descriptions of new varieties, and other informa-tion we thought essential. Nurserymen as a race are not fond of receiving a lot of paper, unless it begins with the word "Pay" and is signed by a customer; the amount of information we send has therefore to be no more than the Registered Growers will happily receive. But plans are in hand to extend a general information service to all prominent Rosarians.

Having come upon the scene to find the tide out, as regards sales of roses in particular, and the strength of business in Britain in general, BARB sought to lay the right foundations for future prosperity. Our 183 Registered Growers are our customers, and a consequence of an Association having customers is to feel more heavily a corporate responsibility for their welfare.

This feeling may be one of some importance in the commercial structure of the country. Acting as an individual, one can deal with a wholesale custo-mer by selling what he wants, as much as you can of it, and leaving him with the responsibility to get on from there. An Association has to go further. We outline a deliberate policy directive for guidance each year. We ask our-selves, what are the prospects for selling the roses budded this summer? If the answer is "poor", we take all the heat out of selling, in order that our customers shall not plunge, suffer loss, and blame us for it in due time. An individual firm remains free to act as it pleases; but so far, BARB's appreciation of the situation has obviously had its influence on the Members. We have been a little amused to notice that in 1974, the pressure salesmanship of new Roses came from breeders who are not members of BARB. We counselled caution, and kept quiet, because of a corporate sense of responsibility to the Registered Growers, and to one another.

We devised a sales scheme, which will be in action in 1976 if the Registered Growers approve. They are exercising their opinions on it as you receive this *Rose Annual*. Briefly, it starts on the assumption that the average nursery catalogue does not contain a balanced selection of varieties, and many are limited to the point of inconveniencing the buyer. Indeed many catalogues deliberately exclude some of the best varieties for one reason or another.

We propose to enlist experts in each field, covering the whole range of roses from novelties to species, to produce lists of the best 100, 200, 300, 400 and 500 roses. The criterion is quality; qualified by considerations such as obtaining a full panorama of the genus, a balanced colour range, and reasonable availability of stock. But quality is first, even to the extent that we are prepared to sponsor varieties of our friends outside BARB.

Then we shall invite Growers to catalogue the best 100 or 200 or however many they like; plus, of course, their own fancies, for nobody will ever agree as to which are the best. But the public will know they can go to a BARB Grower because he stocks the best varieties, chosen impartially. We hope to enlist appropriate RNRS experts to nominate the various classes, and we will nominate the novelties from the BARB and RNRS Trial Winners. The proportions have been worked out at approximately 34 hybrid teas, 33 floribundas, 5 Miniatures, 5 Modern Shrub, 5 Old Garden, 5 Species, 10 Climbers and 3 Novelties per 100, with some adjustments in the 400 and 500 range.

Along with this scheme, which we hope will give confidence to the public in buying roses, we shall provide advertising material of a unique kind, or so we believe, in the Rose Trade. It will be informative and entertaining, and we promise not gimmicky. As this will not be seen until 1976, I cannot go further in revealing it.

Of interest to RNRS Members will be our attitude to Amateur breeders. We believe Amateurs' roses should gain their merited place on the market. We are prepared to offer them to our Registered Growers with the same impartial treatment as the roses of our own members. We have a memorandum, which any amateur may ask for, advising upon the selection of a distributor and the negotiation of terms between distributor and amateur breeder. BARB will with great pleasure pay the same attention and give the same facilities to Mr Amateur's rose being offered by a nurseryman distributor, as it will to Herr Kordes' 'Peer Gynt' being offered by McGredy.

Ever since Albert Norman's 'Ena Harkness', hope of riches has entwined itself around the Amateur breeder's heart like *Polygonum baldschuanicum* smothering a 4-ft cane. BARB is aware of this, and most earnestly advises breeders that there is less money in new roses than is popularly supposed. For one thing, there are far too many for each to find a good market, and it is very common to offer a new rose which does not even earn enough royalties to pay for its Plant Breeders' Rights. The professional breeders, competing in this market, most usually find one variety in ten years which carries the losses of the others; they are more likely to find none than two. Their breeding stations, except possibly a few who rely heavily on cut flowers or other varieties on the Continent, are just not viable business propositions. They continue because the breeder is wrapped up in breeding roses, justifies it by selling his own varieties and welcomes the standing and renown it brings him. Please believe us when we give you the advice not to expect riches. We know of cases where a variety was offered, and not one budding eye sold, not one penny earned.

Perhaps the happiest result of BARB has been a growing sense of fellowship between the Breeders and the Registered Growers. Among the 183 Registered Growers are some of the most illustrious nurseries in general horticulture, names like Cramphorn, Hillier, Jefferies, Notcutt, John Scott, Waterer, Wyevale. Most of the famous retail rose nurseries are with us, naturally the Members' own nurseries, also Bees and Gregory. The big wholesale rose growers include Bentley, John Charles, Collin, Soper and Wharton. Then we go through the entire scale of nurseries, to very small firms growing a few thousand a year, some of them part timers.

Many of these Registered Growers have been visited during the year, and this has extended our knowledge and understanding of one another. Some of the small nurseries are excellent, despite, or perhaps because of being small. One which particularly impressed our representative was David E. Lister of Leeds.

We aim to visit every Registered Grower at least once in three years, and each of our Members is responsible for an area, thus covering the country. The area representative is on call for any problems, with such advice and assistance as he can supply. He is also on the look out for persons who are not Registered Growers, who might find it advantageous to join.

We hold an open day with the Registered Growers and Members each year; here the BARB Trials can be seen, also the varieties of all Members being introduced in the year, and the seedlings of the host Member. The likes and dislikes of the Registered Growers prove a useful guide to future introductions. We have provision for a Council of Registered Growers, but so far this has not been implemented, presumably because the channels of communication described, and through the Secretary to the BARB General Meetings and back to the Registered Growers, have sufficed.

BARB's work and enquiries extend into many other interesting fields, each important in its way, and better omitted until a future article, rather than briefly listed. I should, for example, like to have written about our work in rose nomenclature, and with trade organizations both at home and abroad. But let the temptation subside. At the last count we found ourselves engaged in 31 tasks, of which I have told you nine or ten. I hope you will notice us in the future, and will have no cause to offer us anything but your support, because we are competitors, who work as friends, and each gives without stint, not for himself, but for the improvement of the rose.

I have written this on behalf of the Members of BARB, and if we had a fully attended meeting, you would see: Bill Anderson from Aberdeen, sometimes kilted, usually laughing, always helpful and loyal to his promises; Roger Pawsey from Cants of Colchester, who quietly accepts a lot of detailed work, and contributes common-sense and good humour; Alec Cocker from Aberdeen, emphatic and earnest one moment, and arousing gales of laughter the next; Bob Boswijk from Rearsby, representing De Ruiter, full of practical sense, quick witted, a man of great heart to depend on; Gys de Ruiter from Holland, with an austere air, twinkling eye, and a keen, logical mind; Pat Dickson from Newtownards, our President, persistent to press for the truth, and considerate to every viewpoint; Frank Fryer from Knutsford, he makes us laugh, but we value his shrewd business mind, and his clever appraisal of roses; Jack Harkness of Hitchin, that's me, I am the Secretary, and I have recorded 150 minutes, every single one of them unanimous; Peter Ilsink of Holland, a real go-getter with enough energy for five and business acumen for twenty; Bill Warriner of Jackson & Perkins, U.S.A., a man of quiet purpose, infinite courtesy and high principles; Reimer Kordes of Germany, who will listen for twenty minutes and answer in twenty seconds, because he sifts the wheat from the chaff in this business better than any; Edward Le Grice from North Walsham, whose goodness and integrity look just the same to us in the trade as they do to those outside it—not always the case, that; Alfred Lowe from Beeston, a man of honour and kindness, in whom duty and fairness are high priorities; John Mattock from Oxford, our Treasurer, who has given us a great deal of work—and John's work is valuable because his abilities are great, and his impartiality unshakeable; George Priestly from Tandragee, representing McGredy, quiet, but with a hammer in his hand to drive the nail home, a most valuable member giving us whole-hearted work; Sam McGredy from New Zealand, who of course we don't often see, but wish we did, for he is a great breeder and has the personal power to lift up any company he is in; Niels Poulsen from Denmark, another humorist, but an expert on Plant Breeders' Rights on the Continent; Harold Robinson from Burbage, a great contributor in keeping our meetings going, with his sturdy common-sense and good humour; Alain Meilland, from Antibes, pouring out his vision and his knowledge in an emphatic torrent, generously contributing information and documents from his organization; and Michael O'Dell from Waltham Cross, representing Universal Rose Selection—Meilland, always willing to carry out a task, always doing exactly as he promised, and able to advise us about the British cut flower market.

I wonder what the devil they will say to me at the BARB meeting after they have seen this *Rose Annual*?

Rose Nutrition in a World of Scarcity

E. F. ALLEN, M.A. Dip. Agric.(Cantab.), A.I.C.T.A.
(*Gardener, Naturalist, Agronomist and Fruit-grower*)

I wrote in last autumn's *Rose Bulletin* that I was shocked when, in January, 1974, I was quoted £9.00 for a 1 cwt (50·8 kg) bag of Hoof and Horn fertilizer. Twelve years earlier the same bag would have cost £2·00. Since Hoof and Horn is the standard source of slow-acting nitrogen for the John Innes potting composts I realized at once that this would have a most serious effect on horticulture, whether amateur or professional, so I commenced a short term research project both to assess the immediate problem and also to search for substitute sources of the major plant nutrients.

Price Trends and Future Availability

Inorganic nitrogen fertilizers are largely manufactured in the U.K. and the chief imported ingredient is oil, the usual source of energy. Natural gas would be an even better source. For many years the standard nitrogenous fertilizer on farms has been sulphate of ammonia (21 per cent N) and the price of this, to a gardener, has varied from £1·10 per cwt in 1939, to £2·00 in 1959, then down to £1·60 in 1962 and back to £2·00 in January, 1974. At the time of writing (November) it is about £2·70 but the price trend is upwards.

In recent years proprietary brands of ammonium nitrate have been a better buy for farmers than sulphate of ammonia, but they have not been quoted on the garden market.

Blood Meal has always been a favourite source of nitrogen amongst gardeners but is perhaps now too valuable an ingredient of livestock food-stuffs to be used as a fertilizer. Certain synthetic organic materials are available to the gardener but their prices are high and in a state of flux. Two which I can recommend from personal experience are urea-formaldehyde (Nitroform) and sulphur-coated prilled urea (Gold-N). I suspect that these will soon replace Hoof and Horn in commercially prepared potting composts.

The price trend of phosphate fertilizers is quite alarming. The chief raw material is phosphate rock and some 70 per cent of Britain's consumption comes from Morocco. One year ago its bulk price was increased from $14 to $42 per ton and, in July, 1974, it was further increased to $63, a shattering 450 per cent price rise. Ground Rock Phosphate, as it is known in agriculture, makes an excellent fertilizer in the humid tropics but is much less efficient in drier and colder countries. For UK use it is converted by acid treatment into superphosphate (19 per cent P_2O_5) or triple superphosphate (47 per cent P_2O_5) but the latter has gone off the market while the price of the former is now 250 per cent of that which I paid a few years ago. The gardener's price, per cwt, was 60p in 1939, £1·75 in 1959, £1·35 in 1962, £2·20 in January, 1974 and about £3·00 as I write.

Basic Slag, a by-product of the steel industry, is a valuable indigenous source of phosphate, plus lime and magnesia, but it is more popular with farmers than with gardeners. At the time of writing there seems to have been some panic buying and no supplies are available, although a new product known as Phosphated Slag is said to be in plentiful supply in the U.K.

Bone Meal is a favourite source of phosphate for gardeners, but it is a variable product and the better grades, those guaranteed free from anthrax, seem recently to have been directed to feeding livestock. Sterilized Bone Meal was quoted at £4·60 per cwt in early 1974 but the price trend is upwards. Most of the bones from which bone meal is prepared come from the Indian sub-continent and I find it difficult to condone this traffic, since the exporter's need for plant nutrients must surely be greater than our own.

I cannot overemphasize the long-term vulnerability of this country to possible shortages of phosphates in the future and this has been highlighted recently in an excellent paper (Allaby, Blythe & Hines: *Losing Ground*, July 1974) published by the Friends of the Earth Ltd. As far as rose cultivation is concerned, phosphorus is an all-important element since response to nitrogen is reduced when phosphorus is deficient. Fortunately all rosarians can do something about this shortage.

Until very recently virtually all our potash fertilizer has been imported. Sulphate of potash, the source favoured by rosarians, came mostly from the Stassfurt deposits in Germany. Its price has risen steadily from £1·10 per cwt in 1939, £2·25 in 1959, £2·80 in early 1974 and is now even higher. The form favoured by compounders of liquid fertilizers is nitrate of potash and this is now too expensive for normal garden use. Farmers buy the chloride (muriate), which has a higher analysis (60 per cent K_2O) but even this is £3·30 per cwt at the time of writing. Most of it comes from Israel, having been extracted from the Dead Sea. It has the reputation of being an unsuitable potash source for potatoes, dessert apples and roses. However, provided that it is applied in the autumn, the chloride is leached out by winter rains and no harm then comes to apples so it may be that there is a lesson here for rosarians.

Potassium is present in some abundance in clay minerals and I feel certain that rosarians who garden on heavy soils could quite safely reduce potash fertilizer application by 50 to 70 per cent or more.

Plant and wood ashes are traditional and useful sources of potash but, as will be seen later, their use is not without complications in practice. In fact my search for substitutes for imported potash fertilizers has not met with the same success as for nitrogen and phosphorus. It is fortunate, therefore, that Britain is now on the verge of self-sufficiency in potash. According to an I.C.I. Ltd leaflet (*Our Company*) "the country's only potash mine, sunk in Yorkshire by Cleveland Potash Ltd, will be building up to full production in 1975, saving £20 million in imports every year. The mine will not only satisfy all the requirements of Britain's farmers, but should also yield potash for export".

Magnesium is an important major plant nutrient on light soils and its uptake is reduced by too heavy application of potash. The most convenient fertilizer source, kieserite, is all imported. However, dolomitic limestone is another important source and there are deposits in the midlands and north-east England. Magnesium is also present in wood ash.

If this country were not so heavily industrialized then sulphur would also be an important major plant nutrient. In practice, however, industrial fallout from the atmosphere prevents most parts of the U.K. from needing additional fertilizer. In any case considerable quantities are applied to the soil in sulphate of ammonia, sulphate of potash and single superphosphate, this last containing 50 per cent gypsum. The most important U.K. source of sulphur is that of anhydrite at Billingham, Durham.

So much for the short-term future for the major plant nutrients. Let us now see what the average rosarian can do about this problem.

Novel Sources of Nutrients

Roses appear to have no mycorrhizal sources of nitrogen, such as are available to legumes, many forest trees, alders, *Elaeagnus spp* and certain other plants. Hence, they must be supplied with some form of nitrogen each year. During 1974 I have tested two relatively novel sources with excellent results: one is available to every household as a waste product; the other in many rural areas. These are wool waste, in all its forms, and feathers. Both are composed of a peculiar protein called keratin—the same as that in Hoof and Horn—and my replicated pot trials with roses, maize seedlings and other plants have shown that they can be used, without any special treatment, as a substitute for Hoof and Horn meal. Now the keratin group of proteins are, I think, unique in being entirely indigestible to animals and birds. This means that they cannot be used for compounding livestock foodstuffs.

Domestic wool waste, in my own household, comes mostly from old flannel trousers, worn-out tweed coats and old sea-boot over-socks, such as are used by most gardeners when wearing rubber boots. I find that I discard some 5 lb. of such waste a year, yielding at least 11 oz. of nitrogen. During the winter I shoot pheasants, partridge, wood-pigeon and a few wild duck and these provide me with about 50 lb. of dried feathers. These must be kept dry, until required, in a polythene sack or similar container.

For my pot trials I found it necessary, entirely for experimental reasons, to cut up the wool scrap into small pieces and also to chop up the larger feathers with a pair of hedge shears. Neither operation is necessary for outdoor application since both wool fibre and feathers will decompose readily in the soil with the release of ammonia. Long strips of wool fabric can be positioned half way between rose bushes—in the feeding root zone—and then pushed below soil level with a walking stick or similar blunt instrument. Feathers need to be covered over by a mulch or a thin layer of soil. Mid-March is a suitable season for this operation.

In the growing season I am also a keen trout fisherman and catch about 100 rainbow trout per year. After cleaning these fish I wash them in clear rain water and the slurry of skin slime (an interesting protein), blood and guts, after passing through a sieve, provides me with some 50 gallons of "Trout Tea", a speciality of mine, which makes an excellent liquid fertilizer or foliar feed for the most delicate glasshouse plants. The solid residue and fish heads are buried promptly, one spit deep, in favoured rose beds or given to a few special container-grown camellias and other plants.

These examples are given in some detail as I have been quite appalled in recent years at the feeble helplessness of our urban society when confronted by the sudden withdrawal of labour by refuse collectors. If we exclude large quantities of fats then virtually any edible product can be placed inside a compost heap or trenched in the garden.

Most artificial fibres have no manurial or biological value in the soil. Ardil is one exception and this can be treated as wool. If a pair of trousers contains 60 per cent wool and 40 per cent nylon or terylene then it can still be used in the garden, but only the wool fraction will yield nitrogen. Plastics are mostly, but not entirely, valueless. It appears that some plastic buttons, when ground up finely, will yield a nitrogenous manure, but I have not yet investigated these. In a case of this nature it is important to avoid using more energy in grinding up the buttons than their yield of energy-equivalent as plant nutrient. Perhaps some enthusiastic young member might care to collect these buttons from his neighbours with a view to possible future utilization.

I have already indicated that a potential phosphate shortage would have disastrous consequences for the horticulture and agriculture of this country. Fortunately there is one domestic source in every non-vegetarian household in the country. This is, of course, the considerable quantity of surplus bones of food animals, poultry and fish. Some of these are certainly fed to pets, but mutton, lamb, ham and poultry bones are all unsuitable for dogs and most of these are currently discarded in refuse bins. The domestic manufacture of bone meal is not feasible but if all surplus bones are wrapped up in old news-paper and then either burnt on an open fire in winter or on a small bonfire in summer they are rapidly converted into a brittle bone char which can then easily be powdered, sieved and graded. For grinding I find that two methods work well: either they can be passed through an old-fashioned mincing machine or else placed in a thick plastic sack and beaten with a mallet on a concrete floor. The fine ash, after passing through a brass kitchen-type sieve, yields a rapidly available, high analysis (34 per cent P_2O_5) phosphate fertilizer. Three parts by weight of this bone ash can replace five parts of a top quality bone meal. The coarse fraction can either be used as a slower-acting fertilizer or else added to the next batch for re-grinding.

In the preparation of bone ash two practical considerations are important: wrapping up in old newspaper is advised because the newsprint has some preservation action in delaying decomposition. In cool weather this permits the accumulation of several such parcels before burning. Secondly, it is beneficial not to scrape off all fatty scraps since they help with combustion. If dry woody twigs are collected it is possible to make a small garden fire in summer which will produce very little smoke.

The smaller poultry and fish bones will disappear during burning, but if the ash is mixed in a compost heap the phosphate will be recovered for later garden use.

If any member wishes to test the phosphate availability of bone ash for himself, I recommend that he uses seedlings of a dwarf F.1 hybrid Sweet Corn. For my tests I used the variety 'Early Extra Sweet', pre-germinated in 2-in. plastic pots of pure moss peat and then potted on into the experimental composts in $3\frac{1}{2}$ in pots. This crop is very sensitive to phosphate deficiency in the seedling stage, so it is important to use a loam which is known to be deficient in this element. Most woodland sub-soils are suitable. An experiment on these lines will give a rapid answer and the sweet corn seedlings can then be planted out in the vegetable garden.

Many gardeners know from experience that wood ash is a useful source of both potash and lime. In practice, the high lime content, 32 per cent CaO being a common figure, limits its usefulness to the rosarian, although it is valuable, in rotation, in the vegetable garden and any surplus can always be added to the compost heap. However, there can be relatively few people who use wood unmixed with fossil fuels for domestic heating. I have, therefore, examined in some detail the value of mixed ashes on the assumption that half derives from wood and half from fossil fuel.

It will be seen from Table 1 that coal ashes contain considerable aluminium silicate, together with the basic oxides lime, magnesia and iron, with traces of sulphates, carbonates and phosphates. By comparison, wood ashes contain more alkalis, potash and soda, which are present as the carbonates, with little or no alumina. Judging from the analyses of some American ashes it seems that the soda content usually exceeds that of potash. Clearly coal ashes are much less valuable as a source of plant nutrients than are wood ashes. There is another factor limiting their garden use—the very variable minor elements content of coal. Since these include arsenic and also elements which are beneficial to plant growth only in very small quantities, such as boron, copper and manganese, I have thought it wise to confine my attention to the ash from the smokeless fuel Coalite. My reasons for this are two: first, it is the fuel which we use in our own household, in admixture with wood; secondly, because of its pre-treatment during manufacture there should be an extremely low content of volatile matter and this, in my view, should virtually exclude appreciable danger from volatile arsenic, the "fixed" element being of lesser importance.

In practice, it is the high alkalinity of the mixed Coalite and wood ashes which limits their value to rosarians and, as a result of my pot trials, I now recommend that these ashes be considered primarily as a source of lime and that, when applied to rose beds, subsequent fertilizer applications of potash and magnesia should be reduced by 25 per cent.

In some countries it may be that Steffens waste from the beet sugar industry would be a useful source of potash fertilizer. However, the British Sugar Corporation do not use the Steffens process and no comparable waste product is available from their factories.

TABLE 1: *Ash Composition, by weight, of British Coals and of Wood*

Element as oxide	Coal Typical Analysis	Coal Limit of Analysis	Wood Ash
	%	%	%
SiO_2	40	25–50	low
Al_2O_3	28	20–40	trace
Fe_2O_3	10	0–30	
CaO	6	1–10	32·5
MgO	3	0·5–5	3·5
K_2O	} 4	} 1–6	5
Na_2O			1
SO_3	5	1–12	1
P_2O_5	0·4		2

Practical Considerations

My trials in 1974 were almost confined to pot experiments, both under glass and outdoors. Such trials have the advantage of providing quick answers, since a mistake in fertilizer practice shows up at once. My own potting composts have been based on the John Innes formulae with two modifications derived from practical experience with roses. First, the sand is replaced by an equivalent volume of perlite, which is sold in garden shops in large paper sacks under the proprietary name of Loam-a-Lite. This is an expanded volcanic glass, from the Greek Islands, which is virtually as inert and as non-absorbent as sand, but which weighs eleven times less per unit volume. This huge weight reduction is a great advantage when handling many large potted plants and it also makes it easier to judge, by weight estimation, if a plant in a plastic pot requires watering.

My second modification is to add seven parts by weight of kieserite for every 8 parts of chalk used in the compost. Experience has shown that, with my somewhat light loam, this extra magnesium is of benefit to roses, tomatoes and capsicum in particular. With a heavier loam this addition is perhaps of less importance.

The JIP (John Innes Potting) formulae are usually quoted per bushel (8 imperial gallons) which I find not very useful. At least two designs of soil sterilizer currently available to the amateur gardener have a capacity of $\frac{1}{2}$ cu. ft of loam. It is usually convenient to treat four batches at a time and this yields two cu. ft or 49 quarts of sterilized loam. A standard 5-inch plastic pot provides a convenient quart measure. To this quantity of loam are added 21 quarts of moss peat and 14 quarts of perlite (or sand). This gives a batch of 21 gallons of compost. It is then necessary to add the appropriate fertilizers to provide either JIP.1 or JIP.3. I find that the former mix can also be used as a seed compost, while JIP.2 is obtained by taking equal parts of the other two. The additives required for preparing my different formulae are summarized in Table 2.

TABLE 2: *Nutrient additions in oz per batch of 21 gallons compost:*

INGREDIENT	STANDARD JIP.1	JIP.3	EXPERIMENTAL JIP.1	JIP.3	RECOMMENDED JIP.1	JIP.3
JI.Base	10·5	31·5	—	—	—	—
chalk	2	6	—	—	—	—
kieserite	1·75	5·25	—	—	—	—
Coalite–wood ash	—	—	7·8	23·4	7·8	23·4
sulphate of potash	—	—	—	—	1·575	4·725
bone ash	—	—	2·52	7·56	2·52	7·56
feathers or wool	—	—	4·2	12·6	4·2	12·6
Coalite–wood ash leachate	—	—	23·4	70·2	—	—

My standard formula is the one that has given good results with roses and many other plants for more than ten years. Small seedlings are potted into JIP.1, larger seedlings are potted on into JIP.2, while budded plants go into JIP.3.

My experimental mix, which is somewhat troublesome to prepare, involves adding one quarter of the required potash and all the lime as dried Coalite–wood ash. The remaining three-quarters is mixed in a plastic bucket with rainwater, allowed to settle and the clear supernatant liquid decanted over the compost. This is repeated once. In theory it represents a simple method of extracting the potassium and sodium carbonates from the ash while leaving behind most of the sparingly soluble lime. In practice it has caused some chlorosis with 'Climbing Pink Cameo' and certain other roses, perhaps because the alkali carbonates in solution have a very high pH. No plant toxin seems to be involved because various pelargonium cultivars thrive in the compost. Nevertheless my recommended mix is the better formula to use for roses and it has been my practice to assume that both my wool waste and feathers have a nitrogen content of 14 per cent. Pure wool contains up to 17 per cent nitrogen and this may account for the fact that, on average, rose seedlings grown in JIP recommended composts have grown better and with less Powdery Mildew than those in standard composts.

I am advised by the National Coal Board that ash from Homefire, which is an excellent smokeless fuel, should not be used as a fertilizer ingredient because its boron content considerably exceeds that of other ashes. I have done no experiments with the ash from any other smokeless fuels, so cannot express an opinion on their value.

For use on outdoor roses I recommend the following dressings per ten square yards:

30 oz. Coalite-wood ash or wood ash in November or December.
5 oz. bone ash, also in November or December.
10–12 oz. wool scrap or feathers placed in the soil in March.
4 oz. sulphate of potash broadcast in March or April.
2 oz. kieserite broadcast in March or April.

I suggest that Members should aim at treating one rose bed only for three years and aim at applying proprietary fertilizers elsewhere in the rose garden. This will provide a valuable comparison on which to base future practice. If extra domestic plant nutrients are available, they can be used on parts of the vegetable garden. By this means a considerable national saving should be effected.

Discussion

I make these recommendations in all seriousness at the risk of being dubbed either an alarmist or a crank. It might be suggested that the recovery of a relatively small quantity of plant nutrients from domestic waste materials is not strictly economic. In my view this would be an error. Not being either a politician or an economist, I know exactly how to cure the nation's current inflation. First, one must consume less; secondly, one must produce more. Now rosarians are manifestly public-spirited and responsible people and they can be expected to react with commonsense, provided that the reasons for any particular line of action are expressed clearly. I myself believe that the U.K. is now intolerably vulnerable to possible interruptions in the import of both food and phosphates. To ignore this—to me—self-evident fact is lunacy and it is difficult to forgive the lack of action by recent governments. My thesis, then, is that the situation is now too serious to be left to the government and that members of this Society should set an example. I appreciate that many of you are retired and cannot, therefore, produce more. You can, however, waste less and persuade your immediate neighbours to do likewise. A measure of success would be the weight of refuse bin or bag. If you can also grow more and heavier crops of vegetables, so much the better for your own health and the country's financial standing.

On a medium term basis it seems to me that a considerable quantity of phosphate can be recovered from industry and my proposals for one such project are given in an appendix which may not be of interest to all rosarians.

Appendix

Industries which use steel sheet in quantity, and this includes the motor industry, dip this sheet in a bath of de-rusting and de-greasing liquid which is based primarily on phosphoric acid, with the addition of detergents and buffering agents. The precipitated sludge in these baths seems to consist mostly of insoluble iron phosphate, with traces of zinc, manganese, nickel and perhaps of molybdenum. At intervals the baths are emptied and the sludge and remaining liquid discarded. At least some of this is poured down the drain. In no circumstances, in my view, should this practice be allowed to continue; firstly, because phosphate in lakes and rivers encourages algal bloom in hot weather and this is harmful to most fish and other aquatic life. The second objection is that the waste of phosphate is indefensible in a time of scarcity.

Mr A. L. Day, a senior Engineer in the Austin-Morris Group of British Leyland Ltd, has been kind enough to have a laboratory test made of the practicability of phosphate recovery. This can be achieved by dissolving the sludge in hydrochloric acid and then precipitating out the iron and other heavy metals in various other chemical solutions. Clearly a pilot test on a larger scale would be required to determine the profitability of such a project and it may well be that one of the larger fertilizer companies would be prepared to carry out this research. If such a plant were to be carefully sited within easy reach of several large factories which produce this sludge, they could then draw on considerable quantities of this industrial waste material. I recommend early action on these lines.

'MAMAN COCHET' (Tea) (see page 45)

'GLOIRE DE DIJON', improved form (clg. Tea) (see page 41)

'BARONNE HENRIETTE SNOY' (Tea)

'MERMAID', a recurrent climber (*see page* 140)

Acknowledgements

In preparing this paper I have been helped by discussions with two colleagues on Council—Mr E. V. Elwes and Dr J. T. Watts.

Mr R. Pane, of Coalite and Chemical Products Ltd, and Mr J. Gibson, Director of the National Coal Board's Coal Research Establishment, have both been very helpful indeed.

Mr A. L. Day, as I have already indicated, took great care to provide answers to my awkward questions because of their importance nationally. And to Mr H. V. Mitchell, current Chairman of the Colchester Rose Society, I am indebted for his first indicating the availability of waste phosphate sludge in industry.

As always, I am in debt to my old friend Dr Vladimir Ignatieff, of Canada, for his excellent F.A.O. publication *Efficient Use of Fertilizers* (Leonard Hill Ltd, London, 1952).

(November, 1974)

A Rose Novice and His First Garden

DR A. K. BROWN

(Amateur rose grower)

"It's a fine piece of land for rose-growing," assured the local builder as I gazed with some dismay on the tiny plot on which I was to produce my superb rose garden as well as a house and garage. It was twelve years ago and I had just intimated that my modest ambition was to grow the finest roses in the neighbourhood, or even the whole of the North-West of England, despite the obvious drawback that I had never grown a single rose in my life until then. I was to think on his prophetic words as the long months passed, with the house growing ever so slowly from one seemingly inexplicable delay to yet another. As the bricklayers, plumbers, electricians, plasterers and decorators all came and left their débris, the slow realization had dawned that our house was the last one to be built on the estate and the garden had acquired a huge collection of miscellaneous rubbish.

One evening, as dusk fell, I was once more viewing my precious land when

I came across a good, dark patch of promising loam near the putative site of the front door. I soon regretted the decision to explore, however, as I discovered that the loam was a deep trench with a three-inch thick muddy base, a fact which was found out by the simple expedient of falling in!

Eventually the house was completed, we moved in and I could begin to survey the situation in the virgin garden. The weeds were growing well in most places, but some areas were ominously devoid of any recognisable life forms. I was somewhat embarrassed to be complimented by a partially-sighted walker who mistook a giant thistle for a "lovely bloom" and the oblong area of front garden was rapidly chosen as the main rose bed where I determined to prepare the soil thoroughly before tilting at the supremacy of the local rosarians. The "fine rose-growing land" was not promising. The estate may very well have been built on the site of a splendid orchard as my builder friend suggested, but any subsoil from this outstanding source had long since disappeared and instead, various materials of dubious benefit to roses were unearthed. What roses could possibly flourish in a "soil" comprising a layer of loose shale under which was a layer of numerous different sizes of brick encased in plaster and finally the ultimate in soil problems, a layer of concrete about one inch thick?

Never daunted by the size of a problem, a pick and shovel were used to replace these materials with a large hole which thoroughly intrigued the neighbours. Speculation on the reason for the hole varied, I understand, from a swimming pool (very small!) to a sunken garden, but my secret was soon exposed when my first load of local woodland loam arrived. Unfortunately the lorry driver managed to demolish one of the gate posts while depositing the soil in the main drive and just as he drove away with profuse apologies for the damage, the telephone summoned me to work which meant that, somehow or other, I must clear the drive to get the car out of the garage. Out came the shovel and some twenty minutes later, as I paused for breath and wiped the sweat from my forehead, I was gently chided for working too fast. The mild remonstrance came from a friendly rose grower who had long since learned the art of husbanding his resources and working steadily. Incidentally, he was able to get through far more work in the garden than me, despite long-standing heart disease.

After the liberal addition of horse manure and bone meal I retired behind the glossy catalogues and enjoyed many hours making different permutations of varieties of rose to grace my garden plot. Ultimately I deserted most of the catalogues for the local nurseryman on the advice of my new rosarian friend and this advice I have never regretted.

Other decisions which run contrary to many expert suggestions were to have as many different varieties as possible and, even though this was a minute garden, the roses would not be restricted to compact varieties. The reason for deciding against planting groups of the same rose was simply because my wife and I were eager to try to find roses which would grow best under our conditions and we also felt that variability in height and form would add interest to the rose bed.

Amongst the red varieties, I remember how disappointed I was at the hanging heads of 'Ena Harkness'. The vigour, colour, habit and form were all superb but the let-down when the flowers drooped so miserably was absolute. I have always retained a soft spot for 'Chrysler Imperial', despite the sparsity of blooms and the tendency to fade, but 'Frensham' rapidly "frosted" with mildew and the colour was too flat and dull to be really appealing. 'Josephine Bruce' was a must because of the richness of the velvety red blooms, but the sprawling habit was a poor feature. 'Karl Herbst' was another disappointment, with an abundance of moderately attractive blooms which were ruined by even a hint of rain. About mid-season, 'Montezuma' produced a series of superbly formed blooms which outclassed anything else in the garden, but, try as I might, I have never succeeded so well since and the tendency to ball in the rain should decide me against this variety, but perhaps next year ... 'Dickson's Flame' aroused local comment about the vivid colour but failed to produce enough flowers to preserve its image.

The disasters within the group of predominantly yellow roses were 'Marcelle Gret' which produced a moderate number of blooms which were "blown" within 24 hours and which had particularly poor foliage, and 'Faust', which at first shone in full glory and was a real delight, only to end the season completely mildewed. 'Sutter's Gold' and 'Buccaneer' were the pick of the yellow varieties, but my neighbour had a superb specimen of the latter which dwarfed and outshone my example and I have frustrated myself ever since with attempts to emulate his success.

The pink bushes provided some appealing roses with the old, sweetly smelling 'Madame Butterfly' a real pleasure and 'Queen Elizabeth', which was always an eye-catcher although rather late in the season. 'Monique' and 'Grace de Monaco' were worth their places in the bed, but 'Eden Rose', despite an abundance of flowers, never really appealed because of the rather dark pink colour and 'Pink Peace' was a sad blow with its massive, dark-pink blooms of great inelegance. 'Perfecta' was highly recommended, but the ugly patchwork bud which seemed to stay for ever could not be compensated by the admittedly excellent flowers.

'Virgo' was lovely in bud but rain soon spoiled the flowers, which left 'Iceberg' as the best white representative, with masses of showy blooms, although the stems were spindly.

Of the bicolours, 'Rose Gaujard' and 'Stella' were splendid, but not in the first year, when the former in particular seemed to produce pallid-coloured blooms compared with subsequent years. 'Sultane' was a useful addition, but was no match for later introductions such as 'Piccadilly', and 'Tzigane' had such dull colours it was depressing.

I suppose one becomes more critical of superseded roses over the years, but even so, there are some varieties which I have consistently grown in subsequent gardens because of the sheer pleasure they have given over the years and because I can't bear to be without them. Perhaps a list of these roses will seem mundane to many rose growers, but we all enjoy our roses in different ways and the following are still making me happy each year: 'Peace', 'Buccaneer', 'Sutter's Gold', 'Queen Elizabeth', 'Monique', 'Madame Butterfly', 'Stella', 'Rose Gaujard', 'Virgo', 'Iceberg', 'Montezuma', 'Chrysler Imperial', 'Dickson's Flame'.

A Breeder's Reply

A. P. C. DICKSON

(*Rose nurseryman and breeder*)

Have you ever asked yourself, "Are the rose breeders really producing better roses, or are they just trying to make us believe they are?". It didn't occur to me that such a view existed in anyone's mind; not, that is, until last July when I was confronted by a person with this very question. It was no coincidence that it happened on the morning of the final judging of the City of Belfast Rose Trials, and further, it was being asked by an eminent and respected horticulturist who had just completed his judging. The roses that day were a revelation. I had walked quietly round at a safe distance from the judges, and had been marvelling at the beauty before me. They had been cultivated to perfection. Varieties I knew well were being shown with such splendour that I was both spellbound and proud. Proud that it was in Belfast, with all its troubles, that this garden was established by the Corporation, open for everyone to visit.

Yet here I was, confronted by my friend who believed with conviction and in all seriousness that no advances had been made in rose breeding over the years. I don't think I had been as shocked since the day I read that someone on the Council of the RNRS had suggested that all rose breeders should be removed from the New Seedling Judging Committee as they could not be impartial! I was speechless for what seemed like minutes; my blood pressure rising. I decided I wouldn't defend rose breeders, rather I would attack the validity of the question, and what better way than by using the particular section of breeding in which I have most experience—crimson hybrid teas?

Most people know of 'Crimson Glory' (Kordes 1934). She reigned as supreme garden rose for at least ten years, and played no mean part in the breeding of her replacement, 'Ena Harkness' (Norman 1946)—'Crimson Glory' × 'Southport'. 'Ena Harkness' was brighter, healthier, stronger; altogether superior. Just about this time breeders the world over were getting to know 'Peace', perhaps the most influential variety in the breeding of garden roses. One of her offspring 'Karl Herbst' (Kordes 1950)—'Independence' × 'Peace'—affectionately christened "The Old Bull", played a most important part in the breeding of modern roses, and still to-day, though more indirectly, has a contribution to make, particularly to crimsons.

At this point in our conversation, true to our Irish climate, it began to rain so my friend and I moved to the more comfortable, but still as yet sparsely populated, refreshment marquee. I could see that I was starting to make an impression, but my points needed pressing home. It's always worth a point or two to speak from personal experience, and I felt I had reached the stage where this was possible. I brought in 'Red Devil', introduced in 1967— 'Silver Lining' × 'Prima Ballerina'—well, not quite all 'Prima Ballerina' and perhaps now is as good a time as any to say she did have some help. It's a devil indeed in the wet, though a great plant, with excellent health and lovely foliage. However, it has one major fault—too many petals. A breeder will tell you that it's easier to take petals off than put them on. Seventy-five in the case of 'Red Devil' resulted in thirty-six in 'Red Planet' (Dickson 1970)— 'Red Devil' × ('Brilliant' × Seedling). It's a fine healthy plant and its wet weather performance is a big improvement on its mother's, but it is too dark in colour. 'Precious Platinum' (Dickson 1974)—'Red Planet' × 'Franklin

Engelmann'—is a much better colour with all the other parental qualities, but as yet no award. Plenty of acclaim, though, especially on the Continent. Coming right up-to-date, DIC 8825—'Precious Platinum' × 'Julie'—is a candidate for the 1977 Trials and is, I hope, another step forward. I could not exclude 'Alec's Red' (Cocker 1970) and 'National Trust' (McGredy 1970) from my list, and my friend agreed that we had come a very long way since the introduction of 'Crimson Glory'.

I hadn't realized that the level of our voices had been rather high, and also that the marquee had been rapidly filling up. We had gained an audience of keen rosarians who were not prepared just to listen; they had their own opinions and were determined to make themselves heard. Someone remarked that 'Pye Colour' (Dickson 1972), a scarlet, compact-growing floribunda was on the short list of varieties for the Floribunda Award. A helpful remark, because really excellent varieties, such as 'Marlena' (Kordes 1964), 'Sunday Times' (McGredy 1971) and 'Topsi' (Tantau 1973) have been added to the list of compact-growing floribundas and have removed the need for the dwarf Polyanthas with their limited colour range, poor flower form and tendency to mildew. In fact, in my opinion they have no place in modern roses. Going to the other end of the scale and looking at the Shrub roses, I pointed out that here again there has been a tremendous improvement. In 1972 'Fountain' (Tantau) a bright crimson shrub, or giant-sized hybrid tea if you like, deservedly won the President's International Trophy. It is a great addition to a range of super coloured shrubs such as 'Joseph's Coat' (Armstrong & Swim 1964) orange and gold, 'Fred Loads' (Holmes 1968) vermilion, and 'Chinatown' (Poulsen 1963) yellow, all with floribunda type flowering habits. Although breeders are producing these wonderful varieties they are not generally being used to advantage. With the necessity of keeping down labour costs, the larger gardens are becoming less formal in character. Shrub roses lend themselves to this type of landscaping and they ought to be used to much greater advantage. This also applies to the older, established shrub roses.

My friend broke in here with a very valid point—the annual influx of so-called novelties, the majority of which are certainly no improvement, rather a step backward. Yes, we all make mistakes, myself included, but this is no excuse for the ever increasing number of novelties which are no improvement on existing varieties and do nothing but tarnish the image of the really worthy ones. I believe that the BARB Trials will achieve their object—give a clear indication of what to grow, and discourage those whose varieties fail the Trials from offering them for sale. The RNRS Trials are excellent. However, they are run by an amateur society, and therefore, it is more difficult for them to give directions as to what should or should not be grown. The BARB Trials (as you will read elsewhere in this Issue) are to an extent complementary to the Society's Trials. The performance of each variety is noted and taken into consideration in each case, all with the object of seeing that you are not offered a variety simply because it's new. Varieties carrying a BARB Award will be worthy varieties, and their performance reports will be there for anyone to see.

Perhaps in terms of numbers rose breeding throughout the world is on the decline, partly due to the economic situation, and we can expect no further growth in this country. Nevertheless, it should be recognised that breeders are widening their scope and more, as yet untried, fertile species are being used. Progress may be slow but we are moving forward.

My friend in Dixon Park made me stop and think, and take stock—never a bad thing!

Redouté Redivivus

G. D. ROWLEY

(Lecturer in Taxonomy, Reading University)

No flower paintings have ever achieved wider or longer popularity than the roses of Redouté. One sees them on table mats, tea towels, lamp shades, letter headings and chinaware—often a pale shadow of their original glory but instantly characteristic and acceptable to all tastes. It was in his combination of skills, bringing satisfaction to the botanist as well as to the art connoisseur, that Redouté still ranks among the greatest of flower painters. Such a combination is rare indeed. Many painters dazzle us with the splendour of their compositions, colours and chiaroscuro, but botanical art demands much more than this. A flower must be recognisable in all its diagnostic features, and this requires minute examination, a basic knowledge of morphology and careful layout and design to accent each feature without introducing artificiality or a textbook stiffness. In this ever-so-slight exaggeration of Nature lies the secret of a great flower painting. The balance is critical, and varies even in the work of one artist. Thus, as Stafleu has pointed out, Redouté's style changed throughout his lifetime. His early studies of succulent plants, under the influence of strict botanical training from L'Heritier, are extremely faithful to Nature and make minimal concessions to pictorialism. Towards the end of his life an elegance and flamboyance is more notice-able, in order to appease popular demand and meet his ever-mounting debts. Happily the roses occupy the zenith of his career and the balance is almost ideal throughout.

Redouté painted over 200 different roses, and the sum of his oeuvres has a historical value quite apart from that of the individual pictures. He lived at a period when rapid changes were taking place in garden roses and older groups were becoming eclipsed by new. The influx of China and Tea roses from the Far East was changing the look of the rose as well as extending its flowering period. In the space of a few years many once-popular roses dis-appeared forever or lingered in oblivion, to be resuscitated by a later age as nostalgic souvenirs of the past. The Empress Josephine, who sponsored Redouté's publication *Les Roses*, was in the forefront of this new wave of rose breeding, encouraging the raising of novelties and filling her garden at Malmaison with everything that could be acquired. We can see in the pages of *Les Roses* examples of both the new and the old, as well as the wild species from which they are descended: a unique testament, not only to the origin of garden roses, but to the richness of the garden at Malmaison. The book is, and always will be, indispensable to rose historians and growers seeking to identify survivors of that era.

Pierre-Joseph Redouté was born in 1759 at Saint-Hubert, a most attractive small village in the Ardennes in Belgium. Both his father and grandfather were painters, and he and two of his brothers were destined to follow a similar profession. Redouté left home at the age of 13, and finally settled in Paris when 23. His talents came to the notice of the amateur botanist L'-Heritier de Brutelle, who acted as his Maecenas and launched him on a successful career. He studied further under the famous Dutch flower painter Van Spaendonck, and his fame spread rapidly, undisturbed by the political dramas that flared in France around this period. He painted for the unhappy Queen Marie-Antoinette. He painted for the Empress Josephine, Napoleon's first wife. He painted for the Duke of Orleans, the future King Louis-Philippe and his daughters. Early on he had his own studio where he directed a team of assistants and engravers. Young daughters of the aristocracy clam-oured to attend his classes. His activity seemed limitless. He taught and painted at the Museum, published a succession of mighty folios of plates, and became a member of many scientific societies where he counted among his distinguished friends the Swiss botanist A. P. De Candolle. He gave his last class on 18 June, 1840. A few hours later he died while painting a lily picked for him by his daughter.

While samples of Redouté's art, at second or third hand, have become commonplace in the household, his magnum opus *Les Roses* has become a collector's piece of the utmost value, rarely seen outside the largest museums and libraries where it is zealously guarded behind bars and locked doors. It was originally published in 30 parts between 1817 and 1824, with text written by Claude Antoine Thory and 169 plates printed by Redouté's own modification of stipple engraving with the finer details retouched by hand afterwards. One hundred copies only of the first folio edition appeared; other smaller-sized reissues followed up to 1835. The plates in these are more or less inferior in quality although some additional ones were included. Since 1835 no attempt has been made to reprint the whole work—only tantalizing selections of plates of varying quality. Now for the first time the complete three folio volumes are being reprinted, full size, and with no efforts spared to do justice to the beauty and perfection of one of the most superb and coveted of all flower books.

It would have been nice to have reproduced direct from the original vellums painted by Redouté. Unfortunately, although many flower studies by Redouté survive, few are of roses. Apparently the majority were lost in a fire at the Louvre library in 1871. Hence recourse must be had to the published prints. Of these Stafleu has this to say: "Admittedly the prints cannot convey the more delicate nuances of the originals. It is remarkable, however, how closely the prints do approximate the Redouté style, while the enforced simplification in the print imparts a decorative quality of its own."

So far no mention has been made of the text for *Les Roses*. It was written by Thory (1759–1827), a close friend of Redouté who has unjustly been overshadowed by the name of the artist. He was a methodical and accurate recorder of roses and in 1820 published his own 190-page monograph of the genus. In *Les Roses* he contributes a detailed and critical synonymy, excellent descriptions which add details not apparent from the plates, and historical notes on the origin and affinities of each subject. Even without the illustrations, Thory's text would have its place in history.

The new edition of *Les Roses* will be limited to 500 copies plus 10 which are not for sale. Volume I came off the press in November 1974; Volume II is due to appear in November 1975 and Volumes III and IV by 1976 or 1977. Volume IV is an additional feature which will include an introduction to the reprint by Sir George Taylor, a biography and bibliography of Redouté and Thory by Dr A. Lawalrée, a summary-translation of Thory's text by Mrs L. Glass and myself, and a commentary including modern botanical names by the Baroness de la Roche. In addition, there will be extra colour plates of

roses by Redouté not included in the first edition of *Les Roses*, to make the
venture as complete as possible.

Heading the team of specialists responsible for the reprint is Mr C. De
Schutter, whose firm in Antwerp is justly renowned for the quality of its
colour printing. Each plate coming from his workshop testifies to the
complete mastery of an exacting technique. Further motivation comes from
Mr and Mrs R. De Belder, owners of the Arboretum of Kalmthout, Belgium,
whose collections of plants—roses in particular—are rightly esteemed. Their
library of botanical books includes many treasures, one of the most precious
of which is an exceptionally fine first folio edition of *Les Roses* in which
Redouté has added a note "This is one of the first printing and one of the
most beautiful." It is from this set that the new facsimile is being made.

Sir George Taylor, who writes the opening chapter of Vol. IV, needs no
introduction: for many years he was Director of the Royal Botanic Gardens
at Kew and is a well known figure in the world of botany. Prof A. Lawalrée
of the National Botanical Garden of Belgium has made a special study of the
life and works of Redouté, so is the ideal choice to contribute the biography
and bibliography. One of the most difficult tasks, identifying Redouté's
roses and sorting out their correct status and names today from amid a
plethora of taxonomic confusion, has fallen to the lot of the Baroness de la
Roche. Again the choice could not have been bettered. A connoisseur and
grower of old roses, Mrs de la Roche has devoted an immense amount of
scholarly research to producing her commentary, and this alone would make
Vol. IV indispensable to botanists and earn it a place on the shelf of every
scientific reference library. Finally, Mrs L. Glass combines an uncommon
skill in translating the most tortuous and technical of scientific jargon with a
first-hand knowledge of the subject—so necessary in order to ensure complete accuracy. I am proud to have been associated with such a team of experts.

References

LAWALRÉE, A. & BUCHHEIM, G., "P. J. Redouté". Hunt Institute,
Pittsburgh 1972.

ROWLEY, G. D., "Pierre-Joseph Redouté—Raphael of the Succulents" in
Cactus & Succulent Journal of Great Britain XVIII: 91–93, 101, 1956; XIX:
6–8, 30–32, 36, 54–57, 77, 89–93, 1957.

STAFLEU, F. A., "Redouté—Peintre de Fleurs" in *A Catalogue of Redoutéana*,
Hunt Bot. Library 1963: 1–32.

STAFLEU, F. A., "Redouté and his Circle" in *Bibliography & Natural
History*, Lawrence, Kansas 1966: 46–65.

Roses growing in a boscage of azaleas. 'Lilac Charm' in the foreground (*see page 112*)

Uncrowded, 'Iceberg' stands 5 ft 6 in. among herbaceous plants. In front is the Lancaster geranium, with the author behind (*see page* 114)

A low hedge of roses 'Natalie Nypels' and 'Red Favourite' flanks the drive, with Helianthemum 'Croceum'

The "Hybrid Musk" rose 'Penelope' throws out big swags of blossom on long,
arching stems (*see page* 113)

Roses As Garden Plants

C. E. LUCAS PHILLIPS
(War historian and amateur rose grower)

The title is the Editor's, whom one must obey. Roses are obviously "garden plants", but the editorial intention is to consider how to employ roses to advantage otherwise than in separate, formal beds. Thus my theme will be a garden with lots of roses of all sorts and not merely a "rose garden".

Perhaps I have some qualifications on this subject, because I do not always accept orthodoxy without question and am an inveterate experimenter (by no means always a successful one). Moreover, I now have only a small garden, which my wife and I (both older than the century) tend with very little help, and into this we cram as many of the plants we love as we can. Roses have priority, but have to learn to live sociably with all sorts of other plants.

I start on the classic basis that a garden, of whatever size, should be designed as a picture. It must not be haphazard but should be thought out according to the canons of good design. It must also have due regard to the seasons. Into this pattern the rose has to fit.

One of the first lessons one learns in applying these notions to a small plot (if you have a catholic taste) is that you must crowd things a little. Profusion takes precedence over perfection.

The Hybrid Tea Roses

You come slap up against this notion when you consider hybrid teas. Here one does, indeed, yearn for some perfection of bloom but you will never get it if you overcrowd the very vigorous modern hybrid teas. A bed of hybrid teas on their own has to look just right. Therefore you begin to think of the idea of spacing them well apart and growing other plants, of low stature, between them.

This has all sorts of virtues if you exercise a strict discipline and pick their bedmates with great care and with a very strong preference for those that display themselves before the roses bloom, or those that cover the ground with ample leafage to counterbalance the rose's lack of it at the base. This is too big a subject to enlarge upon here, but I offer the suggestion that, where soil and climate are propitious, gentians are ideal. So are, in any soil, *Viola labradorica*, which quickly spreads a purple-tinted mat, and the common or garden mossy saxifrage. Not heathers, unfortunately. Not bulbs. Not any-

111

thing rampageous or coarse. There are plenty of other low, leafy plants that consort well with roses, such as the Dalmatian and Lancaster geraniums and the little grey-leaved hebe, which we are expected to call *H. pinguifolia* 'Pagei'.

In any such treatment the rose is dominant, but another way of using hybrid teas effectively is to treat them as a plant among other plants, secondary or supplementary to the main theme, whether herbaceous or shrubby. Here we want, as a rule, the really lusty hybrid teas—'Peace', 'Prima Ballerina', 'Super Star', 'Fred Gibson' and so on, but any good hybrid tea goes. This is very much an example of treating roses as "garden plants" rather than formal specialities. With a disciplined selectiveness, the results can be charming, forming the idealist's "picture". It is all a matter of scale and proportion.

The Floribunda Roses

When we come to the floribundas the vista opens widely. Here we have not only their massed splendour when growing all together, but also a wide scope for informal pictures of mixed plantings. My own favourite dodge, having a slightly acid soil, is to interplant them with the low, evergreen azaleas or dwarf rhododendrons; not singly, but each in a cluster of not less than three. The azaleas hide the naked legs of the roses in winter and are a glory of massed blossom in April and May, and in summer their dense greenery is topped by the coloured clusters of the floribundas. Behind them come the taller deciduous azaleas in their brilliant colours and behind them again, beyond a path, rhododendrons, camellias, lilies and more roses. Thus we get a continuity of bloom from March right through to November.

In limy soils the azaleas and rhododendrons can be replaced by the low growing Japanese quinces, *Chaenomeles speciosa* "Simonii" and *C. japonica alpina*, but they are not evergeen.

There are, of course, plenty of other uses for floribundas, formal and informal. They happily fill odd corners, flank a drive and soften the harsh outlines of garages and sheds. The dwarf varieties, of which there is an increasing number, rarely exceed 15 in high and have a special value. In front of one of our sitting-out places we have a jolly bed of 'Tip-top', which allows us an unimpeded view, over its massed pink clusters, across the whole breadth of the garden. We have a few of the charming golden 'Kim' fringing the bronze skirts of a dwarf Japanese maple (*Acer palmatum* 'Dissectum Atropurpureum'), and so forming a refreshing colour harmony. 'Escapade', looking like a sublimated dog-rose, 'The Fairy', stretching out its arms widely, and 'Ballerina' are ideal plants for mixed company and you can grow them anywhere. Many of the floribundas you can grow in quite an appreciable degree of shade and then you want the softer colours—anything but red. Red is a colour to avoid, furthermore, against any very dark background, such as holly or yew.

The Shrub Roses

The very opposite of the floribundas is seen in the "shrub" roses—that unsatisfactory term which simply means a big bush. Gardeners, even on a small scale, should think more about these, both the old and the new, for they are among the finest of "garden plants", suiting themselves to all sorts of situations. The rugosas, for example, challenge comparison with any other type of shrub whatsoever, except the camellia, which is the most beautiful of all hardy shrubs. The dense, dark, rugged drapery of the rugosas, virtually immune to disease, is worn right down to the ground, smothering weeds, and their sumptuous flowers are borne, in some varieties, more or less all the season. The purple-flowered 'Scabrosa' and 'Roseraie de l' Haÿ', in particular, make the finest of hedges and the former is splendidly shown on the flank of the Society's great garden at Bone Hill. Rugosas, however, rarely succeed in lime.

The hybrid musks also come high among the shrub roses. Behaving quite differently from the rugosas, they are sparsely leaved and throw out their big swags of blossom on long, arching stems that are most effective at the back of a border of any sort of flowers or low shrubs. Their tender, pallid hues of pink and yellow and the white of 'Pax' are cool and soothing and look well nodding over such plants as hydrangeas, daphnes, potentillas, fuchsias, hypericums and so on.

Rosa primula is one of the most delightful of garden plants, indeed unique, forming a 6-ft mound of small, dense foliage of aromatic breath, spangled with scented, buttercup-like flowers in May and equipped with large, ruby thorns. It goes well in any place where you would plant a shrub, but is most agreeable at some spot where you would brush against its honeyed leaves as you pass by.

There are plenty of other elegant shrub roses such as 'Canary Bird', 'Erfurt', 'Fritz Nobis' and the unique 'Golden Wings', and several robust modern ones, such as 'Chinatown' and 'Fred Loads', which have a long season of bloom, but are of somewhat restricted use, and we find a greater versatility as garden plants in the beautiful and scented Bourbons.

The peculiarity about the Bourbons is that they do not really go well with all other roses, certainly not with modern ones, but you can put them to all sorts of uses. 'Mme Pierre Oger', for example, with its delicate, shell-like flowers repeatedly borne, is a slim, whippy, elegant creature that will fit narrow places in isolation or in small groups. 'Mme Isaac Pereire' and 'La Reine Victoria', luscious in both flower and scent, are delightful as pillar roses or short climbers, as well as in the form of free-standing, wide-flung, rather floppy shrubs. All go very well indeed with herbacious plants of modest growth and with the dwarf shrubs, such as azaleas, rue, variegated sages, applemint and marjoram, columbines, fuchsias, hostas and true geraniums, all in their due seasons, and are, indeed, far more to be esteemed in such company than as a bed of roses on their own.

Two roses that, I suppose, very few people think of as designed for a bed of roses as such are 'Nevada' and its pink offspring 'Marguerite Hilling'. They have personalities all their own. Their supple limbs, springing out like longbows full-bent, easily extend themselves over 15 ft of ground, so they take their places with distinction in any border or congregation of shrubs. Nowhere, I think, are they more effective than when arching over rhododendrons of moderate growth, giving diversity of foliage and a sustained season of blossom, for they start as the rhododendrons end.

Rose Hedges

If hedges are "garden plants", roses make them specially so. Except for purely utilitarian purposes, there is no reason why hedges should be merely green walls and I prefer to think of them as essentially parts of the garden. You must not, of course, plant anything too violently prickly along a public pavement and must look out for any wandering and wayward shoots. I have already mentioned the rugosas, which are the best of all hedging roses. 'New Dawn' is a perfectly splendid barrier, forming a dense, branching, boyproof, thicket of 6 ft or more and flowering all the summer and, if not a perfectionist, you can clip it with shears; but it is extremely prickly. The few-thorned 'Iceberg' makes a beautiful, all-white hedge of 4 ft or more. I do not consider that 'Queen Elizabeth' is a good hedger; its legs are too bare and its habit too stiff, though these faults can be remedied in part by cutting it down knee-high.

Ground-cover Roses

Many gardens have steep banks or slopes or are on hillsides shored up by stone, brick or concrete walls. In these there is a crying need for plants that will tumble down and form a curtain. Various plants offer their services for this task, but the rose is seldom thought of by the gardener. Yet there are some very good candidates, all either quite prostrate or of lax growth. Good ones for covering slopes are the old hybrid perpetuals with very long canes, such as 'Reine des Violettes' and 'Hugh Dickson', but they need to be pegged down. For general use I would give priority to 'Max Graf' and *R. paulii* and its pink form, *R. paulii rosea*. *R. wichuraiana*, parent of most ramblers, grows absolutely flat, ever-spreading and crowded with white flowers in August. 'Raubritter' makes a pink mound in July and swoops densely out and down. The new climbing miniature 'Nozomi' could also be tried. Such roses are also valuable for covering old tree stumps and other awkward spots, but not manholes (too prickly!)

Rambling and climbing roses

It is scarcely necessary to say that, in their own contexts, ramblers and climbers are among the most splendid of garden plants, taking the garden to its farthest extremities and right up to the house. In addition, we can use them on arches to form a frame for a chosen garden picture, as screens economically dividing one part of the garden from another, such as masking the vegetable garden or the compost corner, and as clothing for a pergola. Many an unlovely shed has been put to decorative use by embowering it in a mantle of roses and in this role I have found the old 'Gloire de Dijon' a delight, almost as happy in a shaded northern aspect as in full sun. 'Golden Showers' and 'Aloha', slim and erect, will neatly fit into the space between two windows. 'Leverkusen' can be trained to look like a tree. Any rose with supple stems can be spread out around a terrace or along a balustrade, performing tasks that very few other plants will undertake.

Finally, there are the remarkable tree-climbing roses, (*R. filipes* 'Kiftsgate', *R. longicuspis*, *R.* 'Polyantha Grandiflora' (*gentiliana*) and *R. helenae*) which will easily climb 20 ft into the branches of their host and then, usually, bend over and hang down, swooning under the weight and voluptuous scent of their massed trusses of white flowers.

The rose that all are praising
Is not the rose for me.

THOMAS HAYNES BAYLY

The Rosarium of Sangerhausen

HUMPHREY BROOKE

(Amateur rose grower, specializing in Victorian Roses)

The Rosarium at Sangerhausen in East Germany contains over 6,500 varieties of roses. It is still adding both old and new ones to the collection and is now the only place where many that are extinct elsewhere in the world may be seen. For example, in contrast to the dozen or so Hybrid Perpetuals available in Britain (and their number has recently been diminishing) there are about 400 at Sangerhausen, and such is the sumptuous beauty of their blooms, their richness of scent and their vigour that it is difficult to make a choice among them. Rose Kingsley in her *Roses and Rose Growing* (1908) lavished particular praise on this class and her comment that "The Hybrid Perpetual must forever prevail" is fully justified by what Sangerhausen has to offer.

I spent from 12–18 July, 1973 in this celebrated Rosarium, being kindly welcomed on arrival by the Director, Herr Vonholdt, with whom I had been in correspondence. Apart from seeing as many Victorian roses as possible, this being the period when so many that I admire the most were raised, I had been encouraged to think that it might be possible to collect budwood[1] from a few of the most outstanding varieties. This latter expectation accounted for my choice of a rather late date.

The siting of the Rosarium on soil more suitable for the growing of conifers was a matter of chance. It originated in a suggestion made by Pieter Lambert, one of the leading German hybridists, raiser of 'Trier', the first Hybrid Musk, in 1904 and other important roses. This was at a meeting of the *Verein Deutscher Rosenfreunde* (roughly the equivalent of our National Rose Society) in 1897. He is reported to have urged the creation of a Rosarium and to have asked for suggestions as to where there was sufficient ground available for such a project. Among a number of possibilities the only one available immediately, through an act of personal generosity on the past of a rose amateur, was an area of 25 acres on the outskirts of the small town of Sangerhausen in a remote area about 40 miles north of Weimar. While the *Deutscher Rosenfreunde* is based on Baden Baden, the Rosarium it created is now a state-maintained institution of the German Democratic Republic on the other side of the Iron Curtain.

---

[1] The pioneer in the propagation of budwood from Sangerhausen has been Mr. L. A. Wyatt (a former Editor of *The Rose*), 20 Connaught Road, Teddington, Middlesex. His Lists of "Roses Lost and Found" are invaluable.

The area itself continues to offer something of the same challenge so effectively faced by Professor Gnau (1853–1943), known as "Rosenvater" Gnau, whose effigy in bronze surveys his creation from its highest point. The Rosarium is narrow and irregular in shape, rising from two carp-stocked lakes to an outcrop of rock. A road flanks it to the north and a forest of pine trees to the south. The soil throughout is undesirably light. The arrangement of the beds (there are 226 groups of roses, some involving several beds) is labyrinthine, with variety added by features such as lily-ponds, willow trees and large shrubs. Typical of the imaginative way roses have been blended into this unusual setting is the enormous double hedge of *Wildrosen*, or species, with their hybrids, screening the Rosarium from its flanking road. There are about 800 different varieties in this one group.

Similarly, but on a smaller scale, a collection of Portland roses, including such varieties as 'Jeune Henry' (1815) and 'Madame Boll' (1859), is isolated among ferns and rocks. As one follows the winding paths, among beds separated by mown grass, the lay-out constantly alters, with hundreds of climbing and rambling roses on tripods to bring massive changes of scale at various points. Perhaps the most surprising feature of all in this botanically important collection is that, when resting in the shade of a tree or on a seat, the atmosphere of one's immediate surroundings is so often that of a private garden. I sensed this in particular on an afternoon spent among one group of 270 early Hybrid Teas, arranged in a triangular shape and almost all dating from between 1867 and 1914.

Evidently those responsible for lay-out, including Professor Gnau, were anxious to avoid both monotony and precise symmetry. This does, of course, result in a visitor interested in a particular class being seldom able to find them all in one group. The Portlands among the ferns are exceptional. The 400 Hybrid Perpetuals are in 10 different groups, some quite widely separated. The number of plants of each variety also varies considerably. But fairly typical are the 8 or so of each of 97 Teas in one very shady bed on the edge of the forest. Here one may see the delicate roses which brought to Europe a new scent, a new, pointed shape and new colours such as pearly white, lemon and peach. They include varieties that used to sell daily at Covent Garden in tens of thousands, such as the almost legendary 'Niphetos' (1843) and 'Souvenir d'un Ami' (1846). One can readily imagine the sensation they caused in the Victorian epoch, when they were mostly grown under glass. In this way, they bloomed over an exceptionally long period. Grown out of doors, as at Sangerhausen, they are mounded over with earth and fir-boughs from November to March. It must be noted that one defect several of them suffer from is a tendency to ball, even in warm weather. Doubtless it was from this source (a Tea parent) that the so-called Bourbon 'Souvenir de la Malmaison' (1843) acquired its notorious defect. Despite this, the family as a whole is of so distinctive and subtle a beauty that its revival, either under glass or out of doors, is surely overdue.

It should be mentioned, for the benefit of anyone intending to visit Sangerhausen and hoping to see roses such as 'Korona' and 'Orangeade', that there is a massive display of floribundas and Polyanthas in a bowl-shaped amphitheatre immediately on passing through the turnstiles. This is a dazzling overture. Its perimeter is fringed with trees and shrubs beyond which the enormous range of Europe's roses since earliest times unfolds.

Another family of roses is grouped separately and at the opposite extremity of the Rosarium. These are known as "Lutea Hybrids" and include the early orange and red bi-colours once called Pernetianas, being all descended from Pernet-Ducher's sensational 'Soleil d'Or' (1900). These roses are grouped in isolation because of their liability to Black Spot, and indeed there was hardly a healthy leaf in the entire group. There is insufficient labour in the Rosarium; the main seasonal tasks are carried out by school children and other casual labour, working in gangs under supervision. For this reason there is no spraying and diseases are controlled by this use of remote areas as isolation wards. Elsewhere the roses of every kind are extremely healthy— remarkably so when one considers the mediocre quality of the soil. They are fed on farmyard manure, of which plentiful supplies are available.

Anyone with a special love of summer-flowering roses should go to Sangerhausen in the second half of June. There are, for example, about 130 different Gallicas and over 100 Mosses. By mid-July, these and the Damasks, Albas and Centifolias are just a mass of dead heads, with an occasional lingering bloom as tempting evidence of the glories that have been. Among these there was an exquisitely cup-shaped, pink Gallica, 'Néron', raised by Laffay in 1841. This was one of the first from which I selected budwood, not only because of its superlative charms, but because it is an interesting example of how Monsieur Laffay, one of the greatest of all hybridists, was introducing Gallicas and other summer-flowering roses at the same time as his Perpetuals. For instance, his famous Hybrid Perpetual 'La Reine' dates from 1843.

Also, by mid-July, a proportion of the Portlands, Hybrid Perpetuals, Bourbons and Noisettes are between crops, although mostly still carrying a few blooms.

In compensation the early Hybrid Teas were still near their best, although conspicuously lacking in the vigour of their predecessors. Several groups of these held much interest. Among many I noted were Lacharme's famous pink 'Captain Christy' (1873), Bennett's flesh-toned 'Viscountess Folkestone' (1886), Dickson's crimson 'Liberty', (1900), and his single pink, 'Irish Modesty' of the same year. There were surprises too, such as the unusual vigour of the pink 'Monsieur Fraissenon', introduced by Gamon in 1911.

Fortunately there were still blooms on certain roses I particularly wished to see, including the red 'Rose du Roi', raised at St Cloud at about the time of Waterloo which may be classified either as a Portland or a Hybrid Perpetual, and the original *R. bourboniana* (1822), a palish pink and semi-double, as in Redouté's plate. Most of our bedding roses of to-day have one or other of these in their remote ancestry.

The general rule at Sangerhausen is for the rigorous cutting down each year of all varieties except the *Wildrosen*. This is dictated by reasons of space. The staff of the Rosarium do not subscribe to the theory that pruning is necessarily beneficial. I was told—and with approval—that Herr Wilhelm Kordes once wrote "Der Schrechliste der Schrechen ist der gärtner mit seine schere" (The worst of all evils is the gardener with his secateurs). The experience at Sangerhausen is that hard pruning reduces the average life of a rose to about 30–35 years. The continuity of the old varieties is secured by maintaining a huge nursery some miles away. Here one sees budded maidens of varieties such as the pink and violet Hybrid Perpetual 'Duchesse de Cambacères' (1867) growing between blocks of many thousands of popular floribundas and modern hybrid teas. The sale of the latter provides for the cost of raising the exotic replacements and also contributes towards the running of the Rosarium. This appears to be an extremely practical arrangement and is doubtless due to the fact that Herr Vonholdt had experience in a nursery business before becoming director in 1949.

The opportunity to make a private visit one evening to this establishment was one of numerous courtesies offered by Herr Vonholdt and his assistant Herr Täckelburg. The latter, on another evening, showed me hundreds of coloured slides mostly made in June.

Within their own range of activities the small permanent gardening staff were all similarly helpful, tolerating questions in the vilest of German and always willing to break off from mowing or weeding in order to locate some particular variety within a large group. Possibly this special degree of helpfulness owed something to the fact that I was the first English visitor since the war. With an average annual attendance of 135,000 there is something inevitably idiosyncratic about someone from so far afield. One sensed a similarly cordial reaction, even when ordering beer and grilled chicken.

The catalogue or *Rosen verzeichnis* is an invaluable work of reference, quite apart from its use during a visit. A single line entry for each variety states the family to which it belongs, together with the date of origin (where traceable) and the name of its raiser—nothing else. It was published by Herr Vonholdt in 1962 and is mainly based on the manuscript notes compiled by Professor Gnau. The other major source is Léon Simon's *Nomenclature de tous Les Noms des Roses* (Paris, 1906). It runs to 143 pages, with an average of nearly 50 entries per page, and includes a map. English readers nurtured on the theory that Gallicas, for example, are especially "old", will be surprised to find that with the exception of *R. officinalis* or "the Apothecary's rose" ("England um 1800") all the 130 Gallicas in the collection may be dated between 'Rosa Mundi' (Vibert, 1835[1]) and 'Violacea' (Paul, 1895). This merely bears out what is stated in Thomas Rivers's *The Rose Amateur's Guide* (1846) and William Paul's *The Rose Garden* (1848). Both of these authorities describe the introduction in their time of "improved forms" of the older varieties, especially by M. Vibert and the other French hybridists. The period of these "improvements" is actually later than the introduction of the early Portlands, Hybrid Perpetuals, Bourbons and Noisettes. An illustrated guide in a more popular format is also on sale, but this contains few traces of the expertise of "Rosenvater" Gnau, Léon Simon or August Jaeger (author of a rose lexicon).

The journey to Sangerhausen can conveniently be made by car from Harwich and the Hook of Holland. The Berolina Travel Agency, 19 Dover Street, London, W.1, specializes in handling travel arrangements for Eastern Europe. The regulations controlling the import of budwood into Britain are less stringent than many suppose. The Ministry of Agriculture permits the free entry of 2 Kilograms of plant material per person as a "baggage concession". Above that weight involves periodic inspection by the Ministry's inspectors. My own consignment was well within this limit as I intended to bring back budwood from only about two dozen roses. In the event my actual selection numbered 29. Had it been possible to anticipate the exceptional drought in 1974, which caused a number of failures, I would have imported more.

It is, of course, the author's hope that this modest and very enjoyable journey beyond the Iron Curtain, following on the recovery of so many Victorian roses from the same source by Mr. L. A. Wyatt (see footnote on p. 116), will be but a prelude to far more important exchanges of budwood by Societies and others.

[1] This improved form is stated to have replaced the earlier one attributed to L'Obel in 1581.

'WEE MAN' (miniature)
'*Little Flirt*' × '*Marlena*'
Raised by S. McGredy & Son Ltd,
N. Ireland
CERTIFICATE OF MERIT 1972
See 1974 *Rose Annual, page* 182

Humphrey Brooke, with 24
varieties of Hybrid Perpetuals
from his garden
(*see page* 116)

'COMTE DE CHAMBORD' (Portland) (*see page* 121)

'Comte de Chambord'

GRAHAM THOMAS, O.B.E., V.M.H.

(Authority on the "Old" roses and Gardens Consultant to The National Trust)

One cannot, in this world, often "eat one's cake and have it". Greed comes into a lot of life's pursuits and one of our greedy desires is to have roses that flower continuously from summer to autumn. This has been achieved by floribundas. My love is for the old-fashioned roses and one of the criticisms levelled against them is that they flower only at midsummer—but we won't go into this, just now. Suffice it to say that 'Comte de Chambord' combines the best of both worlds. It is a true old-style rose, but flowers right through the growing season.

At the end of June it might be taken for a Gallica rose, but though of true soft pink, its rolled petals might cause some doubts about this; and rightly so for they are related from the China rose. It was raised in 1860 and is one of a small race derived mainly from the Autumn Damask and the Hybrid Perpetuals. The Autumn Damask itself was known in Roman times; a hybrid China rose was probably the other parent of its noted derivative—the 'Scarlet Four Seasons' or 'Portland rose'(c. 1800). In those days anything which would flower again in autumn was greatly treasured, and this rose soon gave rise to many seedlings which were the forerunners of the Hybrid Perpetuals, themselves the footstools of the Hybrid Teas. Certain by-blows formed into a little group known as Portland roses; though repeat-flowering, they still had the old style of flower and rough leaf. A few have remained in cultivation and were obtained from the Roseraie de l'Haÿ, the famous rose garden near Paris.

The two best which I have seen are 'Jacques Cartier' 1868 and 'Comte de Chambord' 1860. The latter is a good upright leafy bush, continually pushing up flowering shoots until autumn, Each bloom is very full of scent, a rounded dense array of petals rolled over at the edge, and of a clear soft pink, comparable to 'Mrs John Laing'. There is one character that is common to all the Portland roses and this is what I call the "high-shouldered" effect; the flowers sit on a cluster of leaves which are grouped at the base of the flower stalk. (*See photograph opposite.*)

Beautiful Pot Roses by Use of Growth Retardants

S. K. BHATTACHARJEE,[1] M.Sc.(Ag.), Ph.D.

(Horticulturist)

Growth retarding chemicals are now being commercially used for the dwarfing of several species and varieties of ornamental plants. CCC (2 chloroethyltrimethylammonium chloride) has been found effective for suppressing the height of *Azalea*, poinsettia and *Hibiscus*. B-Nine (N-dimethylaminosuccinamic acid) also markedly retards the height of *Chrysanthemum* and *Hydrangea*.

Roses are the most beautiful popular flowering plants, grown almost throughout the world because of their adaptability to a wide range of soils and climatic conditions. Although roses are largely cultivated in the open ground, in cities and towns with limited ground space they are also grown in pots for decoration. In order to develop dwarf, bushy and attractive pot plants of hybrid tea roses, CCC and B-Nine have been used on seven different varieties of roses—'Avon', 'Chantre', 'Eiffel Tower', 'Inge Horstmann', 'Kiss of Fire', 'Mischief' and 'Super Star'.

CCC and B-Nine were treated as a foliar spray, once with 2,000 and 4,000 ppm (parts per million) solutions when the new shoots attained a height of 5 to 7 cm. after pruning, and twice with 4,000 ppm at intervals of 90 days on a set of plants previously treated with the same concentration. CCC was also used as a soil drench, once with 1,000 and 2,000 ppm and twice with 2,000 ppm 15 days after the first treatment.

Foliar application of CCC showed marginal chlorosis on the leaves in 5 to 7 days after treatment in all the varieties. CCC as a soil drench and foliar spray of B-nine, however, did not develop any sign of phytotoxicity. Treatment with the growth retardants caused the formation of smaller and thicker leaves, darker green in colour as compared with those of untreated plants. Senescence and abscission of the leaves on the treated plants were markedly delayed and the plants showed appreciable resistance to drought.

In all varieties of roses both CCC and B-Nine caused effective suppression of shoot length. Application of growth retarding chemicals twice, on the same set of plants proved more effective than single application, irrespective of the methods of treatment. Among the two methods of treatment of CCC, foliar application showed greater reduction in plant height than soil drench.

[1] Indian Botanic Garden, Shibpur, Howrah (W.B.).

Variation in response to treatments was also recorded in the different varieties of roses. Between the two chemicals, however, B-Nine in general caused greater retardation than CCC and the effect was more pronounced with the increase in concentration. Double application of B-Nine caused maximum suppression of shoot length in all the varieties, and the percentage of retardation varied from 16·3 to 74·4 at 180 days after treatment, depending on the variety. Among the different varieties 'Eiffel Tower' showed maximum percentage of suppression due to the treatment.

Treatment with growth retardants developed a larger number of branches in almost all the varieties. B-Nine was found more effective than CCC in this respect. With the double application of B-Nine 50 per cent increase in branching was recorded in 'Eiffel Tower' and 'Mischief'.

Both CCC and B-Nine markedly improved the size of the flowers, developed the flower bud earlier, hastened opening of the flowers and also prolonged their life. The effect was, however, more pronounced by treatment with B-Nine. The number of flowers was increased with the foliar application of B-Nine in all the varieties and the percentage of increase varied from 20 to 70 depending on the variety. Application of CCC did not appreciably increase the number of flowers, but no adverse effect was recorded in the case of any variety.

The reason for the marked reduction in plant height is due to restricted growth of internodes. Growth retardants induced a greater number of lateral branches in all varieties of roses which not only gave a bushy appearance to the treated plants but also improved flowering by increasing the number of flowering shoots. Greater resistance to drought of the treated plants may be attributed to the presence of a greater number of relatively smaller cells in the treated plants, which are inherently hardier than the bigger cells, and to the decreased rate of water loss from a comparatively smaller surface due to the restricted growth of the shoots.

Application of growth retarding chemicals on different types and varieties of roses can be very conveniently introduced to restrict plants from outgrowing their space in a particular design. Along with all improved cultural practices the use of growth retardants may also be recommended to grow attractive pot plants within a very short span of time. This quick and easy change in growth and flowering behaviour will definitely create great interest among rose growers.

Note by Hon. Scientific Adviser:

CCC is known as Cycocel in the United Kingdom, where it is used by farmers to reduce straw length in crops of oats and wheat and it helps to prevent lodging of wheat. B-Nine (proposed common name daminozide) is much used in commercial pot-plant cultivation and also by apple growers, who know it as Alar. B-Nine should not be mixed with other spray chemicals.

Rose pot plants in tropical countries and also under greenhouse cultivation in this country often tend to become leggy and Dr Bhattacharjee's use of these two growth regulators suggests one way to overcome this problem. I myself have used daminozide to reduce stem length in a pot-grown 'Uncle Walter', but both these chemicals are perhaps too expensive to be of much value to members who grow only outdoor roses.

E.F.A.

The Incomparable Rose

ALINE CHAPMAN
(*Amateur rose grower*)

The name is as perfect and complete as the flower. A rose symbolizes perfection, elegance, romance and love. Its association in legend, ritual and in architecture has always been a happy one.

Over 2,500 years ago Sappho, the Greek poetess of Lesbos, named the rose "Queen of Flowers", while the English poet of the last century, Austin Dobson, said so truly ". . . the rose is beauty . . ."

Who has not been enchanted by Robert Burns' impassioned song "My love is like a red, red, rose . . ." or F. E. Weatherley's ever popular ballad "Roses are blooming in Picardy"? From Shakespeare down to a host of minor poets, all have striven with words to do justice to our lovely rose.

This exquisite flower has been beloved in every country in the world for countless centuries. In the Old Testament, Isaiah prophesied that ". . . the desert shall rejoice and blossom as the rose . . ." while in Christian symbolism, the rose represents perfect virtue. Thus one can easily understand why the Virgin Mary is sometimes referred to as "The Mystical Rose".

Rose fossils more than thirty million years old have been found in the states of Oregon and Colorado. There must be something in the climate eminently suitable to the cultivation of roses in the far west of America, for what Oregonian is not proud of his City of Roses, as Portland is known? The city's experimental rose gardens in Washington Park are the mecca of rose cultivators the world over, and the Portland Rose Festival remains an annual pageant of beauty and originality.

The Persians were familiar with the crimson *Rosa gallica* a thousand years before Christ. This species stakes its claim as the oldest plant known to man which is still to be found in the modern garden. *Rosa gallica*, probably introduced to Britain by the Normans, and grown commercially in the environs of many monasteries, was also called the Apothecary's Rose, being of value for certain medicinal purposes. Delicious conserves also were prepared from its crimson petals.

In most ancient times the rose was widely cultivated in the Middle East where it was required for the extract from its petals known as attar—or otto —of roses. This distinctive perfume comes chiefly from the damask rose *Rosa damascena*—originally a native of the Greek Islands, whose bushes for this purpose were allowed to grow into dense masses without clipping. The damask rose reached Britain at the time of Henry VIII and is still widely grown for its perfume.

Farther east, and occasionally in Europe, water scented with the distilled essence of roses is often sprinkled over the hands after eating—a charming and leisurely custom. Such rose-water is universally used in many cosmetic preparations. Indeed, the ever popular cold cream is a simple rose-water ointment, and an effective hand lotion may be made at home by merely mingling rose-water with glycerine.

The ancient Greeks, and later the Romans, were very fond of roses and firmly believed that the wild variety could cure dog bites—hence the name Dog Rose, still in use today.

Probably the Isle of Rhodes in the Aegean Sea, first settled by the Greeks, was originally the Isle of the Rose. The Roman writers Pliny and Horace made frequent allusions to the flower, and coins dating from 400 B.C. had roses embossed.

Both peoples, and notably the Emperor Nero, used garlands of roses at their feasts, and most lavishly at banquets celebrating their victories. Roman warriors were frequently crowned with rose wreaths, while the petals, sprinkled with their fragrant oil, would decorate special confections and strew the floor at banquets. Rose wine would be prescribed to increase vitality when tired, much as our tonic wines are drunk today.

The persecution of Christians by the dissolute Romans at one time almost gave the rose a bad name, but instead it became the symbol of Christian martyrs' blood, hence its liberal use as an adornment of Cathedrals, Churches and chalices. Jewellery too has often been embellished with rose replicas. In the Mochlos tombs of the Minoan period in Crete, gold pins terminating in single open rose heads have been unearthed.

No school history book could fail to record the Wars of the Roses in England, lasting as they did for thirty years from 1455 to 1485. Each of the warring houses chose a rose as their symbol, *Rosa gallica* being the red rose of the House of Lancaster and the semi-double *Rosa alba*, the white rose of the House of York. An inscription on the Chapter House of York Minster reads "The Rose is the Flower of Flowers—this House is the House of Houses". With the death of Richard III when the rival houses settled their differences, the Tudor dynasty began, and a window was set into the Minster to mark the union of the Houses of Lancaster and York with the marriage of Henry VII to the beautiful Elizabeth of York in 1486.

Once more a rose was chosen by the English as their royal emblem and the Tudor Rose remains to this day a symbol of royalty often employed in heraldry, as well as on the British coinage beside the thistle of Scotland, the shamrock of Ireland and the leek of Wales.

Sovereigns and Presidents alike have been in love with roses. The King of Babylonia, who reigned nearly three thousand years before Christ, ordered some to be planted in his capital and they were also found as motifs on the columns of the later King Nebuchadnezzar's palace. The rose motif appears frequently too on Persian porcelain and woven into their fabulous carpets and tapestries.

In the eighteenth century the Empress Josephine gathered from far and wide a large collection of rose bushes, which she had planted round the Palace of Malmaison near Paris, where she encouraged her nurserymen to improve the various strains. In our day the rose garden of the White House in Washington D.C. is often cited as the meeting place of the President of the United States with famous visitors, being secluded and peaceful.

Many metaphors with rose themes are in common usage, such as "a bed of roses", signifying an easy, soft way of living. This originated from the practice of sleeping on mattresses filled with rose petals—an ancient status symbol! "Under the rose"—or *sub rosa*—has long been a term to ensure secrecy, springing from the custom of certain European monarchs of having a rose suspended over a banquet table when the conversation was regarded as confidential.

Modern dieticians tell us that rose hips are richer even than oranges in the vital vitamin C, and during the last war the habit of gathering this hedgerow harvest, to be made into a delicious syrup, began. The thrifty housewife adds home made rose hip jam to her store.

Perhaps it is not surprising that the popularity of roses has remained so constant from time immemorial when one considers the reward they bestow in beauty and fragrance for the minimum of toil. Roses respond in almost any soil or climate by themselves adapting to their habitat. They can be propagated from seed or cuttings, and by layering, grafting or budding.

Roses increase in popularity every year and at least 200 species, whose blooms range from a tiny half-inch diameter to huge specimens more than seven inches across, are cultivated nowadays in the Northern Hemisphere. Besides some exquisite perfumes, their odour may suggest spices, various fruits, hay or even fresh green tea leaves.

With an incomparable choice for such a modest outlay we would be wise to keep faith with history and to follow the poet Herrick's advice:

> "*Gather ye rose-buds while ye may,*
> *Old Time is still a-flying,*
> *And this same flower that smiles today,*
> *To-morrow will be dying.*"

Awards to Rose Specialists

Our sincere congratulations are extended to the following prominent rose specialists on the honours recently awarded to them:

James Cocker & Sons, Whitemyres, Lang Stracht, Aberdeen have been honoured by having the Royal Warrant conferred on them in the New Year.

Mr Alex Dickson, v.m.h., d.h.m., of Alex Dickson & Sons Ltd., Newtownards, Co. Down, N. Ireland had the Honorary Degree of Master of Arts (Agriculture) conferred on him by Queen's University, Belfast.

Mr Graham S. Thomas, v.m.h. became an Officer of the Order of the British Empire in the New Year Honours.

Observations on Foliar Feeding and Black Spot

F. C. H. WITCHELL
(Amateur rose grower)

The articles in *The Rose Annual* 1974 by E. F. Allen and C. H. Warner on foliar feeding and Black Spot, respectively, and the former's expressed interest in the experiences of other rosarians, prompt me to give a résumé of my own observations.

It is nearly twenty years since I began to experiment with foliar feeds. The first trial was made on 'Peace', 'Karl Herbst' and 'Ena Harkness'. In each case, a number of plants of each variety in the same bed were given weekly overhead sprays, the remaining plants receiving none. All the plants had also received their (then) customary spring mulch of mixed horse and cow manure.

During August, the members of the rose group of the local horticultural society were invited to visit my garden and to identify (if they could) which plants were foliar fed and which were not. They were also asked to name the qualities by which they thought they could identify the sprayed plants. All located the sprayed plants by means of their larger and deeper green foliage and better coloured (*not* larger) blooms. Through the intervening years, my experiments have continued; for the past thirteen of these years, in my present garden in Oxfordshire. For the first seven years, here, no disease control was practised. Then, for two years, Captan and Karathane were used, for the next two years Maneb and, for the last two years, Benlate and Mildothane.

My recorded experiments with foliar feeding in my present garden, for all of which Rose Sangral has been the feed used, are summarized as follows:

1. Newly planted bushes which were given ten to fifteen foliar feeds from May to July (in addition to the normal spring ground feed) made from 20 to 80 per cent more shoots than similar bushes which received no foliar feeds.

2. Identical experiments on established bushes showed recognizable differences in the colour, quality and size of the foliage and in the substance and colour of the blooms. Significant differences in numbers of shoots and of blooms were observed in bushes growing in the poorer parts of the garden, but not in bushes growing in those parts where everything grew well

anyway. The foliar fed bushes did, however, show noticeably better resistance to Black Spot, especially those on Laxa and Multiflora stocks.

3. Experiments with the use of liquid drenches and foliar feeds as the sole means of nourishment, showed that bushes so treated were generally more Black Spot resistant than control blocks of the same varieties on the same stocks which received only dry fertilizers.

Since all my roses are irrigated in dry weather, I would not expect that the tiny additional volume of water given in the foliar feeds (about one gallon to 40 bushes) would alone account for the observed effects. Now to my observations on Black Spot, independent of the effects of foliar feeding. My records tell the following story:

1. During the seven years when my roses received no fungicidal treatments of any sort, the incidence of Black Spot was variable and quite unpredictable. For example, 'Ena Harkness' might contract Black Spot in one year but not in the next, while 'Dorothy Peach' might do the exact opposite.

2. Black Spot was first observed anywhere on a bush except on the youngest foliage.

3. Captan was an ineffective disappointment.

4. Maneb had much better sticking properties and, provided that one resprayed before the cover wore too thin (the interval between sprays being therefore, dependent on rainfall), was completely effective.

5. Benlate applied in 1972 according to the maker's original instructions (i.e. spray at the first sign of disease) was not effective.

6. Benlate applied in 1973 to the pattern; three sprays in quick succession in late May and early June followed by two "topping up" sprays late in July, appeared to be effective both in preventing attacks and halting the spread of infection on some varieties and some rootstocks, but less so on others. For example, 'Diorama', 'John Waterer', 'Ernest H. Morse' and 'Stella' remained clean on both Laxa and Canina. 'Grandpa Dickson' was clean on Laxa and Multiflora and 'Princess' clean on Laxa, but several bushes of both varieties on Canina were seriously infected. An even more interesting case was of two adjacent bushes of 'Paddy McGredy' on Canina stock. One remained clean while the other was severely attacked.

7. It is a waste of both time and money to spray resistant varieties with any fungicide. In my garden, 'Rose Gaujard' has never contracted Black Spot and so it is never sprayed. But, one must discover what is and is not resistant in a particular garden. The same variety is not necessarily resistant everywhere.

8. I go along with Dr Lyle about the germination of Black Spot spores. I believe them to be airborne and to be capable of germinating overnight on leaves wet with summer dew (which may start to settle around 9 p.m., so that the leaves can be wet with static water for something like twelve hours). I believe that, when it rains, many spores are washed off the leaves (as in Roy Hay's sprinkler experiments) but, when the rain ceases, recently fallen spores will germinate if the residual rain water does not dry off quickly.

9. It would be very dangerous to assume that anything that happens in my garden will also happen in any other garden, even the one next door. Each garden has its own complex environment and micro-climate. This was made abundantly clear a few years ago when I was writing for *Amateur Gardening*. I invited readers to tell me of the varieties which contracted Black Spot in their gardens that year. About a dozen readers did so and a more confusing and contradictory set of reports could scarcely be imagined. No variety was reported clean in all the districts concerned but, equally, few varieties were universally infected.

Lastly, Mr Warner mentions mildew. I have yet to discover an effective preventive. 'Lilli Marlene', as an example, has got mildew in my garden every year, whatever preventive I have tried. However, almost anything might, on occasion, have some slight eradicant effect. This probably accounts for the various claims made, from time to time, for such sprays as disinfectants, soap, washing soda, detergents, foliar feeds and the rest.

Having reported my observations, let me add a word or two of warning. First, the observations were made in my own garden and on the particular varieties that I have grown. As I have already implied, these results might not be duplicated in other gardens or on other varieties. Even in my own garden, the deviations were wide enough to make one wary of jumping to firm conclusions. For example, the additional growth made by those newly planted bushes which received foliar feeds ranged from 20 to 80 per cent. That is an extremely wide range and there is no means of knowing the reason. Also, it was observed that differences between the reactions of different varieties were not consistent.

Second, and arising from this inconsistency, is the fact that one commences experiments and keeps records with an eye on certain factors only. I was looking for flower colour and size, numbers of new shoots and quality and size of foliage during the first year of the bushes in my garden. I shall never know what the effect of that first year's foliar feeding might have been (if any) on the long term performance or life span of those bushes compared to bushes which did not receive that treatment, because I did not continue my record keeping beyond the first four years of the experiment.

Continuing with the problem of inconsistency, I can offer no explanation for the variation in reaction of varieties on different stocks. Again, the more positive reaction of roses budded on Laxa and Multiflora applied to some varieties and not to others. Perhaps, too, the results might have been different for lighter or heavier soils or for those blessed with different proportions of the principal or trace elements.

I feel that the only hope of arriving at any valid conclusions would be for about twenty keen rosarians in different parts of the country to make the same series of experiments and to keep identical records (perhaps guided by our Hon. Scientific Adviser) for a number of years. Then, if there was any consistency at all in the results, we might feel that we had unlocked one more small box in the safe deposit of true knowledge of the rose.

Comments by The Hon. Scientific Adviser

Clearly Mr Witchell has more stamina and patience than have I: he applied ten to fifteen nutrient sprays to his roses between May and July whereas I became discouraged after no more than four or five. It does seem, however, that I may have overstated the case against foliar feeding since several rosarians, some very experienced indeed, have told me about their favourable results from this technique.

I am very interested to read that Mr Witchell observed some control of Black Spot from foliar feeding. I suspect that this effect, which has been recorded before, may be greater in regions of high rainfall where there must be considerable leaching of nutrients from the foliage. The average rainfall in my garden at Copdock is 23·52 in (598 mm). It would be of interest if anyone writing on this subject could record their average annual rainfall.

I have never been convinced that rootstock has much direct effect on disease susceptibility. There may be an indirect effect whereby bushes on a vigorous stock, such as *R. multiflora*, might prove more susceptible to Black Spot than less vigorous bushes of the same variety unless they are planted at a wider spacing. This subject is under investigation at several Research Stations run by the Ministry of Agriculture, so perhaps we can await their results.

Many workers have noticed that different races of Black Spot attack different varieties. In my own garden I had never seen this disease on 'Perfecta' until some unsprayed 'Polmeriana' stocks became badly infected.

I remain of the opinion that the practice of foliar feeding is a relatively laborious and time-consuming method of manuring roses.   E.F.A.

Codswallop

E. W. PARNELL, B.Sc., Ph.D.

(*Amateur rose grower*)

The title of this article in *The Rose Annual* may seem a little puzzling to the dedicated rosarian. The etymology of this splendid expletive is a little unclear, but it expressed my sentiments most admirably (I am not usually so rude) when, during a discussion with another rose-grower, he stated that it was necessary to prune a rose shoot at an angle to prevent water entering the cut and thereby leading to die-back. For many years, the constant repetition of this—to me—entirely unreasonable hypothesis has been a source of irritation and has at last driven me to propose an alternative. Of course, my friend is not alone in believing his statement to be true. Many "authorities", not only in the field of rose growing but also in fruit-growing, support him.

Surely a moment's reflection will throw some doubt on his reasoning? On a well grown rose bush, the shoots curve upwards and outwards from the base so that the sloping cut, as usually illustrated, above an outward facing eye, is likely to be *at least as close to the horizontal as one at right-angles to the shoot!*

Why then should we make a sloping cut? Is this incorrect? The answer to the last question is certainly no. Years of experience have taught gardeners that this gives the best results. Indeed, right-angled cuts will lead to a proportion of the shoots developing die-back. To find the answer to the first question we must first observe what happens when a pruned shoot commences to die back. It is instructive to examine a shoot so affected, and especially one that has been pruned some distance above the bud. It will be noticed that the bark turns brown and that the zone of browning creeps slowly towards the bud, but on nearing it, extends further down the side away from the bud rather than on the nearer side. Unless fungal infection develops in the dead tissue, the encroachment of the brown bark ends at an angle to the shoot precisely along the line where it should have been pruned! If infection occurs, the shoot may then continue to die back beyond the bud, but the fungal attack is usually secondary to the death of the tissue. It is, therefore, obvious that to avoid this trouble, a stem must be pruned so as to avoid the death of tissue above the bud. The reason why pruning close to the bud at an angle achieves this, is to be found in the structure of the stem.

The shoot contains groups of tubes, the vascular bundles, which conduct water and nutrients to the upper parts of the plant and translocate sugars and other substances from the leaves in a downward direction. Just below where the vascular bundles approach a dormant bud, branches develop sloping upwards and outwards to the bud. When a shoot is cut at right-angles, the main vascular bundles which no longer lead to actively growing tissue become sealed at the point where the branches leading to the bud separate. The tissue above the branching points can then only be supplied inadequately with water and nutrients by diffusion from neighbouring cells. Thus, a heel of tissue is left opposite the bud which starves and slowly dies, thereby providing a suitable breeding ground for fungi. If a sloping cut is made parallel and close to the branches supplying the bud, only a small layer of tissue is left which can be supplied by diffusion and die-back does not occur.

This explanation seems to me to be consistent with the known facts and provides a sound alternative to the usual statements on pruning at an angle which I am sure must have originated with a distant forbear of Mr John S. Mattock's John Charles Willoughby Smythe-Smythe,[1] that well-known purveyor of Codswallop.

[1] *Rose Annual, 1974*, p. 101.

Note by Hon. Scientific Adviser:

The sloping pruning cut, as recommended by the Society in *The Cultivation of the Rose*, is based on long years of experience by Rosarians of the past. The true reason for many such practices is not always known, but Dr E. W. Parnell has now put forward a theory which I, for one, find more convincing than the traditional explanation suggested by his friend. It remains a fact, however, that the sloping cut made on budded stocks during February would shed rainwater more readily than a horizontal cut.

E. F. A.

> *As though a rose should shut, and be a*
> *bud again.*
> KEATS, *The Eve of St. Agnes*, St.27.

Symposium on the Twelve Best Recurrent Climbing Roses

LEONARD HOLLIS

(Editor and amateur rose grower)

No Symposium has hitherto dealt with the recurrent climbers as such, although two may be said to encroach on some common ground. In *The Rose Annual*, 1943 there was a Symposium on The Twelve Best Roses for growing as Pillars. The only variety successful on that occasion and also in the present exercise was 'New Dawn'. In *The Rose Annual*, 1938 there was a Symposium on The Best Twelve Climbing Roses suitable for growing on Walls and here again, only one, 'Mermaid', which topped the list in 1938, was successful on the present occasion. In neither of these earlier exercises was there any stipulation about recurrent flowering although, of course, the ideal rose, whether for pillar or wall, would need to show this quality to meet the exacting requirements of today.

In the present terms of reference contributors were required to include in their selections only those climbers which, in their experience, are *reliably recurrent*. This will normally rule out the ramblers with the exception of 'New Dawn' and 'Phyllis Bide', as this group does not normally contribute much bloom after the prodigal summer display. It will also rule out most of the climbing sports of hybrid teas and floribundas as here again, after the June flush, many of them cannot be relied on to provide much further colour. A few of them, such as 'Clg. Caprice', 'Clg. Mme. Caroline Testout' and 'Clg. Étoile de Hollande' I have found to be reasonably reliable producers of flowers later in the season and, strangely enough, 'Clg. Sutter's Gold' has yielded a nice crop in the unfavourable autumn of 1974, although normally the blooms are very sparse indeed after June/July. Although these climbing sports were not specifically excluded, only two, in fact, were mentioned by our contributors, in each case by only one, viz. 'Clg. Cécile Brunner' and 'Clg. Rose Gaujard'. It seems quite evident that these groups have now been superseded to a large extent by the modern recurrent climbers of a more moderate growth and much more prolonged flowering capacity.

Contributors were asked to take into consideration such additional qualities as bright and pleasing colour, resistance to disease, shedding of the petals cleanly and fragrance, and to deduct points for very prickly growth, which makes pruning and training more difficult and tends to inflict damage

134

on adjacent plants during gales. It was also made clear in the terms of reference that the description "climbing" embraces those varieties of moderately vigorous growth which, under average conditions, will not clothe a pillar of more than moderate height. Such roses as 'Aloha' and 'Joseph's Coat' fall within this category.

All of our twenty contributors are experienced rosarians; eight of them live in the Northern half of the country and twelve in the Southern half, the dividing line for this purpose running from the Wash to the Severn. Grouped accordingly and arranged in alphabetical order in each group they are: *Northern half*: W. K. Bentley, Leics.; Dr A. Dick, Clarkston, Glasgow; C. W. Gregory, Nottingham; R. E. Rice, Lymm, Cheshire; J. Roscoe, Formby, Lancs.; J. C. Shortland, Otley, West Yorks.; E. Shreeves, Swanland, East Yorks.; Mrs C. Wheatcroft, Nottingham. *Southern half*: E. F. Allen, nr. Ipswich, Suffolk; R. C. Balfour, nr. Chelmsford, Essex; F. M. Bowen, nr. Stroud, Glos.; the late F. Deamer, nr. Brentwood, Essex; F. Fairbrother, Taunton, Som.; S. M. Gault, Barnet, Herts.; Mrs E. Harkness, Hitchin, Herts.; E. B. Le Grice, North Walsham, Norfolk; J. S. Mattock, Nuneham Courtenay, Oxon.; C. Pawsey, Colchester, Essex; Brig. C. E. Lucas Phillips, Oxshott, Surrey; Mrs H. Robinson, nr. Chelmsford, Essex.

A point was scored for each time a contributor mentioned a variety in his best dozen. The overall points scored by the twenty contributors are shown below:

	Position	Name of Variety	Points
Elected	1.	Pink Perpêtue	18
	2.	Golden Showers	16
		Handel	16
	4.	Mermaid	14
	5.	Altissimo	12
		Casino	12
		Danse du Feu	12
		New Dawn	12
	9.	Parkdirektor Riggers	10
	10.	Schoolgirl	9
	11.	Bantry Bay	8
		Swan Lake	8
Not elected	13.	Maigold	7
	14.	Joseph's Coat	6
		Rosy Mantle	6
		Zéphirine Drouhin	6
	17.	Galway Bay	5
	18.	Compassion	4
		Mme. Alfred Carrière	4
		Royal Gold	4

In addition 'Malaga' and 'Parade' scored three votes each; thirteen varieties were favoured by two voters, viz. 'Aloha', 'Autumn Sunlight', 'Copenhagen', 'Coral Dawn', 'Danse des Sylphes', 'Dortmund', 'Etude', Hamburger Phoenix', 'Morning Jewel', 'Phyllis Bide', 'Raymond Chenault', 'Santa Catalina', 'Sympathie'. A further nineteen varieties were mentioned by a single contributor, viz. 'Alister Stella Gray', 'Cécile Brunner' (Clg.), 'Coral Satin', 'Crépuscule', 'Crimson Descant', 'Danny Boy', 'Desprez à fleur Jaune', 'Dreaming Spires', 'Fugue', 'Gloire de Dijon', 'Guinée', 'High Noon', 'Kathleen Harrop', 'Leverkusen', 'Ritter von Barmstede', 'Rose Gaujard' (Clg.), 'Soldier Boy', 'White Cockade', 'Zitronenfalter'.

A breakdown of the overall results between North and South showed the following position:

	NORTH			SOUTH			TOTAL	
	Variety	*Points*		*Variety*	*Points*		*Variety*	*Points*
1.	Casino	8		Altissimo	10	1.	Pink Perpêtue	18
	Pink Perpêtue	8	1.	Mermaid	10	2.	Golden Showers	16
3.	Golden Showers	7		Pink Perpêtue	10		Handel	16
	Handel	7		Golden Showers	9	4.	Mermaid	14
5.	Danse du Feu	6	4.	Handel	9		Altissimo	12
	Schoolgirl	6	6.	New Dawn	8	5.	Casino	12
7.	Maigold	5		Danse du Feu	6		Danse du Feu	12
	Bantry Bay	4	7.	Parkdirektor Riggers	6		New Dawn	12
	Mermaid	4		Bantry Bay	4	9.	Parkdirektor Riggers	10
	New Dawn	4		Casino	4	10.	Schoolgirl	9
8.	Parkdirektor Riggers	4	9.	Galway Bay	4	11.	Bantry Bay	8
	Rosy Mantle	4		Joseph's Coat	4		Swan Lake	8
	Swan Lake	4		Swan Lake	4			
	Zéphirine Drouhin	4						

While 'Schoolgirl' received the votes of six out of eight contributors in the North, only three out of twelve supported it in the South. I imagine that the cooler conditions in the North allow the blooms to show to better advantage, as I find that it flies open quickly in my garden and the best colour soon fades. 'Maigold' scored five votes out of eight in the North, but only two out of twelve in the South. I suspect that this is partially explained by the voting for 'Mermaid' which, probably because it is not completely hardy in severe winters, received only four votes in the North, compared with ten out of twelve in the South. Three of the five who voted for 'Maigold' in the North did not vote for 'Mermaid', and the two who did really live in the Midlands, so it does suggest that at least some of the support for 'Maigold' was due to the suspect constitution of 'Mermaid' in the bleaker areas. Another interesting point is the difference between North and South in support of the veteran thornless Bourbon climber, 'Zéphirine Drouhin'. In the Northern table it scored four points out of eight, but only two out of twelve in the Southern table. Even so, for a rose to be placed joint fourteenth in the overall results after 106 years in commerce (introduced in 1868), in competition with the cream of the modern recurrent climbers, must be ranked as a remarkable achievement. Finally, 'Altissimo', one of the three leaders in the South, with ten points out of a possible twelve, was able to muster only two points out of eight in the North, and one of these two voters lives close to the border-line in the Midlands.

If the overall results are compared with the table of Repeat Flowering Climbers on p. 194 of *The Rose Annual*, 1974, it will be seen that nine of the twelve elected varieties are the same, although in a different order of merit. The three which did not make the grade in The Rose Analysis, 1974 are 'Altissimo', 'Bantry Bay' and 'Swan Lake', and it will be observed that the last two occupied the two lowest positions in the Symposium.

Detailed descriptions of the twelve elected varieties, followed by relevant remarks of our contributors on each, are now provided:

Pink Perpêtue (18 votes). Gregory, 1965. 'Danse du Feu' × 'New Dawn.' C. of M. 1964. Clear pink on the inside, deepening to carmine pink on the reverse. *Mrs Wheatcroft* and *Mr Roscoe* refer to it as a true pink, although this conflicts somewhat with the two-toned effect which *Mr Le Grice* finds lends interest to the flowers. The blooms are full and inclined to be globular. *Mrs Robinson* and *Mr Rice* find them long lasting and *Mr Le Grice* considers them well formed. Fragrance is detected by *Mr Pawsey*, *Mr Le Grice* and *Mrs Harkness*, who describes it as sweetly scented. I must confess that I have never been able to isolate more than a slight fragrance, and the fact that our other contributors do not mention fragrance at all seems to support the view. *Mr Bowen* finds it a little disappointing when cut for the house, as the blooms then soon seem to lose their freshness. Our contributors generally agree on its freedom of flowering and excellent recurrence. *Mr. Gregory* recommends that it be lightly pruned back after the first flush to promote new growth—and who should know better, as it is his seedling? *Mr Le Grice* observes that it shows up well from a distance and several others mention that it is good in the autumn. The flowers are carried in medium sized clusters on rather stiff growth. There seems to be some divergence of views about its habit of growth. Whereas *Mr Pawsey* finds it a rather thorny grower and a little untidy, *Mrs Harkness* mentions its reluctance to spread sideways, thus making necessary firm training of the new shoots. *Mr Shreeves* considers it suitable for all purposes, either upright or horizontally trained, and this also appears to be *Dr Dick's* view, as he describes it as suitable for either pillar or fence. *Mrs Robinson* finds it a moderate grower. The foliage is dark green, glossy and rather small. *Mr Roscoe, Mr Rice, Mr Pawsey* and *Mr Balfour* regard it as healthy and trouble-free, but *Mr Fairbrother* has noticed a little Black Spot. *Mr Shortland* notes that it is weather resistant in Yorkshire, but on the wetter side of the Pennines *Mr Rice* refers to the odd bloom not opening in wet weather. This is an example of a seedling from two varieties, both with places in the best dozen, eclipsing both of its parents, with a clear lead. There seems to be some disagreement about the circumflex accent over the middle "e", which offends some growers' susceptibilities. As, however, the variety was registered with this accent, I have allowed it to stand. (*See illustration facing p. 140.*)

Golden Showers (16 votes). Lammerts, 1956. 'Charlotte Armstrong' × 'Capt. Thomas'. All America Rose Selections and Portland Gold Medal, 1957. Golden yellow, long-pointed buds opening flat quite quickly and paling to cream with age. The flowers are thinly double, weather resistant, fragrant and borne very freely both singly and in clusters on long footstalks, with excellent recurrence. While *Mrs Harkness* refers to the soft lemon coloured blooms opening from deeper yellow heads, *Mr Shortland* prefers daffodil yellow, while *Mrs Wheatcroft* refers to the flowers as a clear pale gold. Actually there is considerable variation at different stages and I find that the old flowers sometimes assume pink spotting and mottling. *Mr Gault* and *Mr Bowen* note that the flowers have not much form when open. All are agreed on its freedom of flowering and outstanding recurrence. *Brig. Lucas Phillips* describes it as constantly and liberally in flower from mid-June to November, while *Mrs Wheatcroft* finds it indispensable for continuity. No contributor mentions the freedom with which it sets seed pods, and these must not be allowed to develop. Growth is moderately vigorous and upright with smooth, almost thornless stems. Most contributors refer to its alternative use as a large, free-growing shrub rose, while *Mr Bentley* also finds it suitable for a hedge. Several contributors refer to it as a slow starter, and *Mr Mattock* advises against free use of the secateurs. *Mr Bentley* finds it needs an extra year to reach 7-8 ft, while *Mr Shreeves* assures us that it will reach this height eventually, but takes longer than most. *Mr Roscoe* confirms that it requires good cultivation and generous feeding to attain 10 ft. *Brig. Lucas Phillips* considers it ideal for a narrow space, especially between two windows, while *Mrs Harkness* and *Mr Gregory* find it quite happy on a wall. *Dr Dick* considers that it makes an excellent pillar. My own mature specimen is just 9½ ft. The foliage is glossy, bronze tinted when young and dark green when mature. *Mr Fairbrother* finds it does not get much Black Spot, while *Brig. Lucas Phillips* notes that it is quite free from this disease, although in my garden, only a few miles from the latter, it needs protection from Black Spot. *Mr Shortland* and *Mrs Harkness* refer to it as completely healthy. It is interesting to find *Mr Shreeves* referring to its marvellous scent; *Mr Gault* considers it has a nice fragrance, but our other contributors do not stress this point. I find that it has a sweet scent for a yellow rose. To sum up, this is a fine rose of compact habit, never exceeding its allotted space, and, therefore, particularly valuable for the small garden.

Handel (16 votes): McGredy, 1965. 'Columbine' × 'Heidelberg'. TGC 1965. Cream, flushed rosy pink at the edges of the petals. Shapely in the bud, opening into moderately full blooms (22 petals), $3\frac{1}{2}$ in. across, which are weather resistant. *Mr Le Grice* refers to the colouring as a lovely confection of ivory and pink, which *Mr Rice*, more materialistic, finds that it reminds him of raspberries and cream. Most of our contributors consider it free flowering over a long season. *Mr Pawsey* has found it particularly good in autumn. *Mr Le Grice* regards it as colourful, even in the wet, while both *Brig. Lucas Phillips* and *Mr Bowen* find it valuable as a cut flower. *Mr Shortland* refers to the petals falling cleanly. There is some difference of opinion about scent. *Dr Dick* notes its fragrance; *Mr Le Grice* describes it as briar scented and *Mr Shortland* can detect some fragrance, although *Mr Shreeves* considers the scent is negligible and I agree with him. The fact that twelve contributors have not considered it worth mentioning is an indication that it is no more than slight. Growth is found to be variable. Both *Mr Roscoe* and *Mr Rice* in the North West find it very strong and vigorous, needing careful training to keep it within bounds. On the other hand, *Mr Le Grice* considers that it needs patience to lead it upwards while *Mr Pawsey* also finds it a neat grower. *Mr Balfour's* reference to using it as a shrub implies a restrained habit of growth. *Brig. Lucas Phillips* refers to its lusty growth, too strong and stiff for a cramped position. My own experience is of growth being neat and restrained. *Mr Le Grice* comments that the main flower stems stand well away from the plant, while both *Mr Gault* and *Mr Shortland* find that it breaks freely from the base. The foliage is semi-glossy, dark green, bronze tinted when young. *Mr Rice* refers to slight mildew, while *Brig. Lucas Phillips* has to fight all the time against Black Spot, which agrees with my own experience. *Mr Allen* and *Mr Bowen* feel it needs occasional spraying against Black Spot, while the experience of *Mr Balfour, Mr Shortland, Mr Fairbrother* and *Mr Shreeves* is that the foliage is free from disease.

All are agreed on the beauty of the flower. (*See illustration facing p. 140.*)

Mermaid (14 votes): Paul, 1917. *R. bracteata* × a double yellow tea rose. Gold Medal, 1917. Primrose yellow, with attractive amber stamens. Very large, single flowers, 4½ in. across or more, produced both singly and in clusters throughout the season. Fragrant. The individual flowers are ephemeral, but there are always more opening. *Mr Le Grice* delightfully describes it as "a water lily strayed from its pool". Several contributors refer to its continuity—unlike many climbers, it does not concentrate on a prodigal early summer flush, but as *Brig. Lucas Phillips* expresses it, it is generously persistent. *Mr Gault* believes that it flowers over a longer period than any other climber, and who will contradict him? *Mrs Robinson's* experience is that it is a late starter in her garden, continuous and generous rather than a smother of bloom. Growth is very strong and vigorous, with brittle and very thorny growth, often growing out at right angles to what one would wish. Several contributors mention that it is difficult to establish after transplanting and not completely hardy in a really severe winter. *Mr Pawsey* regards it as suitable for a North wall; *Mr Le Grice* would prefer a West wall, avoiding an Easterly position, while *Mr Allen* would not regard it as hardy in a winter such as 1963. It is generally agreed that time must be allowed for it to establish itself and start growing freely. There should be as little pruning as possible. *Mr Bentley* has grown it by layering in a bed. The foliage is glossy, oval, medium green, bronze tinted when young and very healthy. *Mr Mattock* considers it so superior to anything else that one hardly dares to mention it in the same breath as other cultivars.

This is not a variety for cold districts and it seems significant that *Mr Roscoe* and *Mr Rice* in the North-West, *Mr Shortland* in the North-East and *Dr Dick* in the West of Scotland have not given it a vote. On a warm wall or a close-boarded fence, however, if one can afford to wait for it to become established and is not too fussy about every shoot being in place, there is nothing else like it; it is almost as popular today as when it headed the Symposium in 1938.

Altissimo (12 votes): Delbard-Chabert, 1967. 'Ténor' × unknown. C. of M. 1965. Rich blood red, with crimson tones. Large, single flowers, 4 in. across or more, embellished with golden stamens and borne both singly and in clusters on stiff stems. No scent. *Mr Mattock* thinks it is probably the largest single in cultivation today. He finds the flowers are long lasting and the colour never fades. *Mr Rice* notes that it is completely rain- and sun-proof

'HANDEL', a recurrent climber (*see page* 139)

'PINK PERPÉTUE', a recurrent climber (*see page* 137)

'SCHOOLGIRL', a recurrent climber (*see page* 143)

and shatters well. *Mr Le Grice* regards it as very free flowering and particularly good as a pillar in full sunlight. *Mr Bowen* recommends it for cutting, as the stems are of such good length. Growth seems to vary considerably. *Mr Bentley* considers it a strong variety and gets growth to 15–16 ft and *Mrs Harkness* finds it vigorous to 15 ft. *Mr Rice*'s experience is that it is not over-tall, while the fact that *Mrs Robinson* and *Mr Le Grice* find it excellent as a pillar, and *Mr Gault* and *Mr Bowen* are disposed to recommend it also as a shrub, indicates that it is by no means rampant. In my own garden, admittedly on shallow flinty soil, it has remained at 6–7 ft for the last six years and has to be protected from Black Spot. *Mr Bowen* also finds this necessary, while *Mr Fairbrother* considers it fairly free from disease. The foliage is matt, dark green and large. Several contributors speak highly of its recurrence; *Mr Gault* mentions that it flowers again in the autumn. My own experience is that it is not conspicuous after the first flush.

Casino (12 votes): McGredy, 1963. 'Coral Dawn' × 'Buccaneer'. Gold Medal, 1963. Rich yellow in the bud, opening to a hybrid tea shape in the young flower. When fully open it is a soft yellow, of medium size, full but rather loosely formed, borne in small clusters and carrying some fragrance. Views differ about the shade of yellow. *Mr Roscoe* considers it bright, *Mr Rice* suggests canary yellow, fading to cream and *Dr Dick* offers pale yellow; *Mrs Wheatcroft* and *Mr Bentley* regard it as a deep yellow. *Mr Pawsey* thinks a richer colour is desirable, while *Mr Shreeves* notes that it fades to primrose. It repeats quite well. *Mr Bentley* thinks it has a long flowering period, while *Mrs Harkness* observes that it is seldom without bloom. *Mrs Harkness*, *Mr Shortland* and *Mr Rice* regard the flowers as weather resistant. Fragrance is the subject of some disagreement. *Mrs Harkness* finds considerable scent; *Mr Shortland* detects a strong fragrance while *Mr Shreeves* is conscious of a rich scent. *Mr Balfour* points out that it is fragrant while the other eight make no comment. I am unable to detect more than a slight fragrance. Growth is vigorous to 9 or 10 ft and suitable for a wall, pillar or close-boarded fence. *Mrs Harkness* obtains growth up to 15 ft, *Mrs Wheatcroft* finds it is extra vigorous while *Mr Balfour* considers it very vigorous. *Mr Rice* has experienced some frost damage, and I lost an established specimen which was killed by severe frosts some years ago. The foliage is glossy, dark green and abundant, but needs protection from Black Spot. *Mr Shortland* feels it may need protection against mildew, while *Mr Pawsey* finds some mildew in the autumn. On the other hand, *Mrs Wheatcroft* regards it as a clean and healthy plant.

Danse de Feu (12 votes): ('Spectacular' in U.S.A.). Mallerin, 1954. 'Paul's Scarlet Climber' × *R. multiflora* seedling. C. of M. 1954. Orange scarlet, "blueing" with age. The flowers are of medium size, 3 in. across, moderately full opening flat and produced very freely in medium clusters. The colour is variously described as orange flame, orange red, vermilion red and bright scarlet as well as orange scarlet, which seems to me as close as one can get. I am surprised that not one of our contributors has mentioned the unpleasant "blueing" of the old flowers; these clash horribly with the young ones and need to be removed regularly. The flowers are not usually of immaculate quality, although *Mr Pawsey* commends its well formed hybrid tea type blooms. Most of our contributors, I feel, regard it as a climber for producing a spectacular display *en masse*. *Mr Bentley*, *Mrs Harkness*, *Mr Shreeves* and *Brig. Lucas Phillips* find that it flowers over an extended period. There is little or no fragrance. Growth is vigorous up to 8–10 ft with strong canes. *Mr Roscoe*, *Brig. Lucas Phillips* and *Mrs Harkness* find it very vigorous. *Mr Bentley* comments that it will grow quite well on a North wall, but as several of our contributors point out, it should not be planted against a red brick wall. *Mr Shortland* considers it essential to train it horizontally from the start, to induce low blooming. The foliage is glossy, medium green and tinted bronze when young. *Dr Dick* and *Mr Pawsey* find that there is a tendency to mildew, but otherwise it seems to be disease resistant and has not given me any trouble with Black Spot.

New Dawn (12 votes): Dreer, 1930. Sport from 'Dr W. Van Fleet'. Flesh pink in the centre, paling to blush or silvery white in the outside petals. The flowers are of medium size, moderately full, borne in clusters on long stems and diffuse a delicious perfume. We planted it as a hedge soon after it was introduced and it never failed to give every satisfaction. The shape of the flower seems to be less immaculate than that of the parent and more inclined to be globular. The petals shatter well and it does not mind rain. *Mr Rice* has found that it takes longer than others to become established. *Mr Gault* mentions its long flowering season, while *Brig. Lucas Phillips'* experience is that scarcely a day passes when you cannot pick its tenderly pink and incensed blossoms. *Mrs Harkness* claims that in a mild season it will bloom into December. *Mrs Wheatcroft* considers it unique for freedom of flowering and giving a long, long show, while *Mr Fairbrother* describes it as most generous in the blooms it gives from June to October. Even the basal shoots bear terminal clusters of flowers in the same season. *Mr Mattock* sums up by saying it is probably nearer to continuity than anything else. Growth is moderately vigorous, probably best on a 6–7 ft fence. *Brig. Lucas Phillips* grows it as an 8 ft hedge, while *Mr Le Grice* thinks it delightful where a plant is needed to droop over a wall or nestle with a clematis against the porch of a house. He would confine it to a height of 6 ft. *Dr Dick* finds it rampant and so healthy and hardy that it thrives everywhere. The foliage is glossy, medium green, small and generally healthy, although *Mr Fairbrother* finds it needs watching for Black Spot, while *Mr Rice* has noticed slight mildew on the flower stems at times. There is some difference of opinion about its value as a cut flower. While *Mr Gault* considers it nice for cutting, *Mr Bowen* feels that its only serious fault is its relative poorness as a cut rose.

Parkdirektor Riggers (10 votes): Kordes, 1957. *R. kordesii* × 'Our Princess'. Rich velvety blood red or deep crimson semi-double flowers, 3 in. across, produced in clusters. There are sometimes white shadings at the base of the petals. No scent. Very free and recurrent flowering if dead heading is practised—otherwise a mass of large seed pods will develop to the detriment of later flowers. *Mr Shreeves* describes the colour as clear ruby red or claret, but it is closer to blood red on my soil and non-fading. Growth is very vigorous to 12 ft with glossy, dark green, leathery foliage. *Mr Roscoe, Mr Dick* and *Mr Pawsey* refer to its rapid growth, making it first class for covering a wall or fence quickly. *Mr Bowen's* experience is that it yields to none as a reliable performer year after year and will grow taller and more vigorously than most, even under poor conditions, and this tallies with my own experience. *Mr Shreeves* recommends it as very good for all purposes and a true cluster rose. *Mr Pawsey* mentions some mildew in the autumn, but over the years I have found it to be one of the healthiest of all climbers. It is difficult to criticise this variety, unless it is that it tends to be somewhat commonplace. Like all the Kordesii climbers, it was bred to withstand the severe winters of Germany and the qualities of extreme vigour, hardiness, recurrence and non-fading are probably more meritorious in a climber than hybrid tea form of flower.

Schoolgirl (9 votes): McGredy, 1964. 'Coral Dawn' × 'Belle Blonde'. Orange-apricot or burnt orange, fading paler, when it may develop some salmon flushes. The flowers are full, large, shapely at first. 4 in. across, fragrant and borne in medium clusters, with good recurrence. *Mr Le Grice* comments that the flowers suffer from rain damage. Growth is vigorous, usually 8–10 ft, with glossy, dark green foliage needing protection from Black Spot in pure air districts. *Mr Rice* finds it very vigorous and tall growing, with very large thorns on the older wood. *Dr Dick* considers it the only climber of this colour which is both fragrant and healthy. *Mr Pawsey* also regards it as free from disease, but *Mr Shortland* prefers it for pillars rather than walls, where there may be a tendency towards mildew. On the other hand, *Mr Bentley* commends it for growing against a wall. *Mr Rice* points out that unless it is carefully trained there is a tendency for it to become leggy, and *Mr Shreeves* refers to it as rather straggly in growth. (*See illustration facing p. 141.*)

Bantry Bay (8 votes): McGredy, 1967. 'New Dawn' × 'Korona'. C. of M. 1967. Light rose pink with a tinge of salmon. Shapely in the bud, it opens to semi-double flowers, some 3 in. across, produced in widely spaced trusses very freely and recurrently. There is little or no scent. *Mr Mattock* compares the flower to a dog rose with its simple charm, but *Mr Rice* regards it as "frilly". Growth is vigorous to 8–9 ft with semi-glossy, medium foliage. *Mr Rice* finds it healthy and trouble-free and *Mr Balfour* describes the foliage as healthy, but *Mr Fairbrother* warns that it must be sprayed against Black Spot. *Dr Dick* considers the flowers are rather similar to those of 'Santa Catalina', but borne on much more vigorous growth. Visitors to Bone Hill will have admired the specimen growing on a brick pillar behind the offices, next to 'Handel'.

Swan Lake (8 votes): McGredy, 1968. 'Memoriam' × 'Heidelberg'. White, tinged pink in the heart. The flowers are large, very full, shapely and borne singly and in small clusters with great freedom and recurrence. *Mr Rice* thinks the flowers are reminiscent of 'Memoriam', but notes that it does not shatter. *Mr Pawsey* comments that it stands bad weather exceptionally well, whereas *Mr Fairbrother*'s experience is that it does not stand up to heavy rain well. *Mrs Wheatcroft* notes that it is late coming into flower and repeats after a longish interval, but that it opens well in all weathers. *Mr Le Grice* points out that it is a little messy viewed closely, but produces a good massed effect. Growth is vigorous to 8 ft with strong canes, clothed with semi-glossy, medium green foliage. *Mr Rice* notes that growth is very thorny. *Mr Le Grice* considers it of medium height and *Mrs Wheatcroft* describes it as a medium tall grower. *Mr Pawsey* comments that there is a tendency to mildew in the autumn, but *Mr Fairbrother* finds that a spray early in the season is sufficient to keep the foliage clean.

It is interesting to observe that of the elected dozen, no less than five were raised by McGredy, while Gregory, Lammerts (U.S.A.), Paul, Delbard-Chabert (France), Mallerin (France), Dreer (U.S.A.) and Kordes (West Germany) contributed one each. The oldest variety is 'Mermaid'.

Is It Really True?

MARTIN WATTS

(Amateur rose grower and successful exhibitor)

One of the many pleasures in growing plants, and roses in particular, is that we can make our own observations and experiments and compare these with generally accepted practices and methods that are detailed in the numerous books and articles on rose growing. Standard methods and practices are essential to beginners, but after one has gained some experience, these must be tempered with one's own observations.

It must have been realised by any keen rosarian that everything we read on rose cultivation is not and cannot be true; otherwise we would not see such a glut each year of new rose books, all differing, even if only slightly, on the best or correct method of doing this or that job. If we have an enquiring mind we must have secretly queried some of the "accepted" cultivation methods, and perhaps tried different ones of our own.

Whenever and wherever rosarians meet, at shows, conferences or meetings the subject is of course roses and rose growing. The time literally "flies", and our wives, or husbands as the case may be, always have the utmost difficulty in dragging us away. The opinions expressed in these conversations vary and hence the interest, giving rise to yet another pleasure of rose growing—communication.

One of the best methods of communication for rosarians is through this *Annual*, which gives us plenty of interest and thought-provoking material for both beginners and experienced rose growers, whereas nearly all other rose literature, books and articles mainly cater for the newcomers to roses.

Let us, then, have a look into some of the generally accepted practices that I, for one, do not entirely agree with and ask ourselves the question, "Is it really true?"

Perhaps the best example to start off with is the so often verbally repeated, in "parrot" fashion "roses like clay soil". Well, we should all know that they will tolerate clay, without actually liking it, and it is what we make of our soil that reflects in the later growth and bloom of our roses. "Do not feed first year rose plants, so that their roots can grow in search of food and thus obtain a firm foundation and well spread system", is another. From my own experience over the years, having mulched and fed new roses in exactly the same manner as older established plants, I have never lost a plant, nor found any visible reason for not treating them the same.

145

Quite often at the end of the flowering season in my garden, it is difficult to pick out the first season plants from the older plants! I believe it would be better to encourage gardeners to get into the habit, right at the start, and feed their roses, as if they are advised not to feed in the first year, this could easily be left for the second and third years, to the detriment of the plants. Enthusiasm can fade, no more so than with the average gardener who only does it from a sense of duty, and because it's there!

Another piece of advice usually given is, "do not feed your roses after the end of July; otherwise this will encourage sappy growth, which will not ripen before winter frosts come, bringing die-back". This is true, but almost in the same breath we are usually told, under the heading of "cutting back in autumn", to cut back to two or two and a half feet high all bush roses, and cut out completely all sappy, red, unripe growths to avoid die-back. This is also good advice, but from the end of July there are about another three or possibly four months of flowers to come, and if we are going to cut out sappy, unripe wood—say—at the end of November, why on earth do we stop feeding at the end of July? Better, surely, to feed for another couple of months, with a high potash fertilizer to help make your blooms weather resistant?

"Do not plant new rose trees in old rose beds which have grown roses for ten years or more, as the soil may have become 'rose sick' and they will not thrive," we often read. This I believe, is true, especially if the rose beds have not been fed or mulched regularly for this period. If they have been looked after I believe this period can be extended by many years, as has been found by quite a number of rosarians, who have not had enough space or spare soil to move to accommodate new plantings.

Some rose books recommend dead heading to the first leaf axil, but those unfortunate beginners who have done this, or not cut back down the stem far enough, will have found that the resulting shoot has prematurely come into bud and flowered with a very short length of stem with hardly any leaves on it! I have at times had this happen even when I have cut strong growers of three to four feet down to eighteen inches from the ground. We must cut at least half the length of the stem off with the deadhead to be sure of obtaining another nice length of flowering stem.

With regard to planting new roses we are always advised to use peat with a handful of bonemeal per bucketful of peat, worked into the mixture. I would suggest that if this method is used when planting large quantities of new roses. it will be very expensive. My own method is to use equal quantities of sifted garden soil and peat with a handful of bonemeal added to each bucketful. I find this is equally good, if not better, as in my opinion the rose plant's roots will easily grow through a wholly peat mixture and "come up against it" when reaching normal garden soil. Whereas if the mixture as suggested is used as a planting medium it is more natural, cheaper and still contains moisture-retaining material (peat) for a good start.

If it is found necessary to water roses in a dry season, the usually recommended rate is one gallon per bush. This is, I believe, essential if no mulch has been used, and the water is applied directly onto ordinary (cracked!) garden soil. If a farmyard manure mulch has been laid the previous April or May, over all the surface of the rose beds, any amount of water is, I believe, beneficial, as it will help moisten or rather re-moisten the mulch. Smaller applications of less than a gallon per bush will not, I am sure, harm the hair roots by bringing them to the surface, providing there is a good thick mulch. I believe that in times of drought it is far better to spray plants with foliar feeds or even clear water, than start watering; it is easier, providing you own a good sprayer, and this can be done two or three times a week. In this way foliage is kept fresh, clean and healthy and your normal insecticides and fungicides can be incorporated into your spray, although it is always best to make sure different chemicals do mix and do not finish by scorching the foliage.

On the subject of budding we are advised that maiden plants be moved to permanent quarters after flowering *in situ* after budding. It is not generally known that plants can be moved after heading back, after the shoot has been pinched back in March, providing care is taken. The plant must be lifted carefully, with soil adhering to the roots and great care must be taken not to knock out the scion. If planted properly and watered in, there is very little set back to the plant's system, and growth will not be very much behind any plants of the same variety left *in situ*.

One of the most often repeated pieces of advice given to exhibitors, is in my opinion one of the most stupid, and that is that after cutting, show blooms should be placed in containers "up to their necks in water" until required for transporting to the show. The reason I state that it is stupid must be obvious to any exhibitor; when removing the stems it would be almost impossible not to shake water over the actual blooms, and, conversely, it is difficult to tip out some of the water from a bucket full of roses without wetting some blooms. I have always only run about six inches of water in buckets used for keeping roses in overnight, and for transporting and have never lost one or had one droop yet!

The foregoing are only a few of the generally accepted truths of rose growing that I believe can, under certain circumstances, be untrue. I have not gone out of my way to be controversial, but have just questioned written advice and practices which have been repeated time and time again.

Beginners with roses obviously must, to start with, go by the book but as they gain more experience they can broaden their outlook and experiment, thus forming their own opinions and gaining more from this wonderful hobby.

The International Rose

MICHAEL GIBSON

(*Amateur rose grower*)

Until recently I was quite convinced that a great number of varieties of hybrid teas and floribundas were equally popular in the majority of countries. There can be no doubt, as the names Tantau, McGredy, Boerner, Le Grice, Kordes, Delbard, Poulsen, Dot, Harkness, Dickson, Cocker, Meilland, Gaujard and so on prove, that rose breeding is a very international business, but how far outside their own countries do most of the products of these breeders spread? All over the place, I would have said, until I had to carry out some research for a book into which roses are *popular* in which countries around the world. I used information provided by national societies, nursery lists and my own extensive library of rose books.

I do not claim that my results are absolutely definitive. I covered as far as possible fifteen countries, from Denmark and Germany in the north down to South Africa, and from France to Japan and Australia in the east, but not all were equally ready or perhaps able to provide the information I needed. However, quite a clear picture did, I think, emerge.

I started off with a basic check list of about 230 hybrid teas common to both the United Kingdom and the U.S.A., and added names to it as it became clear that certain roses were popular in quite a number of other countries, although hardly heard of here. This brought the list up to 266 varieties altogether. There seemed to be far less common ground between the countries with floribundas and my list produced only 139 varieties. More or less the same climbers, ramblers, miniatures and shrub roses appeared for country after country, presumably because there have been fewer new varieties introduced over the years when compared with hybrid teas and floribundas.

Having established the lists of names, I began to break them down and analyse them. Taking the hybrid teas first, only 121 were popular in four or more countries, which came down dramatically to thirty-five popular in seven or more countries.

No prizes for guessing that 'Peace' was the most popular rose, in eleven countries. My margin of error may be indicated here, as I am sure this could well have been fifteen out of fifteen if the response to my quest for information had been 100 per cent.

A number of other old (or oldish) favourites in the United Kingdom also come near the top. 'King's Ransom', 'Michèle Meilland', 'Papa Meilland' and 'Super Star' (10 countries); 'Sutter's Gold' and 'Virgo' (9 countries); 'Bettina', 'Champs Elysées,' 'Chicago Peace', 'Chrysler Imperial', 'Ena Harkness', 'Piccadilly', 'Prima Ballerina', 'Rose Gaujard', 'Spek's Yellow' and 'Uncle Walter' (8 countries); 'Baccara', 'Buccaneer', 'Crimson Glory', 'Dr A. J. Verhage', 'First Love', 'Josephine Bruce', 'Suspense' and 'Tzigane' (7 countries). Of the newer roses, 'Arianna', 'Carina', 'Fragrant Cloud' and 'Pascali' were much liked in 9 countries; 'Maria Callas' ('Miss All-American Beauty'), 'Mister Lincoln' and 'Pharaoh' (8 countries); 'Lady X' and 'Peer Gynt' (7 countries) topped the lists.

Roses both old and new popular in 6 countries were:

'Beauté'	'Mischief'
'Belle Blonde'	'Mojave'
'Blue Moon'	'Montezuma'
'Christian Dior'	'Mullard Jubilee'
'Colour Wonder'	'Peter Frankenfeld'
'Duke of Windsor'	'Pilar Landecho'
'Ernest H. Morse'	'Pink Peace'
'Golden Masterpiece'	'Red Queen'
'Grace de Monaco'	'Samourai'
'Grand'mère Jenny'	'Silver Lining'

'Isabel de Ortiz'
'Karl Herbst'
'Perfecta'

'Tiffany'
'Whisky Mac'
'Youki San'

For 5 countries they were:

'Adolf Horstmann'
'Carla'
'Charlotte Armstrong'
'Charm of Paris'
'Cologne Carnival'
'Confidence'
'Dame de Coeur'
'Diamond Jubilee'
'Eden Rose'
'Gold Crown'
'Intermezzo'
'Interview'

'John F. Kennedy'
'John Waterer'
'Ophelia'
'Red Devil'
'Shannon'
'Silva'
'Soraya'
'Summer Holiday'
'Wendy Cussons'
'Western Sun'
'White Christmas'

There is probably not much benefit in going any further than this, so we turn to the floribundas.

Here 'Queen Elizabeth' is first with 11 countries, followed by 'Allgold' and 'Europeana' (10 countries); 'Orange Sensation' (9 countries); 'Elizabeth of Glamis', 'Lilli Marlene', 'Orangeade', 'Rumba', 'Sarabande' and 'Zambra' (8 countries); 'Alain', 'City of Belfast', 'Evelyn Fison', 'Golden Slippers', 'Iceberg' and 'Redgold' (7 countries); 'Charleston', 'Korp', 'Sea Pearl', 'Spartan' and 'Zorina' (6 countries).

For 5 countries they are:

'Apricot Nectar'
'Bonfire Night'
'Chinatown'
'Circus'
'Dearest'
'Decapo'
'Fashion'
'Frensham'
'Goldilocks'
'Gold Marie'
'Jan Spek'

'Korona'
'Masquerade'
'Paddy McGredy'
'Paprika'
'Pernille Poulsen'
'Picasso'
'Pink Parfait'
'Satchmo'
'Scarlet Queen Elizabeth'
'Violet Carson'

And for 4 countries:

'Ama'	'Irish Mist'
'Betty Prior'	'Ivory Fashion
'Cocorico'	'Marlena'
'Diamant'	'Megiddo'
'Elysium'	'Molly McGredy'
'Esther Ofarim'	'Orange Silk'
'Garnette' (red)	'Saratoga'
'Happy Anniversary'	

I think these results merit a few comments. It is surprising to see 'Papa Meilland' so near the top because of its susceptibility to mildew, in this country at least. Obviously it must reflect our love of a deep, dusky red rose, and this idea is supported by the high placings of older favourites 'Chrysler Imperial', 'Josephine Bruce', 'Crimson Glory' and the much newer 'Mister Lincoln'. 'Super Star' seems to be battling on despite its tarnished reputation and somebody somewhere must be able to persuade 'Red Queen' to produce its first flush before August and its second before Christmas! 'Arianna', 'Carina', 'Maria Callas' and 'Pharaoh' are among the front-runners which are so far not very widely grown in the United Kingdom. Also liked are 'Champs Elysées' and 'Suspense', which have never had the distribution here I think they deserve, the latter probably ousted by the ever-popular (and probably better) 'Piccadilly' in the same red and yellow colour range.

In the floribunda list there are no particular surprises, except possibly to see 'Rumba' so high, as its trusses (in our climate, anyway) age so badly and so quickly. However, in both lists it is roses that we have found to stand the test of time that figure most prominently.

The World's Favourite Rose

Help our Society to select our nomination for the World's Favourite Rose - a competition being conducted by The World Federation of Rose Societies. Send a *post card only* to the Secretary at St Albans, giving the name of your favourite rose (all types included) and your name and address, to reach the office before 30 June, 1975.

Growing Roses in the Cape Peninsula (South Africa)

F. H. L. SAWYER
(*Amateur rose grower*)

Cape Town lies on the lower slopes and around Table Mountain, which rises three thousand feet quite abruptly from the sea and the whole is practically surrounded by the sea as the name Cape Peninsula suggests. In winter we have occasional North-Westerly gales, accompanied by heavy rain and in summer our famous, or infamous, South-Easter ("The Cape Doctor") blows for days on end. Both these winds make rose growing very difficult in parts of the Peninsula, but other parts are well protected by Table Mountain, Signal Hill (a thousand feet high) and Lion's Head. The soil varies a lot, from quite heavy clay and black soil on parts of the lower slopes of the mountain to just about pure sand at areas bordering the sea and on the Cape Flats.

When I moved, six years ago, to Plumstead, a southern suburb some ten miles from the centre of Cape Town, a lot of my gardening friends said "You can't grow roses in Plumstead, far too sandy, not enough clay." Well, being a stubborn sort of fellow, who had three whole years of rose growing behind him, I decided to prove them wrong and, with all due modesty, I feel that I am succeeding fairly well. One of the wisest things I did nine years ago was to join the National Rose Society as it was then called and I constantly refer to my nine copies of *The Rose Annual* and the two handbooks. The two latest additions to my Rose Library are *Xenia Field's Book of Roses* and Leonard Hollis' *Roses*, both excellent.

As far as I can tell by reading about roses in Europe and comparing them with those grown here, the main difference seems to be that the flowering season here is much longer. This is an advantage in one way but a great disadvantage too, as they get very little rest in our fairly short and temperate winter, and very often pruning has to start while they are bearing some late blooms; two or three weeks after pruning they are shooting merrily. Recently my specimens of 'Ena Harkness' had to be disbudded less than a month after they had been pruned. No wonder she is inclined to hang her head later on. Actually I find this robust lass one of the hardiest and most beautiful in my garden. She does not know the meaning of the word disease. Our roses grow taller than in Europe, but possibly the blooms are not so delicate and certainly they are not so scented as yours and do not last as long.

From my experience I feel that pruning here should be far less severe; it is a case of large trees on strong roots. In my own garden the soil is naturally rather sandy which means there are no drainage problems at any rate. I get hardly any of the North-West gales and, although some of the summer South-Easters can be a nuisance, my garden is fairly well sheltered from them. Three feet of soil was removed from all my beds and clay added. I have found that roughly 50 per cent clay and 50 per cent of my own sandy soil is the best mixture. Pruning takes place about the middle of July and they are then well sprayed with Lime Sulphur and mulched with a thick layer of cow manure. Afterwards, except for the odd spraying for Aphids, a little Epsom Salts now and again, a splash of trace element mixture, Iron Chelates if they look as if they need it and liquid manure when they are at their peak, they are left to their own devices. I understand that we suffer from the same diseases as you do, but to date my roses have not heard of Black Spot. About two years ago a couple of my 'Super Star' had a little mildew but that was soon rectified and, touch wood, my plants of 'Frensham' have no sign of it up to date. I have even planted a couple of specimens of 'Dorothy Perkins' this year in spite of dire warnings from my suppliers. In case you are thinking how lucky I am it must be stated that last year, and the year before, two 'Grand'-mère Jenny', two 'South Seas', two 'Coronado' and one of my 'Sutter's Gold' suffered quite severely from Rose Rust. I tried maneb last year, without much success, and will spray with a neutral copper fungicide in about three weeks' time and see if that helps.

I purchase my trees from the Transvaal, a thousand miles away, as I find their framework and root system far stronger than the ones obtained locally, no doubt due to the Transvaal's frosty, dry winters. My finest trees are six 'Elizabeth of Glamis', with masses of blooms on growth up to five feet high. I have read in various overseas books that they are difficult to establish. Others which do particularly well are 'Ena Harkness', 'Percy Thrower', a lovely shape, 'Super Star', a couple of 'Virgo' standards, 'Climbing Spartan', 'Queen Elizabeth' and half a dozen bushes of 'Orangeade' which were transplanted last year. Two failures, or rather partial failures are, surprisingly, 'Peace'. Strangely enough, the bed of 'Peace' in the Cape Town Gardens was also disappointing and the plants have been uprooted. Three weeks ago I planted a dozen 'Iceberg' and six 'Piccadilly' and all seem to be doing well. It may surprise some readers that I do all my own planting and digging and that popular character of South African life, the poor native or Cape Coloured, is not waiting in the background to do all the hard work.

Saint George for Merrie England!
A challenge to our Hybridists

JOSEPH MARSH

(*Amateur rose grower*)

Englishmen and women too, celebrate—or, more correctly, observe—the day of their Patron Saint George on April 23 each year. Mark this date; it has something to do with what follows.

The Irish celebrate, I mean really celebrate, St Patrick's Day, when apart from potheen and porter an important part is played by the botanically humble, but nationally exalted emblem, the shamrock. Plentifully available at the right time, no true Irishman would be without a sprig of shamrock in his buttonhole. Shure and its the "Wearin' o' the Green"!

Likewise the Welsh. Their St David's Day occurs most conveniently when daffodils—or leeks, if you prefer them—are in good supply. And the Welsh too, proudly wear or display their emblems, while the beautiful strains of choral singing echo through the valleys, boyo!

The Scots are expert at celebrating. Gay, hospitable, uproarious and very colourful occasions abound, among which is, of course, St Andrew's Day, when, in the galaxy of plaids and pibrochs, sporrans and skean-dhus, highland flings and haggises (or haggii) there shines above all the national emblem, the thistle. Whether worn bejewelled in a corsage or on a balmoral, or teased from a haystack to decorate a crofter's buttonhole, the thistle is very much to the fore on this day. Och aye!

I return now to St George's Day and the English. Why is it that we—I happen to be English—never seem to be aware of our Patron Saint's day until either the youngsters in from school tell us, or we notice in the six o'clock news that television announcers and reporters are sporting roses—our national emblem—in their buttonholes? This, and maybe a passing reference in the news media, plus a few get-togethers of the faithful at St George's Society gatherings—which do not seem to attract much publicity —constitutes our sober observance of this our national day. No eager anticipation. No excitement. No general display of national pride. No parades. No wholesale wearing of roses!

Now why is this so? Phlegmatic English? Could be. Straightbacked, stiff upperlipped? Maybe. Disinterested? Might be. Frustrated? Yes!!

Frustrated, because of the simple horticultural fact that on April 23, any year, there are no roses in our gardens to gather to decorate our homes or ourselves. Greenhouse roses, florist's roses (so expensive), yes, and even plastic roses (Ugh!), but honest to goodness garden roses—none available! To have a garden rose one could tend and have in bloom for wearing on St George's Day, would not only fill one with a glow of achievement but would also make the day itself more popular. England's Day! St George's Day! Think of tens of thousands of people in streets, in shops, offices, factories and schools, all wearing the national emblem, grown by themselves or their friends. What a gay sight and what a gay day it—the rose—would create! What an incentive to celebrate, our most beautiful flower would provide!

But where is this rose? So far as I know it does not exist.

Such a situation at once poses a great challenge to our rose hybridists—or rose breeders if you prefer it—particularly English hybridists, i.e., to produce a rose that will bloom outdoors during April. It should of course be a red rose, fragrant, hardy, of small size for buttonhole wearing—something like the old 'Richmond'—and bear a name—say, 'St George's Rose' or 'Rose of England' or simply 'The English Rose.'

A fairly tall order, you will say, but a breeding line might be sought amongst the few hybrid teas, shrubs and species roses that already bloom in May. Perhaps by a manipulation of genes of these, the result might be still earlier blooming, and once this has been established, other things like colour and vigour could follow.

Climate, and the natural cycle of blooming of the rose, are features one cannot ignore completely, and we in England—well, we learn to live with the vagaries of our climate and also accept that our flushes of bloom will come in June, with generally a second blooming in the autumn. In other parts of the world, however, roses bloom at various times and somewhere, I suppose, is a rose that blooms naturally in April. If so, is it possible, I wonder, that such a rose could be crossed in a way that, whilst the time of blooming would remain permanently fixed, the other characteristics necessary for maintaining health and vigour in this country could be bred in?

It's just a thought, and I can hear loud cries from the botanists, geneticists, and what have you, saying "the man's mad" and then going on to quote facts to prove it!

But hybridists—do not be put off. I have outlined the problem. Go to and solve it for St George of England's sake. Fill the void that exists on his day. If you tell me "it's impossible" I'll say the same was thought before someone flew the Channel, or landed on the moon, and would most humbly and with respect, remind you that a yellow rose, not all that many years ago, was thought impossible.

The Decorative Classes

JULIA CLEMENTS, V.M.H.

(International judge, lecturer and author on Floral Art)

An exciting schedule and better staging seemed to draw more entries than ever in the decorative section of the Summer Show, and the fact that we had experienced such a very dry spring and early summer seemed to make no difference to the crowds that flocked into the Royal Horticultural Society's Halls for this very popular two-day event.

The public just love these classes and it is often enlightening to stand around listening to the remarks made. "They're all the same," said one woman. I wondered where she had been looking, for there was such a diversity of exhibits that I spent three hours just taking my notes.

Mrs K. Pitman of north London, who entered eight classes, was successful in winning three first prizes and the Queen Alexandra Memorial Cup for the best table decoration which had to illustrate "Entertaining Clients". She used an olive green sateen cloth, in the centre of which a silver candelabra with green candles was placed on a silver tray which was filled with fruit. At each end of the table was an arrangement of red roses, well executed—the accessories being four green plates on which were placed red napkins. It was a well-balanced table and seemed acceptable to all who saw it.

Mrs J. Ward of Kent came second with a polished and well-staged table, showing a brown cloth (to the floor) with gold braid edges. Her yellow centre-piece of roses was stood on a similarly covered brown base surrounding a beige Wedgewood, black patterned urn in which fruit was placed. Flanking the central arrangement stood two modern black iron swerved candlesticks holding black candles—very sophisticated. The napkins were gold coloured and the decanter and upturned glasses were placed with expertise.

In the class for "The Good Old Days" Mrs K. Pitman took first prize, showing an exhibit featuring old-fashioned roses on a sea green over blue base, backed with a picture of Queen Elizabeth I and a model of a Galleon (the Armada). There were some good exhibits in this class, Mrs K. Wells featuring her old roses in a model of a hansom cab, but Mrs G. E. Woollard took second prize with a pewter filled bowl of old roses placed on lace over green and purple velvet. A Victorian posy and long kid gloves were accessories.

I liked very much the exhibit of Mr W. Field in the men only class. He made an excellent design of red roses behind a figurine standing on slate with lonicera, privet and hosta foliage. He came only third, the first prize going to Mr F. Staples who displayed a trugful of yellow roses with scissors and a show schedule.

Mrs D. Scanlon of Hamble deservedly took first prize with a magnificent pedestal arrangement in the "Conference Hall" class. She used *Lonicera nitida* at the sides with pink and red roses, nicely recessed, adding Bergenia leaves and golden privet in the centre.

Class 96 for a modern arrangement of roses featuring "Glass" was well entered and well won by Mrs E. M. Woodcock of Essex, who placed two large pink roses atop a tall blue glass bottle with one rose fixed low down to the stopper. All stood on a white glass square on a black base and were united by twisted cane. Mrs K. Wells came second in this class with a tall swerve of white roses placed in a large glass swan staged on a mirror base which stood on pale green chiffon. Blocks of cut glass surrounded the swan. Mrs K. Pitman, although not a prizewinner, showed originality in this class by using two empty cylindrical glass vases with her roses grouped low down around them.

The class for an arrangement of roses with any foliage to represent "In the Year 2000" drew a lot of comment. Certainly the exhibit of Mrs J. Ward stopped most onlookers in their tracks, for she showed a model missile platform surrounded by roses low down and from which, high up, shot out a long branch on the end of which was one rose. Her title was "The First Rose on the Moon". However, it was Mrs A. C. Doughty of Edgware who took first prize in this class, with a well-designed exhibit featuring a dull black round base, holding a tin, holding in turn a midnight blue/black branch at the top of which were two rings holding two 'Super Star' roses, followed by two low down with hosta and pittosporum leaves.

Some of the exhibitors did not seem to get the atmosphere of "Al Fresco" into their exhibits. Meaning, in the open air, some of them made arrangements which were too formal. Mrs G. E. Woollard got the right idea with yellow roses bursting out of a pottery cockerel container on a brown check cloth.

"Dignity", a class for a vertical arrangement, gave us many variations, with Mrs J. Ward taking first prize. She used white roses in a tall design in a white figurine vase with tall variegated privet and small hosta leaves—very dignified. Mrs K. Wells came second with five red roses in white alabaster on a red base with looped flax leaves.

In the class for "Conflict and Harmony" Mrs Wells came first and Mrs Ward second. This called for two arrangements. And in the class for "Colour

Madness", which obviously called for a riot of colour, one visitor said quite out loud: "Goodness, those awful colours, don't they know how to blend?" I pointed out that the class called for a clash of colours. "Oh, I don't know about the classes, I only know what I like," she said. This all brings me to state again that one should view the decorative classes with a schedule in one's hand, or else study the very well-placed class titles that are always on display. Of course not everyone is so unobservant, for many look at the class title before assessing the exhibits, and that is how it should be. Mrs Pitman won first in this class with cerise, pink, flame and red roses standing on a shocking pink base backed with orange linen. Mrs Field was second and Mrs Ward came third.

The first prize winning exhibit in the Club class entitled "World of Music" was won by Southgate with a superb exhibit of red roses surrounded by clefs and five bars with crochets made out of black cane. This led the eye to a globe with accessories of a music sheet, baton and white tie.

The Autumn Show

Rain and gales prior to the show date reduced the number of trade entries at the Autumn Show, so the decorative classes took the centre of the floor at the Royal Horticultural Society where the show was held. I visited the show on its second day, and was pleasantly surprised to notice how fresh all the arrangements were. Obviously the competitors are well trained in conditioning their roses.

The hall was crowded and everyone seemed interested in the "Nursery Rhyme" class which won for Mrs K. Wells of Dover the first prize and challenge trophy for the best exhibit in the decorative classes. She interpreted "Old King Cole" by using red roses in a throne-like wooden container, draped in gold-edged red velvet. A pipe and a bowl of fruit were displayed on one side and three smaller arrangements, each one interspersed with a small fiddle, were composed on the other side. A crown was supported somehow over the "throne" and the verse displayed among the roses read "Old King Cole was a Merry Old Soul and a Merry Old Soul was he, he called for his pipe, he called for his bowl, and he called for his fiddlers three". It was well thought out and very well executed. Mrs Woodcock came second with an interpretation of "Hey diddle, diddle, the cat and the fiddle . . ." Mrs M. Woodcock, who lives in Essex, told me that when she was carrying her roses into the hall at midnight, a camera and her food were stolen from her car. However, after starting her entries, she slept on a collapsible bed and finished her exhibits before the judges arrived next morning. She was rewarded with two firsts, one second and a third. One of her firsts was in a class entitled "Caprice", an arrangement of roses incorporating a fan. She used mauve roses and trails of variegated honeysuckle in a green oriental vase on a green silk base, a mauve pink silk fan being inserted high up.

Others in this class I liked very much were those entered by Mrs Mascall and Mrs Pitman. Mrs Mascall made a low arrangement of coral coloured roses placed behind and in front of a black lace fan on grey chiffon, whilst Mrs K. Pitman used pastel coloured roses in pink, mauve and cream with a fan interspersed. Roses seem to lend themselves to this kind of class and I must say they looked most appealing as reminders of a more genteel age.

Mrs K. Field came first in the class for Roses and Rose Heps in a basket; she also took a first in the "Get Well" class which called for an arrangement of roses and rose foliage only. Many made their arrangement too large or too tall for the title of the class, Mrs Field making hers very daintily in an all round basket which could easily have been stood on the top of a locker. A get well card was allowed.

First prize in the class entitled "Economy", using not more than five roses, went to Mrs A. W. Downey who made a Hogarth curve outline of broom with five roses in a cupid type vase standing on a green base. She also took a first in "The Jewel Box", using multicoloured roses flowing out of the open drawers of a jewel box, the roses being interspersed with beads, pearls and other jewellery.

Mrs J. Ward of Herne Bay, Kent, has skilled hands when it comes to making accessories. She took a first in the "Carnival" class, having made a gay merry-go-round from which hung miniature posies of roses. Accessories included a blue-ribboned straw hat and a blue decorated frame on which were the words "Oh dear, what can the matter be, Johnny's so long at the fair".

"As I Like It" was the title of the class reserved for those who had not previously won a prize. This was won by Mrs B. Jackson, who used a green soapstone vase in which she made a lovely swerved design. She will soon move up.

Mr W. Field's work is very good. He took second in the "Carnival" class using two bronze dancing figurines, surrounded by red roses on a red drape base with black mask; in fact, most of them in this class showed great artistry.

The schedule was excellent and I felt it must be difficult to vary this each year, just as I find it difficult to vary my notes each year! I try to describe the exhibits in order to interest those who do not see them.

Book Reviews

Shrub Roses of Today by Graham Stuart Thomas. New and Revised Edition, 1974. Published by J. M. Dent & Sons Ltd., London. Price £4.50.

While re-reading Graham Thomas's book *Shrub Roses of Today* in the revised edition, the Muslim proverb came into my mind, "A good book is like a garden carried in your pouch." After the publication of his book *The Old Shrub Roses* Graham Thomas was acknowledged in the English-speaking world as the authority on old garden roses. The sequel to his first book is *Shrub Roses of Today* which follows on where the first book ended—after the introduction of China roses into Europe and the effect these roses had in the development of the repeat-flowering Bourbon roses.

Shrub Roses of Today is divided into three sections. The first part traces the history and the evolution of the single, wild rose, to the doubling of the flower, the changing shapes of the roses—as one style was perfected another emerged to suit the change in fashions and the increased range of colours introduced into garden roses by selection and hybridization. The shrub roses are grouped into two parts; the first concentrates on species, their garden forms and first generation hybrids. Their uses in the garden landscape, their value as ground cover plants, the beautiful and varied foliage, decorative heps and autumn leaves as well as the blooms are fully described. The second part is devoted to shrub roses which have affinity to the China rose; they include China roses, Hybrid Perpetual roses, Poly-poms, Hybrid Musk roses and shrub roses of the twentieth century. Added to the revised edition are the descriptions of three new shrub roses: 'Autumn Fire', 'Golden Chersonese' and *Rosa macrophylla* var. 'Master Hugh'. Almost all the Hybrid Teas and Floribunda roses have been left out because a shrub rose has come to mean to gardeners, if not to lexicographers, something different from a bush rose. However, it was Graham Thomas who rescued from neglect the first Floribunda rose, 'Gruss an Aachen' and reintroduced this scented, creamy-coloured rose to many gardeners. The rose is illustrated in *Journal des Roses*, August 1912.

The book is beautifully illustrated by the author's water-colours, pencil drawings and, with four exceptions, his own photographs of roses. The drawings of 'Cécile Brunner' and 'Bloomfield Abundance' with its elongated calyx lobes should help gardeners to identify these two similar roses, although grown on rich soil the calyx on 'Cécile Brunner' is longer than on the rose illustrated. Postscripts have been added at the end of the introduction and some other chapters giving additional information. An article by Capt. C. A. E. Stanfield, R.N., in the *Rose Annual* for 1972 has convinced Graham Thomas that 'Bloomfield Abundance' is a sport from 'Cécile Brunner', which contradicts the parentage given in McFarland's *Modern Roses*. The author gives references to rose illustrations to be found in other books and compares their quality.

From my own experience I have found that a number of Hybrid Perpetuals are very susceptible to the rose disease Rust and we have only three H.P.s in the garden;

Class 101 at the Summer Show. "Conflict and Harmony." Two arrangements of roses with any foliage. First Prize: Mrs K. Wells, Dover. (*See page* 157)

Class 55 at the Autumn Show. "Carnival." An arrangement of roses, any foliage.
First Prize: Mrs J. Ward, Herne Bay. (*See page* 159)

therefore, I might have echoed the sentence on page 131: "Today there are very few of the thousands of H.P.s still in cultivation and perhaps it is as well, for many were undoubtedly only fit for the bonfire", if I had not seen the vigorous Hybrid Perpetuals growing at "Lime Kiln", Claydon. With exactly the same good cultivation Hybrid Teas struggled to survive in this chalk garden. The growth and roses of the H.P.s planted and cherished by Humphrey Brooke have to be seen to be believed; a bucket of his "soil" looks to me like a bucket of dusty chalk; that being so, gardeners on chalk may be only too pleased to rescue some H.P.s from the bonfire.

Mention is made of the RNRS display garden at Bone Hill and the National Trust's rose collection at Mottisfont Abbey. I had hoped the revised edition would have solved my problem about *Rosa pendulina plena (flore pleno)*. The nursery from which I bought it and 'Morlettii' has recently published an erudite manual in which *Rosa pendulina flore pleno* is given as a synonym of 'Morlettii', but the two roses I planted are quite distinct. Graham Thomas writes: " 'Morlettii'. Morlet 1883. *Rosa inermis morlettii*. Also found under the name of *R. pendulina plena*, which is of doubtful authenticity."

There are chapters on fragrance and on cultivation and pruning; the author is in no doubt that the rose owes its popularity through the ages to the flowers' scent. Each chapter is headed with a verse or prose extract about roses from poets or authors. Gordon Rowley, former keeper of the National Rose Species collection at Bayfordbury, is responsible for chapter 15; he has compiled a key to the main groups of garden roses and drawn three useful diagrams on: a simplified genealogy of the main groups of garden roses, the origins of Kordes' hybrid Rubiginosas and modern hybrid Spinosissimas, respectively. The botanist also on page 200 contributes a most interesting list of rose species for which double-flowered mutants have been recorded. There is a printer's error on this page; *Rosa virginiana* should not be listed under Platyrhodon with *Rosa roxburghii* but with *Rosa carolina* under Cinnamomeae.

The index is excellent and in this edition six more additions have been made to the interesting Bibliography which makes a valuable reference for further reading. The date of *Plus Belles Roses* has been corrected to 1912 and other minor corrections to the first edition have been made.

Shrub Roses of Today is a most important book; it is a reference book for present and future generations. But it is more than a comprehensive handbook, a work of careful research, since the author has made the shrub roses he has grown and described blossom into literary permanence.

T.E.A.

Roses, by Leonard Hollis. (Second edition November, 1974)
240 pp. Published by The Hamlyn Publishing Group Ltd.
Collingridge Standard Guides. £3.50.

Here we have a revised edition of Leonard Hollis' book on roses, first published in
1970. The text of this second edition is nearly similar to that of the first which is
rightly considered as being an outstanding contribution to rose literature. There are
significant additions in the new book.

A chapter on Nomenclature gives a very interesting exposition by the author of
the history and difficulties of this subject. He points out that it is not a trivial matter
but one "in which a little more thought might well be given by the world's leading
rose breeders having regard to spelling and pronunciation." Mr Hollis reminds us in
this connection of two bygone tongue-twisters 'Gloire de Chédane-Guinoisseau' and
'Souvenir de Denier Van der Gon'. The latter, he points out, had a raw deal by reason
of its clumsy name, as it was in fact an excellent garden rose.

Two new chapters by Ena Harkness, "Roses in Flower Arrangement" and "Products of the Rose" are, to a mere male reviewer, very well done and will be of great
appeal to the ladies. The chapter on "Products of the Rose" includes 12 recipes for
perfume and wine etc. from various sources including one from each of the 14th,
15th and 16th centuries. There will be some strange, and no doubt delicious, smells
in the homes of many rose lovers.

Interest in Shrub Roses and Old Garden Roses appears to be growing and, recog-
nising this, Mr Hollis now deals more fully with the subject.

The detailed lists of varieties have been ruthlessly culled of those which are not now
available and brought up to date with new varieties, some of which, when the book
was written, were not yet on the market but which are now in commerce. A valuable addition to this list of varieties is that any awards made after exhaustive trials
by The Royal National Rose Society are now under the description of the variety.

There are 59 colour pictures, the standard of which is fair, some very good and
others not so good. Those who understand the immense difficulties of exactly producing the colours of nature on paper, will find them generally acceptable. It is good
to see that black and white photographs of rose blooms and foliage have been used
with restraint for in most cases these reproductions render the illustrations almost a
waste of time. Earlier publications (not those of Mr Hollis) have suffered from this
weakness and with the improvement in colour work it is to be hoped that the old
black and white will take a back seat. On the other hand, the line drawings and the
photographs which are in support of the text are most admirably done and add a
great deal to the understanding of the operations described.

At the present-day reasonable price of £3.50 this book is of superb value, and from
the amateur point of view, coming from so distinguished a rosarian with his fluent
and forthright style of writing, is surely the best buy on the subject of roses, to date.
It is a beautifully proportioned book, a delight to handle and a most attractive
addition to any collection.

R. L. PALLETT

Plant Breeding—Some New Challenges and Prospects

The 26th Amos Memorial Lecture, with the above title, was delivered at East Malling Research Station on 7 November, 1973 by Professor D. Roy Davies, who is Director of the John Innes Institute at Norwich and also Head of the Department of Applied Genetics at that Institute.

Although Professor Davies was addressing an audience largely interested in some aspects of top fruit, he discussed the technology of plant breeding in a much wider context and went on to define four stages in a breeding programme:

1. Recognition of defects in the particular crop plant.
2. A search for forms which show improvements in these respects or which could be expected to produce superior progeny.
3. The generation of such superior progeny by an intercrossing programme.
5. Finally, the evaluation of the new population of hybrid progeny.

One example was quoted of how a defect—a leafless pea—could be used for crop improvement. In this race the photosynthetic area is provided by the pods and tendrils. The lack of foliage would be an advantage when harvesting a pea crop for processing during inclement autumn weather.

In the search for improved characters the plant breeder must guard against genetic erosion—namely, the progressive loss of variation present in wild ancestors. One remedy is the establishment of so-called gene banks and the Society's collection of wild rose species can be considered such a bank.

Professor Davies digressed briefly to consider the importance of generating variation by mutation (sporting) using radiation or chemicals. Colour varieties in many ornamental plants have been produced by this means but, in a breeding programme with *Streptocarpus*, the range of variation produced by X-irradiation was much smaller than that generated by hybridization.

The mechanism of incompatibility was then considered in some detail and much of this may make difficult reading for some rose breeders, but they should nevertheless remember that one particular source of incompatibility can be overcome by the use of gibberellins in *Rosa*.

Some new and speculative techniques in plant genetics were then considered, but the speaker emphasized that these would be unlikely to replace conventional methods based on sexual hybridization. Tissue culture techniques are now familiar to carnation and orchid growers and breeders and Professor Davies quoted *Brassica*, *Lilium*, *Hordeum* and *Freesia* as four genera for which tissue culture had been used effectively.

Pollen culture has recently attracted much interest as haploid plants of *Datura* and *Nicotiana* have been produced by this means. If a haploid rose were to be produced it would have only seven chromosomes and would be sterile. However, colchicine treatment might then be used to produce a fertile diploid which would be homozygous (true-breeding). Two such diploids, crossed together, would then yield F.1 hybrid rose seed. Perhaps I should add that this speculation is mine and not Professor Davies's.

The full text of this fascinating lecture is published in the East Malling Research Station Report for 1973.[1]   E. F .A.

Studies on seeds and seedlings of some oil-bearing and spontaneous species of roses for breeding and propagation of roses, by R. Tsvetkov, Research Institute of Roses, Aromatik and Medicinal Plants, Kazanlik, Bulgaria.

Partly because the production of attar is such an important industry in Bulgaria, authorities at the above Institute decided to carry out some experiments with various things in mind; to see what stocks were most suitable for the Kazanlik Damask rose and how they affected production of attar and also the suitability of other stocks in the climate of Bulgaria for use in budding modern roses. The experiments covered the maturing of the seeds and stratification, also the treatment of them by acids, temperature and humidity before sowing. Seeds were saved of the Kazanlik Damask, and the following *Rosa canina* clones: 'Pollmeriana', 'Broggs', 'Schmidt's Ideal' and 'Inermis'. The production of growth and bloom was carefully watched and it was found that 'Schmidt's Ideal' and 'Broggs' grew well and bore abundant fruit. Also that these two and 'Inermis' were most vigorous, while 'Pollmeriana' and 'Inermis' provided the best root collars. 'Broggs' seemed to suit the Kazanlik Damask best and also the Climbers and Hybrid Teas; 'Pollmeriana' proved most suitable for the Polyanthas, and 'Schmidt's Ideal' and 'Inermis' suited Floribundas. None of the stocks mentioned produced suckers when used for budding the Damask rose.

While the Damask rose at Kazanlik is used in great bulk for the production of attar, *Rosa alba semi-plena* is also used in smaller quantity but does not produce so good an extract. Some years ago Dr V. N. Staicov of the Research Institute kindly sent me a pressed sample of the Damask rose and it proved to be almost, if not quite, identical with the rose over here known as *Rosa damascena trigintipetala*. He also very kindly sent me a tiny sample of attar; its delicious fragrance made me realise at once from what the delicate flavour of the pink portions of Turkish Delight and Marshmallow originated. Astronomical quantities of blooms have to be picked very early in the morning to be conveyed to the vats for distilling and it takes about three tons of flowers (well over a million) to produce 2 lb. of attar.

                                                                    G. S. THOMAS

Rosen, Rosen, Rosen, by Gerd Krüssmann, Published by Verlag Paul Parey. May 1974. 460 pages. Price DM. 158.

This is probably the most comprehensive encyclopedia on the rose which has yet been produced and the publishers suggest that nothing comparable has been available since

[1] Obtainable from East Malling Research Station, Maidstone, Kent, ME19 6BT, price £1·50 $5·00) post free.

Th. Nietner's work of 1880. The author, Gerd Krüssmann, is Director of the Dort-mund Rosarium. He has spared no effort in bringing together a remarkable collection of facts and figures about every aspect of the rose, for which the research work has taken more than four years. The author has had the benefit of the co-operation of Wilhelm and Reimer Kordes in checking the text, particularly in relation to the section on hybridization.

The work is divided into sixteen main groups covering everything from the history of the rose in earliest times to a systematic description of the species *Rosa*; from notes on the various rose societies across the world to details and illustrations of roses used on international coinage.

Some of the early groups contain fascinating information on the rose in art and literature. For example, he illustrates the secret Jacobite emblem in the shape of a rose on which was inscribed the names of the "martyrs" of the '45 rebellion and in another section describes the coat of arms of the town of Eye in Suffolk, with its two crossed stems of white roses. To the serious student of the rose in history these sections will be a source of endless interest and delight.

The text throughout is liberally illustrated with line drawings and half-tone blocks of good quality. There are, in addition, about forty colour plates of modern varieties. These appear somewhat over-bright and harsh, though their definition is excellent.

Dr Krüssmann deals at length with the classification and description of the species *Rosa*. This section is well represented with drawings and maps giving the geographical distribution of the main groups.

The list of modern varieties which occupies the final 125 pages of the book, com-prises those cultivars which are to be found growing in the five great German display gardens at Dortmund, Insel Mainau, Uetersen, Weihenstephan and Zweibruecken. The author details the main works of reference in which the roses are described but unfortunately has omitted to show the international awards which they have gained.

From the point of view of the British reader the book has two drawbacks. Firstly its price, which is approximately £25·75 at the current rate of exchange. Secondly, there is at present no English translation and therefore an adequate knowledge of German is necessary to enjoy to the full all that this outstanding work has to offer.

H. N. R.

La Rosa Nel Giardino (*The Rose in the Garden*) by Stelvio Coggiatti, illustrated by Anna Maria Trechslin. 180 pp. Published in collaboration with the Giornale d'Agricultura. Price L3.500

The author is well known to readers of our *Rose Annual* and the artist has gained the title "Redouté of the XXth. Century."

It is a fascinating little book, though "little" is scarcely appropriate, for Signor Coggiatti has packed into it a mass of information for the novice and interest for the expert all amplified, simplified and enhanced by Signorina Trechslin's line-drawings which must be seen to be believed, especially the pert little 'Mme Hardy' (Damascena) which pops up in nine odd corners and has five whole pages to herself.

There are fifteen chapters. The first deals with the evolution of the rose from "twenty to thirty million years before man." Beginning with the famous fossils and, after mentioning Herodotus, Pliny, Virgil and others, it reaches present day with 'Lady X' and ends with questions about the future.

Chapter II gives a very clear "genealogical tree", the branches being *R. canina*, *R. gallica*, *R. damascena*, *R. chinensis* and *R. moschata*, and with interesting historical and hybridizing details, ultimately produces the modern hybrid tea. Fourteen lovely drawings illustrate this chapter.

Chapter III deals with the "anatomy" of the rose and the various deviations according to type.

Chapter IV gives an account of the International Conferences that are held annually at twelve European centres to evaluate the new roses. The first such meeting was in Paris (Bagatelle) in 1907 and naturally this present volume is chiefly about the subject in Rome itself. Tribute is paid to those public-spirited citizens who, since 1928, have worked to make the rose really international. Two sketches here show the Display Garden on one side of the road and the Trial Ground on the other, both with the ruins of Ancient Rome in the background.

Chapter V, after a short list of recommended varieties according to colour, explains and illustrates the different groups—multiflora, polyantha, floribunda, grandiflora and miniature (Lillipuziana!).

Chapter VI deals with Climbers (Rampicanti) of all types, the earliest date mentioned being 1793 with a species from Central China which eventually produced 'Mermaid.'

Chapter VII—"le rose piccole" begins with 'Perle d'Or' and its sister 'Cécile Brunner' followed by 'Bloomfield Abundance'. After a list of seventeen lilliputians there is mention of Tantau's 'Garnette' of 1950.

Chapter VIII gives 18 pages, including 21 illustrations, of information about planting roses.

Chapter IX gives 21 pages, including 26 illustrations, of information about pruning, disbudding, feeding etc.

Chapter X deals with reproduction either from seeds or by budding or by cuttings with or without hormone.

Chapter XI is for the hybridist, while Chapter XII is for the artist by the Artist, with 18 exquisite pictures for the garden, from a pergola to a flower-pot.

Chapter XIII is headed "principali nemici dela rosa" and in thirteen pages there is an account, each with a picture, of sixteen of the pests and plagues, bugs and beetles, "anomalies" and "monstrosities" that beset the rose and the rosarian.

Chapter XIV is a dictionary of 122 rose terms, while Chapter XV is a useful index. This is a beautifully produced handbook.

ARBEL M. ALDOUS

Turn on the Fountains. The Life of Dean Hole, by Betty Massingham, 256 pp. Published by Victor Gollancz Ltd. 1974. Price £5.00 net.

This is a delightful and absorbing biography of a great Victorian, Samuel Reynolds Hole, D.D., first President of The (Royal) National Rose Society who graced that office from its inception in 1877 until his death in 1904. The title is from a remembrance of Dame Sybil Thorndike, who spent much of her childhood at Rochester and knew the Dean through his close association with her grandfather who was a Canon of the Cathedral. In fulfilling an invitation from the Duke of Rutland to look over the gardens of Belvoir Castle whenever he wished he arrived unannounced and sought the head gardener who conducted him round. Subsequently realising the visitor was a knowledgeable gardener and a dignitary of the Church he asked the pleasure of his identity. "The Dean of Rochester, Dean Hole" was his reply; whereupon the head gardener called through his cupped hands down through the gardens to the under-gardeners "Turn on the fountains! Turn on the fountains!"

As Betty Massingham says in her author's note, "It is the object in this biography to show Dean Hole in the general circumstances of his life, as a person, not only in his connection with the rose world, but also to see his work in the light of the times". It reveals a man of wide interests, devoted to his family, who enjoyed life to the full. He was of no mean literary attainment and became a frequent contributor to *Punch*. He was an outstanding preacher and preached in St Paul's Cathedral on some fifty occasions.

The many strands selected from a considerable bibliography, along with contemporary and family correspondence and diaries, have been woven together with consummate skill by the author and we are indebted to her for this most readable account of the life of Dean Hole.

W. A. JAMES

The Man Who Painted Roses by Antonia Ridge. Published by Faber & Faber, May 1974. 409 pages. Price £2.65.

Biographical work on the painter Pierre Joseph Redouté is conspicuous by its absence and any attempt to fill the gap is a matter for profound gratitude from those interested in the painting of flowers and the history of art.

Mrs Ridge, who is well known already for her chronicle of 'Peace', has undoubtedly gone to great lengths to obtain as much factual detail as possible about Redouté. It is therefore to be regretted that the end product of her labour is not written in a more serious and scholarly way. She seems to have adopted a style that is a mixture of the romantic novelist and nursery governess and this, inevitably, somewhat detracts from the value of the research work which she has had to undertake in order to compile the book.

It also seems unnecessary to fill in so much comparatively trite background detail of the period, which only serves the purpose of prolonging the book without enhancing the value of the information. It would have been preferable to have given the reader details of Redouté's engravers and their method, subjects which she leaves unmentioned.

There is only one illustration, a coloured frontispiece, of *Rosa bifera officinalis* and it is unfortunate that this should appear with a misprint in the title on the contents page.

In a work of this nature it is strange that there should not have been additional illustrations in monochrome and one thinks particularly of the main protagonists in the story and also of the places mentioned. For example, the portrait of Redouté himself, Prud'hon's portrait of the Empress Joséphine and Garneray's fine picture of Malmaison come quickly to mind.

Lastly, from the student's point of view, it is a missed opportunity not to have included, at the end of the book, a bibliography of the sources of information. Acknowledgements are made to various collections of archives and it would have been most helpful to have had well-documented evidence of the source material.

Nevertheless, Mrs Ridge has attempted a work for which there has been a great need for many years and, although scholars may find fault with her approach, the general reading public will have reason to be grateful for an entertaining chronicle of the greatest painter of roses ever to have lived.

H. N. R.

Articles for *The Rose Annual* should be submitted to the editor by the end of August, addressed to him at The Royal National Rose Society's Offices, Bone Hill, Chiswell Green Lane, St. Albans, Herts. They should be the author's own work, should not have been accepted by any other publication and should be typed in double spacing or, if hand-written, the lines should be well spaced. Black and white photographs of good definition, featuring items of general interest to members, are also welcomed.

Members are asked to note that any enquiries addressed to contributors to *The Rose Annual* should be accompanied by the appropriate postage, or in the case of overseas members, Commonwealth or International Reply coupons for surface or air-mail reply.

The Summer Rose Show

PETER WOOD, N.D.H.

The weather prior to a flower show has a great influence on its success, particularly for the summer show of the RNRS. This year the weather was hot and dry until two days before the show when there was very heavy rain—conditions hardly ideal for showing prize blooms. This reflected in the quality of blooms on display, and certainly in the New Hall of the Royal Horticultural Society, the trade exhibits were decidely "thin on the ground." Nevertheless, R. Harkness & Co. won the Championship Trophy for the best exhibit, the 40th occasion they have done so, which is surely a wonderful record. In addition, they took the Coronation Trophy for the best exhibit over 450 sq. ft and a Large Gold Medal. As a neutral foil for their vases they used what looked like rush matting material to screen the wall behind and for the base. Here were roses in excellent condition and a well represented collection of old and new varieties. For instance, they showed "oldies" such as 'Cécile Brunner', 'Mermaid' and 'Cornelia' as well as "mods" including 'Pineapple Poll', 'Moon Maiden', 'Kim', a dwarf floribunda, 'Just Joey', 'Alec's Red' and 'Seven Seas'.

Cants of Colchester won the Queen Mary Trophy for the best exhibit over 300 sq. ft, and not exceeding 450 sq. ft, and a Large Gold Medal. Their large display against a wall had a green base and a pale blue background. Low blue tables and silver bowls were used to display their blooms. Prominent was 'Alpine Sunset', their new hybrid tea introduction for 1974. The creamy-yellow, pink-flushed blooms are fragrant and it looks a promising new rose.[1] I also admired on their stand the deep red climber 'Altissimo' as well as varieties such as 'Fleet Street,' 'National Trust', 'Tenerife', 'Esther Ofarim', 'John Waterer', 'Red Devil' and 'Yellow Pages'.

The China Trophy for the best exhibit between 151 and 300 sq. ft went to Warley Rose Gardens, together with a Gold Medal. They had an island exhibit with blooms shown at two levels, each level having a blue skirt and a grey base. There were white stands as well as black bowls to display the roses. These included the hybrid tea 'Baroness Rothschild', 'Whisky Mac' and 'Josephine Bruce', in excellent condition, 'Red Devil', 'Youki San' and 'National Trust'. They also showed well known miniatures such as 'New Penny', 'Pink Gem', 'Darling Flame' and 'Pour Toi'.

The Norman Rogers Cup is awarded to the best exhibit of 150 sq. ft or

[1] It has since been awarded a Trial Ground Certificate. [Ed.]

less. This year it went to E. B. Le Grice (Roses) Ltd, who also received a Silver Gilt Medal. Their island group consisted of a grey base and silver containers. Their purple floribunda 'News' was very prominent and was well displayed with the pink floribunda 'Agreement', lavender 'Ripples' and deep lilac 'Overture'. 'Red Sprite' is one of their new floribundas in deep red and appears to have great potential as a low bedding rose.

I do not think John Mattock's exhibit could have pleased the judges as they gave it only a Large Gold Medal. As a background they used pleated fawn hessian, and a green hessian base. It was simple but perhaps a little drab for a really effective display. Grey urns were used to hold the blooms and shrub roses were placed in the background. Here were 'Great Maiden's Blush', 'Mme. Plantier', 'Charles de Mills' and their new variety 'Rainbow' combining yellow-orange and coral. I also admired their new miniature 'Gold Pin', which should become popular as a buttonhole rose. 'City of Belfast' was among their floribunda roses and also the new 'Matangi', vermilion with silver shading beneath the petals.

The Waterer Group won a Gold Medal. Their staging was similar to what we have seen in the past, using golden bowls placed on a base of large black and white tiles. There were obvious signs of weather damage among their representative collection of hybrid tea and floribunda roses including 'Allgold', 'National Trust', 'Chanelle', 'Rose Gaujard', 'City of Leeds' and 'Irish Mist'.

C. Gregory & Son also won a Gold Medal. Their staging was similar to that of last year. White pillars were placed on a black base and the roses were shown in black vases on the pillars. The latest varieties were given prominence, being displayed in separate groups on polished wood. Some of the novelties they showed included the red hybrid tea 'Royal Show', orange and flame 'Doris Tysterman' and 'Cock o' the North', another red hybrid tea.

Dicksons of Hawlmark had a small island group and won a Silver Gilt medal. Their staging was effective; a shining black base with white containers and white shelving in sharp contrast. Among their new varieties on display were 'Coalite Flame', 'Futura' and 'Precious Platinum'.

Harry Wheatcroft Gardening Ltd had a wall exhibit for which they received a Silver Gilt Medal. 'Sir Harry Pilkington', a red hybrid tea, was prominent and so were the brightly coloured 'Harry Wheatcroft', soft pink 'Lady Helen', and the pink and white 'Candy Stripe'.

Mark Court Nurseries and George Longley & Sons Ltd are the recognized winners in the box classes for nurserymen. This year the results went as follows: Mark Court Nurseries took the William E. Harkness Memorial Trophy for the best bowl of roses, the Kilbee Stuart Memorial Cup for 24 blooms, distinct varieties, in a box and the A. C. Turner Challenge Cup for 15 distinct vases. G. Longley & Sons Ltd took the John Hart Memorial Cup for 48 specimen blooms, distinct varieties, in a box. They were all good roses, of excellent show standard.

Amateurs

All the amateur exhibits were staged in the Old Hall of the R.H.S. and once again F. E. Owen was the most successful exhibitor in classes 16–29 and 26–39 inclusive, winning the Courtney Page Memorial Cup. He also won the Edward Mawley Challenge Cup in Class 16 for a box of 12 superb blooms, distinct. They included 'Akebono', 'Goliath', 'Grandpa Dickson', 'Red Devil', 'Ernest H. Morse', which was particularly good, 'Embassy', 'Royal Highness', 'Peter Frankenfeld', 'Red Lion', 'Honey Favourite' (very good), 'Pink Favourite' and 'Amatsu Otome'. Mr Owen also won the S. W. Burgess Memorial Cup for six vases of hybrid teas in six varieties. The blooms were all evenly matched, beautifully clean and included 'Grandpa Dickson', 'City of Gloucester', 'Charlie's Aunt', 'Royal Highness', 'Red Devil' and 'Peter Frankenfeld'.

The Robert Shipman Memorial Class is for a bowl of old garden roses introduced prior to 1910. This was won by N. P. I. Hadow with 'Tuscany', 'William Lobb', 'Rosa Mundi', *R. gallica officinalis*, 'Charles de Mills', 'Camaieux', 'Fantin Latour', 'Souvenir de l'Impératrice Josephine', 'Chapeau de Napoléon'. My impression here was that there were too few roses.

In contrast, Mr and Mrs E. F. Allen had a beautiful display of old roses, winning the W. C. Thorn Memorial Cup. Among their varieties were *R. gallica versicolor*, 'Général Jacqueminot', 'Tour de Malakoff,' 'Lady Mary Fitzwilliam', *R. centifolia bullata*, *R. rapa*, 'William Lobb', 'Président de Sèze', 'Rose du Maître d'Ecole', 'Perle d'Or', 'Ispahan'.

I also liked D. R. Thorne's vase of climbing roses which won the Frank Naylor Memorial Class. His varieties were 'Handel' and 'Swan Lake', all in beautiful condition. A RNRS Trophy is offered in class 23 for three vases of floribunda roses, distinct. The winner was Miss E. Pritchard who showed three lovely vases of 'Europeana', 'Santa Maria' and 'Arthur Bell'.

Mrs F. M. Pugh is a well known rose exhibitor and this year she won the Lindsell Cup for the difficult box of 24 blooms, distinct, class. It was an outstanding box, all the blooms being very even and only slightly marked by the weather. Her 24 varieties were: 'Perfecta', 'Red Devil', 'Fragrant

Cloud', 'Alec's Red', 'Charlie's Aunt', 'Fleet Street', 'Bonsoir', 'Pink Favourite', 'Peter Frankenfeld', 'Elizabeth Harkness', 'Red Lion', 'City of Gloucester', 'Ernest H. Morse', 'Admiral Rodney', 'Chicago Peace', 'Bob Woolley', 'Femina', 'Embassy', 'Grandpa Dickson', 'City of Bath', 'Fred Gibson', 'Gavotte', 'Norman Hartnell' and 'Royal Highness'.

Captain C. A. E. Stanfield, R.N. is another name that is always prominent in the list of winners. This year he took both the Nicholson Challenge Cup and the Alfred Hewlett Memorial Class. For the first trophy he showed a good box of 12 specimen blooms, distinct. 'Apogee' was a little blown but most of the others were good; they included 'Jimmy Greaves', 'Bob Woolley', 'Admiral Rodney', 'Croft Original', 'Ernest H. Morse', 'City of Bath', 'Silver Lining', 'Grandpa Dickson', 'Red Devil', 'Akebono' and 'John Waterer'.

The Brayfort Challenge Cup was won by A. J. Goodgame with a box of six nice blooms. The largest bloom was 'Pink Favourite', but 'Peace' was on the small side; there was also 'Royal Highness', 'Stella', 'Eden Rose' and 'Red Devil' which was marked.

Most of the blooms shown by H. V. Mitchell in class 36 were showing signs of weather damage, but despite this they won the H. R. Darlington Memorial Cup. Commendable for their evenness in size they included 'Fred Gibson', 'Montezuma', 'Pascali', 'Isabel de Ortiz', 'Red Devil' and 'Anne Letts'.

M. L. Watts did well in Division C for amateurs with not more than 500 rose trees. He took the Sam McGredy Challenge Cup for a box of 12 specimen blooms, with 'My Choice', 'Gavotte' (2), 'Ernest H. Morse', 'Dorothy Peach', 'Papa Meilland', 'Royal Highness' (2), 'City of Bath', a huge 'Red Lion', 'Silver Lining' and 'Red Devil'. He also took the Edward J. Holland Memorial Cup for three distinct vases of hybrid tea blooms. 'Royal Highness' was the best, 'Gavotte' was marked and 'City of Bath' small. He also won the Edward Mawley Memorial Medal for the highest aggregate points in classes 40–48 inclusive. Once again M. E. Bullen won the Rev. H. Honeywood D'Ombrain Memorial Cup for the best bowl of floribunda roses in classes 25, 39 or 46, and the Gardeners' Company Challenge Cup for the most successful exhibitor in classes 75 to 89 inclusive was won by T. A. Jones.

The Gilbert Burch Memorial Class in Division D is for amateurs with not more than 250 rose trees and was won by F. C. H. Witchell. His blooms showed signs of weather damage and included 'John Waterer', 'Montezuma', 'Royal Highness', 'Grandpa Dickson (2)', and 'Red Devil'.

In the same division the Slaughter Memorial Cup for three vases of hybrid tea roses was won by R. Farmiloe with 'Royal Highness' which was marked, 'Red Devil' and 'City of Gloucester'.

The Charles Rigg Cup in Division E is for amateurs with not more than 150 rose trees. R. C. Price's box won the cup with 'Montezuma', 'Pink Favourite' (poor), 'Royal Highness', 'Chicago Peace' and 'Red Devil' (2).

The Cocker Cup is for a vase of six specimen blooms and it was won by J. S. Hancock with 'Fred Gibson', 'Gavotte', 'Royal Highness' (2), 'Grandpa Dickson' and 'Red Devil'. They were good blooms although some showed signs of damage. Division F is for amateurs with not more than 100 rose trees. The important class here is the Kathleen Louise Mahaffy class for a box of six blooms. H. V. Gannon showed six very nice, evenly matched blooms of 'Red Devil'.

E. W. A. Perry won the Albert E. Griffith Memorial Class in Division G for amateurs with not more than 50 rose trees, but his blooms of 'Isabel de Ortiz', 'Rose Gaujard' and 'Royal Highness' were small and badly marked.

In the Affiliated Societies section there were no entries in class 90 for the Hereford Centenary Cup. The Franklin Dennison Memorial Cup in class 91 was won by the Woodham Park and New Haw Horticultural Society. Their bowl of floribundas included 'Evelyn Fison', 'Queen Elizabeth', 'Iceberg', 'Orange Sensation' and 'Europeana'. They were all nice and clean. Among their hybrid teas were 'Fred Gibson', 'Red Devil', 'Pink Favourite' and 'City of Gloucester', all of good size and well matched.

The best bloom in the amateur section was 'Grandpa Dickson'. It was shown by K. E. Poole in class 62 and came as a surprise, as it did not match the standard of recent years.

The Northern Rose Show

I. O. MATTHEWS
(*Assistant Hon. Secretary, North Western Group of RNRS members*)

The return of the Show to Roundhay on 16 and 17 July, after last year's change of venue was like a homecoming. In my experience it was a rewarding show.

Trade Exhibitors' Section

Judging was in progress when I arrived and our President, Mr R. C. Balfour, was very much in evidence, tackling the job as conscientiously as he has carried out his many presidential duties.

The Roundhay Horticultural Society Trophy, the Premier Award and the Brotherton Trophy went to Nostell Priory Rose Gardens, who were also awarded a Large Gold Medal for a theme dominated by the eye-catching floribunda 'Fred Loads'. Their effective centrepiece of bi-colour hybrid tea 'Piccadilly' was flanked by popular varieties such as 'Rose Gaujard' and 'Grandpa Dickson', whilst in complete contrast their new dwarf floribunda 'Novia' was set strategically at the front of the display. Fryers Nurseries Ltd were also awarded a Large Gold Medal and the RNRS Trophy for an exhibit not exceeding 200 sq. ft. The display featured their new floribunda/H.T. type 'Sunsilk', with bowls of 'Bobby Charlton', 'Cheshire Life', 'Oriana' and 'Miss Harp'.

C. Gregory & Sons and R. Harkness & Co. of Hitchin also received well merited Large Gold Medals, while E. B. Le Grice (Roses) Ltd, Lowe & Son Ltd and Rosemount Nurseries were worthy recipients of Gold Medals. It was good to see the stands of Charles Kershaw, David E. Lister and F. W. Shaw & Son Ltd gain Silver Gilt Awards.

E. B. Le Grice displayed his new hybrid tea 'Great News', a much deeper purple than we have previously seen. Also featured was their new fragrant dwarf floribunda, 'Red Sprite'. Gregory's new hybrid tea roses 'Cock o' the North' and 'Lady of the Sky' made good bowls complementary to the dazzling floribunda 'Bengali', cool, gentle 'Fleur Cowles' and dashing 'Sir Lancelot'. Harkness placed orange-vermilion 'Alexander' to good effect, surrounded by 'Elizabeth Harkness', 'Northern Lights' and bi-colour 'Royal Albert Hall'. 'Arakan' and 'Gold Bonnet' made a fine background with lilac mauve 'Seven Seas' placed in front.

Rosemount's effective pyramid displayed many popular varieties, among them the 1958 Gold Medallist 'Highlight'—still a good 'un. The gay coloured 'Harry Wheatcroft' took the eye and 'Red Devil', of immaculate exhibition form, looked well. David Lister's display with grey upper background and lower black tiers made an ideal setting for baskets and bowls of 'City of Leeds', 'Kerryman' and 'Liverpool Echo'. Kershaw's 24 bowls included 'Duke of Windsor', 'Gold Crown' and 'Whisky Mac', while compact 'Tip Top' and 'Topsi' looked very happy together. Shaw's Roses had varieties to suit all tastes, ranging from miniature 'Wee Man' to shrub rose 'Fountain'. 'Burma Star', 'Tony Jacklin' and 'Elation' were there.

Amateur Section

The judges, splitting up into groups, dealt efficiently with the five divisions of 50 classes which were well supported with 300 exhibits from a wide ranging area of Britain. F. E. Owen again won the Jubilee Trophy to bring this year's championship into his sights. He was first in Class 204 for a box of 12 superb distinct specimens, including an attractive 'Oxfam'. F. L. Birch, Stafford and H. A. Thompson, Lincoln were placed second and third respectively. F. L. Birch reversed the order in Class 205 with his box of 6 which included two noteworthy specimens of 'Admiral Rodney'. Fred Owen's winning exhibits in the hybrid tea and floribunda bowl classes were excellent, and 5 stems of 'Fred Loads' gained him another first in Class 210. Another successful entrant in Division A. was J. I. M. Naylor of Leeds, with a vase of 'E. H. Morse', 'Grandpa Dickson' and 'Bonsoir'. A fine impression was created by D. Charlton of Billingham with seven firsts, five of them in Division B, in his first attempt at National level. His vase of 3 'Royal Highness' and 3 'Grandpa Dickson' with perfect foliage was outstanding.

In Division C, M. L. Watts, Northampton accounted for five first prizes; his bowl of 12 hybrid teas included 'Akebono' and 'Kronenbourg' and his bowl of floribundas was furnished with good stems of 'Molly McGredy'. M. o'Loughlin, Kendal, gained a first with a vase of six specimens which included two fine blooms of 'Perfecta Superior'. C. Medley, York, staged three spotless stems of 'Liverpool Echo' to win Class 232.

In Division D, the honours went to D. G. Langdale, Lincoln, R. N. Venables, Streetly, P. N. Wesson, Sutton Coldfield, F. Poole, Hartlepool, C. Medley, A. E. Straw, Horsforth and T. G. Foster. Division E firsts were gained by W. R. Crawforth, K. Waddington, J. Woolway, Mrs. M. L. Anderson, T. G. Foster, D. Charlton and Mrs J. M. Bartle.

Congleton & District Horticultural Society under their captain, A. J. Brindley, are to be congratulated on again winning both Affiliated Society classes, Leicester and Leicestershire Rose Society running a worthy second.

In Classes 212–215, restricted to amateurs living within 20 miles of Leeds, J. Hardacre, Hobley retained the Roundhay (Leeds) Cup but was hard pressed by J. I. M. Naylor. The Silver Gilt Medal for the Best Bloom was awarded to D. V. Pearson's 'Jimmy Greaves', a bloom that held well on the second day of the show.

The Autumn Rose Show

ROY HAY

It was just too bad that the Autumn Show, like the Summer Show, was plagued by bad weather, but at least, if they did but realize it, the visitors were seeing the varieties that could stand up fairly well to really bad weather.

In 1973 R. Harkness & Co. Ltd, pipped John Mattock Ltd. for the best trade exhibit, but at the 1974 show Mattock's swept back magnificently to win the Autumn Roses Challenge Cup, the Lewis Levy Memorial Cup for the best exhibit of over 450 sq ft, and naturally, a Large Gold Medal. It was a really beautiful exhibit of remarkable quality, especially considering the buffeting from the wind and rain which the flowers had undergone.

Among their most outstanding varieties were the floribundas 'All Gold', 'Bonfire Night', orange scarlet and yellow, 'Esther Ofarim', orange red and yellow and 'Korp', vivid orange, and the hybrid teas 'Whisky Mac', amber, 'Diorama', yellow and orange and 'National Trust', crimson.

The D'Escofet cup and a Large Gold Medal for an exhibit between 300 and 450 sq ft went to C. Gregory & Son Ltd. They showed good popular varieties including 'Piccadilly', yellow and red, 'Peace', 'City of Leeds', salmon, 'Beauté', old gold, and 'Doris Tysterman', a new orange hybrid tea rose. Gregory's also had a charming exhibit of miniature roses which included the orange red and yellow 'Little Flirt', 'Lavender Lace', 'Rosina', yellow, and 'Pour Toi', white, tinted yellow.

The RNRS Challenge Cup for the best exhibit between 150 and 300 sq ft and a Gold Medal were won by E. B. Le Grice (Roses) Ltd. Among their floribunda roses were 'Flashlight', orange scarlet, 'Satchmo', crimson, 'Plentiful', pink and 'Orange Sensation', while the vermilion 'Duke of Windsor' stood out among their hybrid teas.

On this occasion R. Harkness & Co. had to be content with a Large Gold Medal, and it was well deserved with fine blooms of 'Grandpa Dickson', yellow, 'Wilfred Norris', salmon and 'Alec's Red' among the hybrid teas, with 'Arthur Bell' golden yellow, 'Stephen Langdon', crimson, and 'Moonraker', pale yellow, showing up well among the floribundas.

Another Large Gold Medal went to Cants of Colchester, who had fine blooms of 'Molly McGredy', cherry red with a silvery reverse, 'Super Sun', orange and scarlet with a paler reverse and 'John Waterer', crimson, among the hybrid teas, and 'Living Fire', an orange scarlet floribunda.

The Jubilee Trophy for an exhibit 150 sq ft or less, and a Silver Gilt Medal was won by Warley Rose Gardens Ltd, who showed fine blooms of the floribundas 'Meteor', scarlet and 'Tony Jacklin' ,deep salmon, with 'National Trust', 'Mala Rubinstein', pink, and 'Red Devil' among the hybrid teas.

Fryers Nurseries Ltd received a Silver Gilt Medal for their exhibit which concentrated on their novelties, including the hybrid tea 'Cheshire Life', orange vermilion, and 'Sunsilk', a lovely yellow floribunda, H.T. type.

A. Dickson & Sons Ltd also received a Silver Gilt Medal, and showed among other recent introductions 'Coalite Flame', salmon, and 'Alec's Red'.

Garnette Holdings and C. Newberry, awarded Silver Medals, both showed Garnette roses. The RNRS exhibit of rose hips was, if my memory serves me, an innovation which might well be repeated at this show and possibly at some of the autumn shows of the RHS. It aroused a good deal of interest. It is now a foregone conclusion that Mark Court will win the A. C. Turner cup for 15 vases and the classes for 24 blooms of 12 varieties, and for a box of 12 blooms, distinct. Once more they gathered in these prizes.

The Amateur Classes

Turning now to the amateurs' exhibits, it was obvious that despite the usual efforts to protect their blooms, the exhibitors had been hard put to it to find enough blooms of show standard.

To the lay observer like me, there seemed to be a greater disparity than usual in the size and quality of blooms in the various entries. There is normally a considerable difference between the entries, say in the novices classes or for amateurs with only 75 rose trees, and those that make the running for the amateur championship, but this year there appeared to me to be a greater variation in quality between entries in the same section and in the same class.

These disparities were epitomized by 'Red Lion' which varied enormously in size and colour in the various exhibits. I know this is a notoriously variable rose, but I think it showed greater variations at this show than any other variety. The bloom shown by J. S. Jellyman of Stroud, which was adjudged the best bloom in the show, was really enormous but a good deal paler than some of the specimens shown in other exhibits. The nearest that any other variety that I saw came to equalling this great disparity in size, was 'Royal Highness'. This blush white rose is not, I admit, one that moves me to ecstatic admiration, but it is nevertheless very popular with exhibitors.

Presumably there has always been the tendency for exhibitors to show in the main the same varieties because these are potential winners, and if, for example, we see 'Grandpa Dickson' time and time again in the exhibits, it is because it is a season that has suited 'Grandpa Dickson'.

Of the varieties that were shown frequently at last year's Autumn Show, the following appeared in fair numbers at this year's show too: 'Gavotte', 'Red Devil', 'Red Lion', 'Red Queen', 'Royal Highness', 'Embassy', 'Norman Hartnell', 'City of Bath', 'City of Gloucester' and 'Akebono'.

Turning now to the varieties that appeared again and again in this show, in addition to those already mentioned, there were the following floribundas: 'Fred Loads', 'Elizabeth of Glamis', 'Korona', 'Anne Cocker', 'Redgold', 'Sea Pearl' and 'Dorothy Wheatcroft'. There were, of course, others which won prizes as well.

For the record, here are some representative winners and some of the varieties they won with. It should be noted that these are incomplete because of considerations of space.

Section 4. Division A—open to all amateurs

Six specimen blooms 3 varieties, F. E. Owen, Tamworth—'Gavotte', 'Isabel de Ortiz', 'Grandpa Dickson'; Six specimen blooms, 4 varieties, Mrs F. A. Pugh, Pembrey—'City of Bath', 'City of Gloucester', 'Fred Gibson', 'Femina'; Six specimen blooms, (vase) F. E. Owen—'Red Devil', 'Gavotte'; A bowl of HTs, 18 stems, L. E. J. Wood—'Montezuma', 'My Choice', 'Bonsoir', 'Akebono', 'Gavotte', 'Grandpa Dickson', 'Wendy Cussons', 'Royal Highness', 'C. F. Warren', 'Red Devil', 'Peace'; Bowl of HTs, 12 stems, His Honour Judge Gage, Saffron Walden—'Embassy', 'E. H. Morse', 'Perfecta', 'Norman Hartnell', 'Gavotte', 'Chicago Peace', 'Kronenbourg', 'Northern Lights', 'Klaus Störtebeker', 'City of Bath'; Bowl of floribundas, 12 stems, L. E. J. Wood—'Dorothy Wheatcroft', 'Anna Wheatcroft', 'Firecracker', 'Korona', 'Paddy McGredy', 'Anne Cocker'.

Division B—amateurs with not more than 500 rose trees

Box of six specimen blooms, 4 varieties, B. S. Pearce, Sutton Coldfield— 'Red Devil', 'Embassy', 'Princess Margaret of England', 'Isabel de Ortiz'; Vase of six specimen blooms, 4 varieties, J. H. Anthony, Walsall—'Isabel de Ortiz,' 'Red Devil', 'Grandpa Dickson', 'Gavotte', 'Embassy', 'Silver Lining'; Bowl of HTs, 12 stems, M. L. Watts, Northampton—'Charlie's Aunt', 'Pink Favourite', 'Grandpa Dickson,' 'Red Devil', 'Red Lion', 'Gary Player', 'Gavotte', 'Alec's Red', 'Anne Letts', 'City of Bath'; Three vases of HTs, RNRS Cup, J. H. Anthony—'Royal Highness', 'Red Devil', 'Gavotte'; Bowl of floribundas, 9 stems, M. L. Watts—'Joyfulness', 'Fred Loads', 'Evelyn Fison', 'Princess Michiko', 'Scented Air', 'Elizabeth of Glamis', 'Stephen Langdon'.

Division C—amateurs with not more than 250 rose trees

Box of 6 specimen blooms, F. C. H. Witchell, Thame—'John Waterer' (very good), 'Royal Highness', 'Stella', 'Dorothy Peach', 'Montezuma'; Vase of 6 specimen blooms, J. S. Hancock, Orpington—'Royal Highness', 'Red Devil', 'Perfecta', 'Pink Favourite', 'Gavotte', 'Fragrant Cloud'; Bowl of floribundas, 5 stems, Mrs R. L. Souter, Pinner—'Sea Pearl', 'Elizabeth of Glamis', 'Queen Elizabeth', 'Heidelberg'; Bowl of floribundas, 1 variety, R. P. Court, Ramsgate—'Kimono' (very nice).

The Provincial Display Gardens

S. MILLAR GAULT

My Rose Tour for 1974 began at Harlow Car when Geoffrey Smith, the superintendent of the Northern Horticultural Society's Garden, was one of my colleagues judging at the "Great Yorkshire Show". This well known show is held at Harrogate, so I thought the opportunity too good to miss. I was informed the roses were later than usual as a severe frost on 29 June, the latest recorded in the area, had very obviously had a retarding effect. Some days later Mr Turner and I had another look when we were in attendance at the Leeds Flower Show. Roses were to be seen but Jupiter Pluvius having intervened in the meantime, I found inspection and note taking somewhat difficult. Weather becoming more settled, we set off on our "Grand Tour" northwards to Redcar, arranging there to see the roses on 2 August. I met Mr Rowe, the District Superintendent, with Mr Jackson, Supervisor and Mr Phillips who is foreman of Borough Park. A new fence surrounded the garden, a decided improvement, and as the roses were looking well and flowering freely I was very pleased. I was informed that a lot of interest was taken in the display by rosarians over quite a large area and as the garden is well looked after, I'm sure they must appreciate seeing new roses doing so well in a somewhat exposed area.

Edinburgh was the next port of call and here I met Mr Wood, the assistant Horticultural Director, with Mr McKay, Horticultural officer, Mr Paterson, District Superintendent, and Mr Loney who not only looks after the roses but takes a close interest in them. As usual in Edinburgh I enjoyed a visit to the Saughton Park Rose Garden, where some of the older roses continue to give great pleasure as they have on previous occasions. 'Mullard Jubilee', 'Garvey', 'Mischief', 'Piccadilly' and 'Dearest' were first-class and 'Whisky Mac', as one might expect, was apparently very much at home.

Glasgow was next, where Mr Oldham, the well known Director of Parks entertained us to lunch with the Horticultural officer Mr Gilmour also there. Mr Gilmour, took us on to Pollok Park where Dr Dick awaited us and the District Superintendent, Mr Mullard, and Mr Hastie who looks after the roses. This is a well designed garden, but the roses have not as yet attained the same standard as at Saughton Park but will, I hope, soon catch up. Beds of 'Mala Rubinstein' and 'Anne Cocker' were already moving in this direction and I look forward to others doing the same.

Southwards next, quite a long haul down to Taunton where on leaving the M5 we got enmeshed in the local traffic and found the three or four miles required to reach Vivary Park a frustrating experience, as indeed it turned out to be for Mr and Mrs Fairbrother, whom we met there. As usual we met Mr Verrier, now Parks Superintendent of a larger area, The Taunton Deane District Council, and the Head Gardener of Vivary Park, Mr Reynolds. Roses had grown well and given a lot of interest to visitors but unfortunately Black Spot is something of a nuisance there. 'Fred Loads' has always excelled in this garden and continues to do so. 'Golden Chersonese' was carrying quite a good crop of flowers for the second time. I have not seen this occur before with this variety, while 'Climbing Iceberg', often addicted to slight mildew here, was twelve feet high and quite free. 'Korp' was the finest I have seen and had aroused a lot of attention because of its striking colour.

Over the Severn Bridge next to Cardiff and Roath Park, where I met the District Superintendent Mr Rees and the Head Gardener Mr Jewell. I was amazed at the transformation which had taken place in the roses since I visited Roath Park in 1973. Mr Rees had been associated with the late Mr Whitney, who took great pride in the Rose Garden and informed me that regular spraying with Benlate had been carried out since mid-April. This combined with a good mulch of peat had made a tremendous difference and I was glad to hear this confirmed by members of Council later in the season, so I cannot be accused of wearing rose-coloured spectacles for the occasion. Amongst older roses there 'Pink Supreme', 'Helen Traubel', 'McGredy's

Yellow' and 'Blessings' were remarkably good, but I give the palm for garden display to 'Violinista Costa', planted in 1952.

After such a feast I returned home as Southport Show was in the offing and I paid my usual visit to the Botanic Garden on the previous evening. The roses looked well in the main but in this garden there is not enough room to keep the older varieties. Mr Boocock, the Park's Director, was as usual busy with the show, but I was able to compliment him on the way the roses are looked after. By this time my eye was "well in" so I decided that another visit to Harlow Car would give me a fairer picture of the roses there, and I was pleased to find a much better display. 'Evangeline Bruce' seemed much more at home here as did the climber 'Malaga'. Rust had reared its ugly head and in spite of persistent spraying had affected 'Nan Anderson', also 'Mala Rubinstein' to a lesser degree. Mr Smith informed me that he had resigned, so that I would not see him at Harlow Car on my next visit. Thanking him on behalf of the R.N.R.S. for the interest he had taken in the new roses I wished him good fortune in the future with the hope that our paths may cross again sometime.

My next visit was to Nottingham in company with Mr Turner, this being the first visit to see the roses, planted there in the Arboretum. We met Mr Stanion, Director of Parks, Mr Holland the Area Superintendent and Mr Gregory, who of course knows this area well. The lay-out is very pleasing, semi-circular beds in an amphitheatre-like setting with a pergola in the background. The roses had established themselves very well, and we were quite inpressed, as on our previous visit it was difficult to visualize the garden as construction had only begun.

In wet October, Mr Turner and I went to Norwich to complete my tour. There we met the Parks Officer, Mr Fogarty, the Area Superintendent Mr Youngs, and Mr Rudd, a young man trained in the Parks and who is responsible for the Rose Display Garden at Heigham Park. We were very pleased with this garden, formerly an herbaceous border which had been grassed down and reshaped and looked quite impressive, even on a wet day. Dull when we left St Albans, the sun shining at Thetford forest where the autumn colours were a delight, there was rain by the time we reached Norwich, which continued unfortunately all the time we were there as well as on our way home. It only remains for me now, with my visits over for another year, to thank those who have helped. So many have done so that it would be invidious to mention names so I hope they will accept this brief "thank you".

THE PROVINCIAL DISPLAY GARDENS

AWARDS, 1971	Cardiff	Edinburgh	Glasgow	Harlow Car	Norwich	Nottingham	Redcar	Southport	Taunton
The President's International Trophy and Gold Medal									
'Fountain'	2	2	(NS)	2			2	1 (VG)	2
Henry Edland Memorial Medal									
'Lily de Gerlache' (Joint) & T.G.C.	1	2	2	2	1		1 (VG)	1	
'Truly Yours'	2	3	2	2	1	(NS)		2	3 (BS)
Certificate of Merit									
'City of Gloucester'	2	1	3	2				2	1 (BS)
'Kerryman'	1	1 (VG)	1	1 (VG)			1	1	1 (BS)
'Korp'	1	1 (SM)	1	1			2	1	1 (VG)
'Stephen Langdon'	1	2	1	1			1	1	
'Topsi'			3 (BS)	1 (VG)	3	(NP)	1	2 (SBS)	2 (BS)
Trial Ground Certificate									
'Korbell'	1 (VG)	1 (VG)	1	1 (VG)	1 (NP)		1 (VG)	2 (VG)	1 (SBS)
'Bonfire Night'	1 (VG)	1 (VG)	2	3 (BS)	(NP)		1 (VG)	1 (VG)	2 (BS)
'Coventry Cathedral'	1 (VG)	2 (BS)	2	3 (BS)	1		2	2	
'Evangeline Bruce'	2	2	2	1 (VG)	2	3	1	1	1
'Just Joey'	1	2	1	1	2	1	1	1 (VG)	2 (SBS)
'Malaga'	2	2 (BS)	3	1 (VG)	2	2	2		1
'Mala Rubinstein'	1	2 (BS)	1 (VG)	1 (BS&R)	2	1		1 (VG)	3
'Nan Anderson'			2	3 (R)	2	2	2		1 (VG)
'Poppy Flash'	1 (VG)				1	1	1 (VG)	1 (VG)	1 (VG)
'Southampton'	1 (VG)	1 (VG)	2	2	1	1		1 (VG)	1 (SBS)
'Yellow Pages'	1			1	1				

1 Very good (Addition of VG means even better)
2 Good
3 Only fair

BS Black spot
SBS Slight Black Spot

SM Slight mildew
NS Not seen
NP Not planted

R Rust

The Trial Ground and Display Garden, 1974

L. G. TURNER

(*Secretary*)

The unusually high rainfall, particularly from June to September when we recorded 12·65 inches, must be held responsible for what will undoubtedly be considered as one of the most disappointing rose seasons for many years. There were few periods when the gardens were bathed in sunshine with the roses at the peak of perfection, but those visitors who braved the elements were at least able to discover the varieties that would withstand such weather —a most important factor when selecting roses for growing in our unpredictable climate.

This report is being written in November and to date we have recorded 32·57 inches of rain, compared with 18·34 inches for the whole of 1973 and 22·29 inches the previous year. The unusual amount of rain may possibly have had compensations for, whereas in 1973 disease incidence was exceptionally high, this past year it has been just the opposite. Considerably fewer varieties were removed from the trials and for the greater part of the season the roses in the display garden were kept clean. It is rather a sad indictment of our flower that it is necessary to spray to keep disease at bay, but it is the unpalatable truth and possibly the sacrifice we have to make for progress in this modern society.

On several occasions this report has mentioned the concern felt at the amount of disease present in the trial ground, and various methods have been tried to improve the situation without giving too much protection to disease-prone varieties. Last year the roses in their first season of trial received identical treatment to those in the display garden, but in the second and third years they were treated only up to the end of June and thereafter any variety becoming badly infected was removed. It would be premature to suggest that the method of control has improved the situation; as I have already mentioned, the unusually high rainfall could have been a contributory factor.

It is often said, and indeed some authors have made quite a feature of it in their articles, that too many new varieties are being introduced and the Society has at times been called to task for giving these recognition. As far as I am able to check, this is a fallacy when compared with a four-year period forty years ago; 1931–1934 produced 23 Gold Medals, 45 Certificates of Merit and 62 Trial Ground Certificates. During 1971–1974 there were only 4 Gold Medals, 13 Certificates of Merit and 39 Trial Ground Certificates. In

1933, in fact, no Trial Ground Certificates were awarded owing to lack of rain and too much sunshine—on the South coast over 1,000 hours of sunshine were recorded between June and September! The method of judging for these awards has, of course, changed but the fact is that over twice as many awards were made and the majority of those varieties were named and, it is reasonable to presume, were put into commerce. What familiar names were revealed when making the comparison—'Phyllis Gold', 'Christopher Stone', 'Karen Poulsen', 'Betty Prior', 'New Dawn', 'Comtesse Vandal', 'Picture', 'The Fairy', 'President Hoover'. I suppose it is fair to say that of these only 'New Dawn' and 'The Fairy' are still popular.

Trials of new roses were commenced by the Society so that all members and the general public would have an opportunity to know the value of novelties when they were put on the market. It was never the intention that the ground should be made available to anybody who produced a new rose merely for the satisfaction of seeing his 'baby' growing at St. Albans, or for the Society to grow a number of varieties for a raiser and advise him which were the best. Unfortunately, this is the situation that has tended to develop and with present day costs of maintenance and materials the Committee has decided there is no alternative but to restrict entries. The tentative scheme being adopted for the current season allows an amateur to submit one variety and a nurseryman three varieties; in addition, one extra variety may be sent for every award received during the preceding seven years, with a maximum of 15 varieties per raiser. The last thing the Committee wishes to do is discourage the keen hybridist or restrict the successful professional, and this scheme should ensure this does not happen. A further innovation is that no variety will be able to gain a Gold Medal or Certificate of Merit until it has completed three flowering seasons.

The newly constructed Sunken Garden for miniature and china roses was much appreciated by visitors, who possibly found this sheltered position a haven from the wind. Work is now proceeding in the adjoining gardens, although at the time of writing this report we are sadly held up by rain.

The only Gold Medal awarded and also the President's Trophy went to 'Matangi', one of the "hand painted" varieties from Sam McGredy Roses International, illustrated in the 1974 *Rose Annual*. It well deserved the award, having been healthy throughout the trial in spite of being surrounded by varieties affected by disease, and in late October it was still carrying a mass of blooms, which is one of the particular attributes of its parent, 'Picasso'. 'Sugar Sweet', raised by John Sanday (Roses) Ltd.—a seedling from 'Wendy Cussons' × 'Prima Ballerina'—received the Henry Edland Memorial Medal

'ALPINE SUNSET' (H.T.)
'Dr A. J. Verhage' × *'Grandpa Dickson'*
Raised by Cants of Colchester Ltd
TRIAL GROUND CERTIFICATE 1974
See page 186

'OLD MASTER' (floribunda)

[('*Evelyn Fison*' × (*Tantau's Triumph*' × R. macrophylla coryana)) × ('*Hamburger Phoenix*' × '*Danse du Feu*')] × ['*Evelyn Fison*' × ('*Orange Sweetheart*' × *Frühlings-morgen*')]

Raised by Sam McGredy Roses International, New Zealand

TRIAL GROUND CERTIFICATE 1973

See 1974 Rose Annual, page 183

for fragrance. 'Mary Sumner', named in honour of the Founder of the Mother's Union, also raised by Sam McGredy Roses International, was awarded a Certificate of Merit.

Once again I cannot conclude this report without paying a warm tribute to my colleague Don Maginnis for the tremendous amount of work he contributes to make the gardens the show piece they now are. His unflagging interest in his work and seemingly endless energy are an example to his men.

The Awards to New Roses in 1974

* Denotes varieties for which it is understood protection is being sought under the Plant Varieties and Seeds Act 1964

The President's International Trophy for the Best New Seedling Rose of the Year and Gold Medal were awarded to:

MATANGI (Flori.). *Raiser:* Sam McGredy Roses International, New Zealand. *Distributor:* Sam McGredy Roses, N. Ireland. Trial Ground No. 2577. [('Little Darling' × 'Goldilocks') × ['Evelyn Fison' × (*R. macrophylla coryana* × 'Tantau's Triumph')]] × 'Picasso'. Bloom: Orange vermilion, silver eye and reverse, moderately full (23 petals), slightly fragrant, borne singly and several together. Growth: vigorous, upright. Foliage: glossy, dark green, tinted copper when young. (*See illustration in 1974 Annual, facing p. 120.*)

The Henry Edland Memorial Medal, awarded to the most fragrant rose on trial, irrespective of country of origin, and Trial Ground Certificate were awarded to:

SUGAR SWEET (Flori. H.T. type). *Raiser:* John Sanday (Roses) Ltd., Bristol. Trial Ground No. 2665. 'Wendy Cussons'× 'Prima Ballerina'. Bloom: soft carmine pink with pale yellow centre, semi-double (13 petals), very fragrant, borne several together. Growth: vigorous, branching. Foliage: matt, medium green. (*See illustration facing p. 5.*)

Certificates of Merit were awarded to:

MARY SUMNER (Flori.). *Raiser:* Sam McGredy Roses International, New Zealand. *Distributor:* Sam McGredy Roses, N. Ireland. Trial Ground No. 2571. ('Orangeade'× 'Margot Fonteyn')× ['Elizabeth of Glamis'×('Little Darling'× 'Goldilocks')]. Bloom: orange salmon, moderately full (23 petals), slightly fragrant, borne several together and in trusses. Growth: very vigorous, tall and upright. Foliage: glossy, medium green, bronzed when young. (*See illustration facing p.* 16.)

*THE SUN (Flori.). *Raiser:* S. McGredy & Son Ltd., N. Ireland. Trial Ground No. 1993. ('Little Darling'× 'Goldilocks')× 'Irish Mist'. Bloom: vermilion, lighter reverse, moderately full (18 petals), slightly fragrant, borne several together. Growth: vigorous, upright. Foliage: semi-glossy, medium green. (1972 award).

Trial Ground Certificates were awarded to:

*ALPINE SUNSET (H.T.). *Raiser:* Cants of Colchester Ltd., Colchester. Trial Ground No. 2749. 'Dr. A. J. Verhage'× 'Grandpa Dickson'. Bloom: peach pink flushed yellow, full (30 petals), globular, fragrant, borne singly and several together. Growth: vigorous, upright. Foliage: glossy, medium green. (*See illustration facing p.* 184.)

BONNIE HAMILTON (Flori.). *Raiser:* J. Cocker & Sons, Aberdeen. Trial Ground No. 2705. 'Anne Cocker'× 'Allgold'. Bloom: vermilion orange, moderately full (19 petals), borne several together. Growth: moderately vigorous, bushy. Foliage: semi-glossy, medium green, coppery red when young.

*DAME OF SARK (Flori.'). *Raiser:* R. Harkness & Co. Ltd., Hitchin. Trial Ground No. 2916. ('Pink Parfait'× 'Masquerade')× 'Tabler's Choice'. Bloom: golden flushed scarlet, full (36 petals), borne in trusses. Growth: very vigorous, upright. Foliage: glossy, medium green.

DUBLIN BAY (Clr.). *Raiser:* Sam McGredy Roses International, New Zealand. *Distributor:* Sam McGredy Roses Ltd., N. Ireland. Trial Ground No. C216. 'Bantry Bay'× 'Altissimo'. Bloom: scarlet-crimson, full (26 petals), slightly fragrant, borne several together, recurrent flowering. Growth: vigorous, upright. Foliage: glossy, dark green. (*See illustration facing p.* 197.)

EYE PAINT (Flori.). *Raiser:* Sam McGredy Roses International, New Zealand. *Distributor:* Sam McGredy Roses Ltd., N. Ireland. Trial Ground No. 2579. [('Little Darling' × 'Goldilocks') × ['Evelyn Fison' ×(R. macrophylla coryana × 'Tantau's Triumph')]]× 'Picasso'. Bloom: scarlet with white eye and pale reverse, pronounced stamens, single (7 petals), very free-flowering, borne in trusses. Growth: very vigorous, upright. Foliage: semi-glossy, medium green. (1973 award.) (*See illustration facing p.* 196.)

International Awards 1974

ROME

LARGE FLOWERS
Certificate	'Evening Star'	Jackson & Perkins Co., U.S.A.

The other awards went to unnamed seedlings.

SMALL FLOWERS
Gold Medal	'Matangi'	Sam McGredy Roses International, New Zealand
First Certificate	'Las Vegas'	W. Kordes, Germany
Certificate	'Old Master'	Sam McGredy Roses International, New Zealand

MONZA

ROSE OF THE YEAR (H.T.)
Gold Medal	'Vivre'	Georges Delbard, France
Silver Medal	'Louis Armand'	Paul Croix, France

The other awards went to unnamed seedlings.

ROSE OF THE YEAR (FLORI.)
Gold Medal	'Yesterday'	R. Harkness & Co. Ltd., England
Silver Medal	'Bordure Rose'	Georges Delbard, France
First Certificate	'Träumerei'	W. Kordes Söhne, Germany

The other award went to an unnamed seedling.

THE MOST BEAUTIFUL ITALIAN ROSE
Prize	'Pironticritow'	Nicola Pironti, Italy

MADRID

Gold Medal and Prize of the City of Madrid	'Bordure Rose' (flori.)	Mme. Marie Delbard, France
First Certificates	'Julischka' (flori.)	Math. Tantau, Germany
	'Paris 2,000' (H.T.)	Georges Delbard, France
Second Certificates	'Presidente' (H.T.)	Paul Croix, France
	'Montana' (flori.)	Math. Tantau, Germany
	'Jockey' (flori.)	Mme. Marie Delbard, France
PERFUME CUP	'Meilanein' (H.T.)	L. Meilland, France

GENEVA

LARGE FLOWERS — All awards went to unnamed seedlings.

SMALL FLOWERS
Gold Medal and Prize	'Légion d'Honneur'	Georges Delbard, France
Silver Medal	'Bordure Rose'	Georges Delbard, France

The other awards went to unnamed seedlings.

CLIMBERS
Gold Medal and Prize	Pironticritow'	Nicola Pironti, Italy
Certificate	'Eddy'	J. Laperrière, France

COURTRAI

Silver Medals	'Lucrecé' (H.T.)	J. Gaujard, France
	'Feuerzauber' (H.T.)	W. Kordes, Germany
	'Lydia' (H.T.)	W. Kordes, Germany
	'Tornado' (poly.)	W. Kordes, Germany
	'Sankt Anton' (pol.-mult.)	H. Delforge, Belgium

The other Silver Medals and the Golden Rose 1974 award went to unnamed seedlings.

THE HAGUE

HYBRID TEA
First Certificate 'Cheshire Life' Fryer's Nurseries Ltd, England
FLORIBUNDA
First Certificate 'Chorus' Meilland, France
The other awards went to unnamed seedlings.
In the beds of roses planted out in the Westbroekpark the International Jury awarded the *Golden Rose of the Hague* to 'Esperanza' (flori.) raised by S. Delforge, Belgium; *First Class Certificates* to 'Prins Willem Alexander' (flori.) raised by H. A. Verschuren & Son, Holland and to 'City of Belfast' (flori.) raised by Sam McGredy IV, Northern Ireland; *Second Class Certificates* to 'Nicky' (flori.) raised by R. V. S. Melle, Belgium and to 'Mullard Jubilee' (H.T.) raised by Sam McGredy IV, Northern Ireland; *Silver Medal for Fragrance* to 'Grande Amore' (H.T.) raised by W. Kordes, Germany.

BADEN-BADEN

Gold Medals	'Schweizer Gold' (H.T.)	W. Kordes, Germany
	'Friesia' (flori.)	W. Kordes, Germany
	'Bordure Nacrée' (poly.)	G. Delbard, France
Silver Medals	'Carinella' (H.T.)	Meilland, France
	'Scherzo' (flori.)	Meilland, France
Bronze Medal	'Marbella' (H.T.)	W. Kordes, Germany

The other awards went to unnamed seedlings.

NEW ZEALAND

'Gold Star of the South Pacific' and Certificate of Merit, also award for the 'Most Fragrant Rose'	'Pink Silk' (H.T.)	C. Gregory & Son, England
'Gold Star of the South Pacific' and Certificate of Merit	'Coventry Cathedral' (flori.)	Sam McGredy Roses International, New Zealand
Certificates of Merit	'Avril Sherwood' (flori.)	G. Sherwood, New Zealand
	'Yesterday' (poly. type)	R. Harkness & Co., England
	'Rusticana' (flori.)	U. R. S. (Meilland), France
	'Bobby Dazzler' (flori.)	R. Harkness & Co., England
	'Lolita' (H.T.)	W. Kordes & Son, Germany
	'Alexander' (H.T.)	R. Harkness & Co., England

The other awards went to unnamed seedlings.

ROEULX

LARGE FLOWERS

Silver Medal	'Freude'	R. Kordes, Germany
Certificates	'Clairette'	Mme. J. Croix, France
	'Presidente'	Mme. J. Croix, France

The other awards went to unnamed seedlings.

SMALL FLOWERS

Gold Medal	'Träumerei'	W. Kordes, Germany
	'Las Vegas'	W. Kordes, Germany
Silver Medal	'Prestige de Bellegarde'	André Eve, France
Certificates	'Tornado'	R. Kordes, Germany
	'Ersatz'	P. Gaujard, France

The other awards went to unnamed seedlings.

Prize for the most Fragrant Rose	'Clairette'	Mme. J. Croix, France

BELFAST

HYBRID TEA		
Gold Medal and Prize	'Alexander'	R. Harkness & Co., England
"Uladh" Award for		
Fragrance	'Harriny'	E. B. Le Grice, England
Certificate	'Typhoon'	Kordes, Germany
FLORIBUNDA		
The "Golden Thorn"		
Award	'Southampton'	R. Harkness & Co., England
Certificates	'Ripples'	E. B. Le Grice, England
	'Bangor'	Alex. Dickson & Sons, N. Ireland
	'Tony Jacklin'	Sam McGredy Roses International, New Zealand
CLIMBER		
Certificate	'Diablotin'	G. Delbard, France

ORLÉANS

FLORIBUNDA		
Golden Rose of the	'Arnaud Delbard'	Delbard-Chabert, France
City of Orléans		
First Certificate and Special Prize	'Virginia'	J. Leenders, Holland
Certificates	'Anabell'	W. Kordes Söhne, Germany
	'Korrigan'	Poulsen, Denmark
	'Rusticana'	Louisette Meilland, France
	'Coventry Cathedral'	Sam McGredy Roses International, New Zealand
	'Happy Wanderer'	Sam McGredy Roses International, New Zealand
	'Danse des Etoiles'	G. Maurice, France
	'Ribambelle'	Paul Croix, France
"GRANDIFLORAS"		
Silver-Gilt Plaque	'Mabella'	W. Kordes Söhne, Germany
First Certificate	'Ginette'	G. Maurice, France
Certificate	'Colour Sergeant'	R. Harkness & Co. Ltd, England
CLIMBERS		
Certificates	'Clg. Zambra'	Louisette Meilland, France
	'Westerland'	W. Kordes Söhne, Germany

The Rose Analysis

L. G. TURNER

It would appear that this year's comments on the Rose Analysis should be sub-titled "Constancy". On checking back on one or two tables some interesting facts have arisen. 'Albertine' has headed the table for Wichuraiana, Climbing and Rambling Roses since 1961 and, with one exception, all the varieties listed in that year are still included. The missing variety is 'Easlea's Golden Rambler' which has been replaced by 'Sanders' White'. 'Danse du Feu' has held a similar position in the list of climbers suitable for wall or close-board fencing since 1967. 'Handel', the cream edged rose pink climber, is now one of the most popular and versatile varieties—for the 4th year it tops the list of repeat flowering climbers, is 2nd to 'Danse du Feu' in the wall and closeboard fencing section and this year is 8th in the group for open fences.

'Queen Elizabeth' is another variety which remains 'top of the garden pops'. In 1961 it entered the list for hedges over 5 ft in 7th position; the following year it was voted number one and there it has remained.

Even in the Audit of Newer Roses constancy is the theme with 'Alec's Red' at the top of the hybrid tea section for the 3rd consecutive year. 'Tenerife', 'Troika' and 'Typhoon' have climbed the ladder of success and are now in the first twelve. 'City of Bath' and 'Embassy' have left this section because of age and have joined the tables for specimen blooms. 'Elizabeth Harkness' has been transferred for the same reason and is proving her worth as a garden rose in both Northern and Southern sections. For the second year running 'Anne Cocker' is placed first in the Floribunda section. 'Topsi' has risen from 12th to 2nd place and 'Southampton' has jumped ten places to 3rd. 'Korp' and 'Korbell' have moved up into the first twelve, replacing 'Stephen Langdon' and 'Molly McGredy' which re-appear in the general floribunda list. 'Lively Lady', however, has not been so favoured.

In the general floribunda audit 'Iceberg', 'Evelyn Fison' and 'Queen Elizabeth' have held the top three places without changing since 1969.

One cannot help wondering whether the method by which these tables are prepared is presenting a true picture of popularity of varieties. Perhaps the voters tend to be too representative of one section of the membership, or possibly the tables are too long for serious consideration. Whatever the reason, it seems questionable that 'Queen Elizabeth', with its tendency to legginess, should still be at the top of the list for hedging. I doubt whether visitors to Bone Hill who were welcomed by the wonderful hedge of *R. rugosa* 'Scabrosa' would agree! By next year possibly another method of evaluation will be tried; one in which many more members can participate.

The Publications Committee is most grateful to all the members who so conscientiously complete the tables each year and without whose assistance the analysis would not be possible.

THE ROSE ANALYSIS

AUDIT OF NEWER ROSES—FLORIBUNDAS

This table includes only varieties introduced in this country since 1 January, 1970

(Maximum points possible—634)

Position	Number of points	NAME	Introduced	COLOUR
1	467	Anne Cocker	1971	Dutch vermilion
2	383	Topsi	1972	Glowing orange-scarlet
3	371	Southampton	1972	Apricot-orange
4	343	Megiddo	1970	Scarlet-red
5	268	*Pineapple Poll	1970	Orange yellow, flushed red
6	266	Rob Roy	1971	Scarlet-crimson
7	261	Picasso	1971	Carmine, silvery reverse
8	252	Kerryman	1970	Cream deepening to pink
9	230	*Michelle	1970	Salmon pink
10	213	Korp	1972	Signal red, scarlet reverse
11	194	Korbell	1972	Salmon-orange
12	174	Esther Ofarim	1971	Orange, red and yellow

* Most fragrant

FLORIBUNDA ROSES

This table includes only varieties introduced in this country before 1 January 1970

(Maximum points possible—1281)

Position	Number of points	NAME	Introduced	COLOUR
1	1113	Iceberg	1958	Pure white tinged pink in bud
2	912	Evelyn Fison	1962	Vivid red with scarlet shading
3	894	Queen Elizabeth	1955	Clear self pink
4	861	City of Leeds	1966	Rich salmon
5	805	*Elizabeth of Glamis	1964	Light salmon
6	716	Allgold	1956	Unfading golden yellow
7	707	*Orange Sensation	1960	Light vermilion
8	639	Pink Parfait	1962	Medium pink, yellow base
9	578	Lilli Marlene	1959	Scarlet-red
10	554	*Arthur Bell	1965	Yellow to creamy yellow
11	553	Orangeade	1959	Bright orange-vermilion
12	552	*Dearest	1960	Rosy salmon
13	512	*Escapade	1967	Magenta with white reverse
14	467	City of Belfast	1968	Bright red
15	433	Molly McGredy	1969	Rose red, reverse silver
16	411	Paddy McGredy	1962	Carmine, lighter reverse
17	400	Anna Wheatcroft	1959	Light vermilion
18	356	Dorothy Wheatcroft	1960	Bright orient red
19	327	News	1968	Beetroot red shading to purple
20	311	Sea Pearl	1964	Pale orange and pink, with yellow
21	309	Europeana	1963	Deep crimson
22	298	Irish Mist	1967	Orange-salmon
23	292	Stephen Langdon	1969	Deep scarlet
24	274	Circus	1955	Yellow, pink and salmon

AUDIT OF NEWER ROSES—HYBRID TEAS

This table includes only varieties introduced in this country since 1 January 1970

(Maximum points possible—769)

Position	Number of points	NAME	Introduced	COLOUR
1	585	*Alec's Red	1970	Cherry red
2	426	Alexander	1972	Vermilion
3	414	City of Gloucester	1970	Yellow shaded gold
4	377	*Mullard Jubilee	1970	Cerise pink
5	375	National Trust	1970	Red
6	372	Tenerife	1972	Coral-salmon, peach reverse
7	319	*John Waterer	1970	Deep rose red
8	307	Troika	1972	Light apricot to orange
9	290	Red Planet	1970	Crimson
10	282	Bob Woolley	1970	Peach pink. apricot base, lemon reverse
11	254	Typhoon	1972	Coppery orange-salmon
12	253	*Mala Rubinstein	1971	Pink

* Most fragrant

HYBRID TEA ROSES PRODUCING LARGE SPECIMEN BLOOMS SUITABLE FOR EXHIBITON

This table includes only varieties introduced in this country before 1 January 1970

(Maximum points possible—484)

Northern Counties

Position	Number of points	NAME	Introduced	COLOUR
1	444	Grandpa Dickson	1966	Yellow, fading to creamy yellow
2	388	*Red Devil	1967	Scarlet, reverse lighter
3	379	*Royal Highness	1962	Soft light pink
4	377	Pink Favourite	1956	Deep rose pink
5	316	*Ernest H. Morse	1965	Rich turkey red
6	286	*Fragrant Cloud	1964	Geranium lake
7	264	*Red Lion	1966	Deep cerise pink
8	263	*Wendy Cussons	1959	Cerise flushed scarlet
9	261	Peace	1947	Light yellow edged with pink
10	257	Gavotte	1963	Light pink with silvery reverse
11	247	Stella	1959	Carmine shading to cream
12	241	Chicago Peace	1962	Phlox pink, base canary yellow
13	235	Perfecta	1957	Cream, shaded rose red
14	209	*Bonsoir	1968	Peach pink, deeper at base
15	192	Fred Gibson	1968	Amber yellow to apricot
16	187	Isabel de Ortiz	1962	Deep pink with silver reverse
17	175	Norman Hartnell	1964	Deep cerise
18	161	Memoriam	1960	White, tinted pale pink
19	151	*Super Star	1960	Pure light vermilion without shading
20	146	Embassy	1969	Light gold, veined and edged carmine
21	123	Princess	1964	Vermilion
22	122	*Silver Lining	1958	Pale rose with silver reverse
23	117	Red Queen	1968	Cherry red
24	115	City of Bath	1969	Deep pink, paler reverse

SOME ROSES FOR INDOOR DECORATION

NAME	Introduced	COLOUR
*Ernest H. Morse	1965	Rich turkey red
Pascali	1963	White
Mischief	1960	Coral salmon
*Super Star	1960	Pure light vermilion without shading
Grandpa Dickson	1966	Yellow fading to creamy yellow
*Fragrant Cloud	1964	Geranium lake
*Wendy Cussons	1959	Cerise flushed scarlet
Queen Elizabeth	1955	Clear self pink
*Sutter's Gold	1950	Light orange shaded red
*Blue Moon	1964	Silvery Lilac
Peace	1947	Light yellow edged pink
*Whisky Mac	1967	Bronze-yellow and orange

* Most fragrant

HYBRID TEA ROSES PRODUCING LARGE SPECIMEN BLOOMS SUITABLE FOR EXHIBITION

This table includes only varieties introduced in this country before 1 January 1970

(Maximum points possible—840)

Southern counties

Position	Number of points	NAME	Introduced	COLOUR
1	728	Pink Favourite	1956	Deep rose pink
2	725	*Red Devil	1967	Scarlet with lighter reverse
3	698	Grandpa Dickson	1966	Yellow, fading to creamy yellow
4	642	Fred Gibson	1968	Amber yellow to apricot
5	628	*Ernest H. Morse	1965	Rich turkey red
6	526	*Royal Highness	1962	Soft light pink
7	503	*Wendy Cussons	1959	Cerise flushed scarlet
8	488	*Red Lion	1966	Deep cerise pink
9	441	Perfecta	1957	Cream, shaded rose red
10	438	*Bonsoir	1968	Peach pink, deeper at base
11	433	Peace	1947	Light yellow edged with pink
12	429	Gavotte	1963	Light pink with silvery reverse
13	419	*Fragrant Cloud	1964	Geranium lake
14	402	Isabel de Ortiz	1962	Deep pink with silver reverse
15	372	Memoriam	1960	White tinted pale pink
16	339	Embassy	1969	Light gold, veined and edged carmine
17	256	Princess	1964	Vermilion
18	255	Charlie's Aunt	1965	Cream, heavily suffused rose
19	243	Honey Favourite	1962	Yellowish pink, base yellow
20	241	Stella	1959	Carmine, shading to cream
21	231	City of Bath	1969	Deep pink, paler reverse
22	227	Rose Gaujard	1958	White, flushed rich carmine
23	215	*Silver Lining	1958	Pale rose with silver reverse
24	204	Chicago Peace	1962	Phlox pink, base canary yellow

REPEAT FLOWERING CLIMBERS

(Maximum points possible—660)

Position	Number of points	NAME	Introduced	COLOUR
1	499	Handel	1965	Cream, edged rose pink
2	430	Danse de Feu	1954	Orange-scarlet
3	420	*Golden Showers	1957	Golden yellow
4	342	Pink Perpêtue	1965	Clear pink with carmine pink
5	{ 253	*Schoolgirl	1964	Orange-apricot
	253	Mermaid	1917	Primrose yellow
7	250	*New Dawn	1930	Pale flesh pink
8	222	Casino	1963	Soft yellow, deeper in bud
9	{ 209	Parkdirektor Riggers	1957	Blood red
	209	*Zéphirine Drouhin	1868	Bright carmine pink
11	208	*Maigold	1953	Bronze yellow
12	178	Royal Gold	1957	Deep yellow

The following varieties may also be recommended: *'Aloha', 'Bantry Bay', *'Compassion', *'Copenhagen', 'Dortmund', 'Galway Bay', 'Hamburger Phoenix', 'Parade', 'Raymond Chenault', 'Swan Lake', 'Sympathie' and 'White Cockade'.

* Most fragrant

HYBRID TEA ROSES FOR GENERAL GARDEN CULTIVATION

This table includes only varieties introduced in this country before 1 January 1970

(Maximum points possible—618)

Northern counties

Position	Number of points	NAME	Introduced	COLOUR
I	402	*Fragrant Cloud	1964	Geranium lake
2	400	Piccadilly	1960	Scarlet, yellow reverse
3	395	Grandpa Dickson	1966	Yellow, fading to creamy yellow
4	393	*Wendy Cussons	1959	Cerise, flushed scarlet
5	391	*Ernest H. Morse	1965	Rich turkey red
6	345	Mischief	1960	Coral salmon
7	328	Peace	1947	Light yellow edged pink
8	327	Pink Favourite	1956	Deep rose pink
9	316	*Super Star	1960	Pure light vermilion without shading
10	294	Chicago Peace	1962	Phlox pink, base yellow
II	293	*Whisky Mac	1967	Bronze-yellow and orange
12	247	*Prima Ballerina	1958	Deep pink
13	207	King's Ransom	1961	Rich pure yellow
14	205	Diorama	1965	Apricot yellow, flushed pink
15	190	Rose Gaujard	1958	White flushed rich carmine
16	169	*Duke of Windsor	1968	Orange-vermilion
17	146	Stella	1959	Carmine shading to cream
18	136	Pascali	1963	White
19	132	Peer Gynt	1968	Yellow, flushed pink at edges
20	74	Perfecta	1957	Cream, shaded rose red
21	62	*Silver Lining	1958	Pale rose with silver reverse
22	55	*Josephine Bruce	1952	Deep velvety crimson scarlet
23	51	*Blessings	1967	Light coral pink
24	49	Elizabeth Harkness	1969	Off-white to creamy buff

WICHURAIANA CLIMBING AND RAMBLING ROSES— SUMMER FLOWERING

Suitable for pergolas and fences

Position	Number of points	NAME	Introduced	COLOUR
I	418	*Albertine	1921	Salmon opening to coppery pink
2	289	Paul's Scarlet Climber	1915	Bright scarlet crimson
3	219	American Pillar	1902	Bright rose with white eye
4	212	Emily Gray	1916	Rich golden buff
5	178	Dorothy Perkins	1901	Rose pink
6	175	Excelsa	1909	Bright rosy crimson
7	174	*Albéric Barbier	1900	Yellow to creamy white
8	158	Chaplin's Pink Climber	1928	Bright pink
9	118	*Sanders' White	1915	White
10	114	*Dr W. Van Fleet	1910	Pale flesh pink
II	92	Crimson Shower	1951	Crimson
12	56	Crimson Conquest	1931	Deep scarlet, white base

* Most fragrant

HYBRID TEA ROSES FOR GENERAL GARDEN CULTIVATION

This table includes only varieties introduced in this country before 1 January 1970

(Maximum points possible—798)

Southern counties

Posi- tion	Number of points	NAME	Intro- duced	COLOUR
1	541	Pink Favourite	1956	Deep rose pink
2	515	*Wendy Cussons	1959	Cerise flushed scarlet
3	473	Peace	1947	Light yellow edged pink
4	441	*Ernest H. Morse	1965	Rich turkey red
5	430	Grandpa Dickson	1966	Yellow fading to creamy yellow
6	407	Piccadilly	1960	Scarlet, yellow reverse
7	404	Mischief	1960	Coral-salmon
8	401	*Fragrant Cloud	1964	Geranium lake
9	360	Rose Gaujard	1958	White flushed rich carmine
10	280	*Prima Ballerina	1958	Deep pink
11	{ 259	Pascali	1963	White
	{ 259	Fred Gibson	1968	Amber yellow to apricot
13	242	*Bonsoir	1968	Peach pink, deeper at base
14	240	Diorama	1965	Apricot yellow flushed pink
15	232	*Red Devil	1967	Scarlet with lighter reverse
16	210	*Blessings	1967	Light coral pink
17	191	*Super Star	1960	Pure light vermilion without shading
18	176	King's Ransom	1961	Rich pure yellow
19	168	Elizabeth Harkness	1969	Off-white to creamy buff
20	157	Stella	1959	Carmine, shading to cream
21	144	Peer Gynt	1968	Yellow, flushed pink at edges
22	136	*Josephine Bruce	1952	Deep velvety crimson scarlet
23	130	Gavotte	1963	Light pink with silvery reverse
24	127	*Silver Lining	1958	Pale rose with silvery reverse

SHRUB ROSES—REPEAT FLOWERING

NAME	COLOUR	Height in feet
*Chinatown	Yellow, sometimes tinted pink	6
*Fred Loads	Vermilion-orange	5–6
*Penelope	Creamy salmon	5
Joseph's Coat	Yellow, orange and red	5–6
*Ballerina	Pink with white eye	4
Nevada	Pale creamy white, sometimes with pink	6
*Cornelia	Pink with yellow base	5–6
Heidelberg	Bright red	5–6
Dorothy Wheatcroft	Orient red with deeper shades	4–5
Kassel	Scarlet red	6
Bonn	Orange-scarlet	6
*Fountain	Rich velvety blood red	5

* Most fragrant

'EYE PAINT' (floribunda)

[('*Little Darling*' × '*Goldilocks*') × ['*Evelyn Fison*' × (R. macrophylla coryana × '*Tantau's Triumph*')]] × '*Picasso*'

Raised by Sam McGredy Roses International, New Zealand

TRIAL GROUND CERTIFICATE 1973

See page 186

'DUBLIN BAY' (climber)
'Bantry Bay' × *'Altissimo'*
Raised by Sam McGredy Roses International, New Zealand
TRIAL GROUND CERTIFICATE 1974
See page 186

CLIMBING AND RAMBLING ROSES FOR SPECIAL PURPOSES

Position	NAME	Introduced	COLOUR
	Suitable for walls or closeboard fencing		
1	Danse du Feu	1954	Orange scarlet
2	Handel	1965	Cream edged rose pink
3	Pink Perpêtue	1965	Clear pink with carmine pink
4	Mermaid	1917	Primrose yellow
5	★Golden Showers	1957	Golden yellow
6	★Maigold	1953	Bronze yellow
7	★Albertine	1921	Salmon opening to coppery pink
8	Parkdirektor Riggers	1957	Blood red
9	Royal Gold	1957	Deep yellow
	Suitable for open fences		
1	★Albertine	1921	Salmon opening to coppery pink
2	Danse du Feu	1954	Orange scarlet
3	★New Dawn	1930	Pale flesh pink
4	Pink Perpêtue	1965	Clear pink with carmine pink
5	★Maigold	1953	Bronze yellow
6	Parkdirektor Riggers	1957	Blood red
7	Paul's Scarlet Climber	1915	Bright scarlet crimson
8	Handel	1965	Cream edged rose pink
9	American Pillar	1902	Bright rose with white eye
	Suitable for pillars		
1	Handel	1965	Cream edged rose pink
2	★Golden Showers	1957	Golden yellow
3	Danse du Feu	1954	Orange scarlet
4	Casino	1963	Soft yellow, deeper in bud
5	Pink Perpêtue	1965	Clear pink with carmine pink
6	Joseph's Coat	1963	Yellow, orange and red
7	★Schoolgirl	1964	Orange-apricot
8	★Zéphirine Drouhin	1868	Bright carmine pink
9	Royal Gold	1957	Deep yellow

SHRUB ROSES—SUMMER FLOWERING ONLY

NAME	COLOUR	Height in feet
Canary Bird	Rich yellow	6
★Frühlingsgold	Clear light yellow	6
R. moyesii	Deep red	8–10
Golden Chersonese	Yellow	6
Frühlingsmorgen	Deep pink to yellow, maroon stamens	6
R. rubrifolia	Pink, foliage tinted mauve and grey	6
★Celestial (Alba)	Pure pink	5
R. gallica versicolor	Crimson striped pink and white	4
R. hugonis	Yellow	5
★Mme Hardy	White	6
★Maiden's Blush (Alba)	Warm pink shading to cream pink	5
★Fritz Nobis	White, reverse reddish salmon-pink	5

★ Most fragrant

REPEAT FLOWERING ROSES FOR HEDGES
Up to 5 ft

Posi-tion	NAME	Intro-duced	COLOUR
1	Iceberg	1958	Pure white tinged pink in bud
2	*Chinatown	1963	Yellow sometimes tinted pink
3	Queen Elizabeth	1955	Clear self pink
4	Peace	1947	Light yellow edged pink
5	*Fred Loads	1967	Vermilion orange
6	Ballerina	1937	Pink with white eye
7	Dorothy Wheatcroft	1960	Orient red with deeper shades
8	Frensham	1946	Deep scarlet crimson
9	*Penelope	1924	Creamy salmon
10	Scarlet Queen Elizabeth	1963	Orange scarlet
11	Masquerade	1950	Yellow, pink and red
12	*Super Star	1960	Pure light vermilion

REPEAT FLOWERING ROSES FOR HEDGES
Over 5 ft

Posi-tion	NAME	Intro-duced	COLOUR
1	Queen Elizabeth	1955	Clear self pink
2	*Fred Loads	1967	Vermilion orange
3	Joseph's Coat	1963	Yellow, orange and red
4	*Chinatown	1963	Yellow, sometimes tinted pink
5	Uncle Walter	1963	Scarlet with crimson shading
6	Nevada	1927	Pale creamy white, sometimes with pink
7	Heidelberg	1958	Bright red
8	*Golden Showers	1957	Golden yellow
9	Roseraie de L'Haÿ	1901	Purplish crimson
10	Kassel	1958	Scarlet red
11	Bonn	1949	Orange scarlet
12	*Zéphirine Drouhin	1868	Bright carmine pink

WEATHER RESISTANT ROSES—HYBRID TEAS

NAME	Intro-duced	COLOUR
Peace	1947	Light yellow, edged pink
*Ernest H. Morse	1965	Rich turkey red
Grandpa Dickson	1966	Yellow, fading to creamy yellow
Mischief	1960	Coral salmon
*Wendy Cussons	1959	Cerise flushed scarlet
Piccadilly	1960	Scarlet, yellow reverse
Rose Gaujard	1958	White, flushed rich carmine
Stella	1959	Carmine, shading to cream
Pink Favourite	1956	Deep rose pink
*Super Star	1960	Light vermilion without shading
Chicago Peace	1962	Phlox pink, base canary yellow
*Fragrant Cloud	1964	Geranium lake

* Most fragrant

WEATHER RESISTANT ROSES—FLORIBUNDAS

NAME	Introduced	COLOUR
Evelyn Fison	1962	Vivid red with scarlet shading
Iceberg	1958	Pure white tinged pink in bud
Allgold	1956	Unfading golden yellow
Queen Elizabeth	1955	Clear self pink
Lilli Marlene	1959	Scarlet red
Orangeade	1959	Bright orange vermilion
City of Leeds	1966	Rich salmon
*Elizabeth of Glamis	1964	Light salmon
Dorothy Wheatcroft	1960	Orient red with deeper shades
*Orange Sensation	1961	Orange vermilion
*Fred Loads	1967	Vermilion orange
Paddy McGredy	1962	Carmine, lighter reverse

MINIATURE ROSES

Mostly of about 6–9 in. in height, rarely more

Position	NAME	COLOUR
1	Baby Masquerade	Yellow and red
2	Rosina	Sunflower yellow
3	Coralin	Coral red to orange red
4	Pour Toi	White, tinted yellow at base
5	Starina	Orange scarlet
6	Easter Morning	Ivory white
7	Cinderella	White, tinted carmine
8	New Penny	Salmon, turning pink with age
9	Little Buckaroo	Bright red

HISTORICAL (OLD GARDEN) ROSES

This table is restricted to varieties introduced prior to the Hybrid Tea and which are particularly suitable for use in a garden of average size.

NAME	Classification	Introduced	COLOUR
Rosa Mundi (R. gallica versicolor)	Gallica	Before 1800	Crimson, striped pink and white
*Mme. Hardy	Damascena	1832	White
Cécile Brunner	Hy. china	1881	Pale pink
*Cardinal de Richelieu	Gallica	Before 1840	Maroon purple
*Celestial	Alba	—	Pink
*Mme. Isaac Pereire	Bourbon	1881	Purplish crimson
*Boule de Neige	Bourbon	1867	Creamy white
*Charles de Mills	Gallica	—	Purplish crimson to maroon
Maiden's Blush	Alba	—	Warm pink to cream pink
*Tuscany	Gallica	—	Deep maroon
*Mme. Pierre Oger	Bourbon	1878	Cream shaded pink
La Reine Victoria	Bourbon	1872	Soft lilac pink

* Most fragrant

WHY ROSES?

Why do we buy
Those thorny stems
With straggly roots?
We see them with the inner eye,
That's why we buy.

Though eyelids close
On colour massed,
There yet remains
The subtle anaesthetic of the nose
That is the rose.

We love so much
To feel the soft
Veined velvet bloom.
Each petal's joy and sadness, that is such
Balm to the touch.

What is the truth—
The real allure?
I do believe
We couple thoughts of roses with our youth
In simple truth.

Townley Johnson.

1976

will be

THE YEAR
OF THE ROSE

Now is the time to commence your planning to ensure your garden is "with it" for our centenary celebrations.

Bare root rose trees are now available and may be planted during March and April; roses for autumn delivery should be ordered early to ensure you get the varieties you require.

Only first quality trees are supplied by the nurseries advertising in this section.

Anderson's
fragrant Scottish roses
from Royal Deeside

The North's Premier Nursery where we concentrate on growing fragrant roses.

Our Free Catalogues are now available.

WHISKY MAC

We grow almost two million rose bushes annually therefore if you wish the choice of the best in the rose world send now for our free 58 page catalogue with 76 colour illustrations.

from **£3·95**

per dozen + 35p c & p

Select from over 175 varieties

PLEASE SEND FREE COPY OF YOUR FULL COLOUR CATALOGUE

Name _____

Address _____

Anderson's
Fragrant Scottish Roses

Anderson's Rose Nursery 22 CULTS ABERDEEN

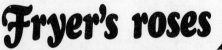 

BIG CHIEF

A huge, bright crimson flower with 30 petals. This is a MUST for the keen exhibitor. (H.T.)

NANA MOUSKOURI

Ivory white. A strong and healthy plant which flowers and grows freely. (Flori)

DICKSONS HAWLMARK · **NEWTOWNARDS, N. IRELAND.**
(REG.)
Incorporated by Alex Dickson & Sons Ltd.

209

Cure and Prevent Mildew. Control Black Spot

with
Murphy Systemic Fungicide

The new multi-purpose fungicide which cures and prevents mildew on roses, chrysanthemums, michaelmas daisies, etc., grey mould on strawberries, apple and pear mildew and scab, lawn diseases and a host of other troubles.

Murphy Systemic Fungicide comes in four sizes:—

SIZE 1	SIZE 2	SIZE 3	SIZE 4
(4 Sachets)	(12 Sachets)	(20 Sachets)	(750 gramme tin)

Murphy is a Trade Mark

Murphy Chemical Limited, Wheathampstead, St. Albans, Hertfordshire. Tel: Wheathampstead 2001 (STD Code 058 283)

Rose upon Rose upon Rose at BLABY.

We extend an invitation for you to visit our nursery during the summer and see the wonderful selection of over 250 varieties, both old and new, which will delight the eye. If a personal visit is not possible, then please ask for our fully illustrated catalogue which will be sent to you completely free of charge.

Blaby Rose Gardens Garden Centre

We are on the main A426 road between Lutterworth and Blaby and have ample parking space for 600 cars.

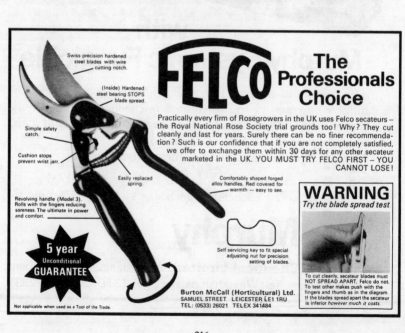

216

Sam McGredy

DOES IT AGAIN!

His new "Hand-painted" Floribunda
'MATANGI'
won the President's Trophy and Gold Medal
of the
Royal National Rose Society

Latest Introductions :

Typhoo Tea, Geoff Boycott, Old Master

Send for your free colour brochure to:

SAM McGREDY ROSES
McGredy Ltd., Royal Nurseries, Tandragee,
Portadown, N.I.

Would you believe it! A nearly black rose from 'Iceberg' – in fact the bud stage is black opening to very dark scarlet. Nice compact growth, about 2 feet, a fine and unusual floribunda. The name is **BLACK ICE.**

ANGELA'S CHOICE is a beautiful new double pink floribunda borne in large clusters on strong, upright, disease free growth. Ideal for cut blooms. Both of these varieties will be available in autumn 1975 at 60p each.

At the same time we offer the new yellow floribunda **GOLDEN SHOT,** which gained a R.N.R.S. Trial Ground Certificate, and my word what a mass of clean growth and what an abundance of flowers! May we ask is there any other yellow floribunda that makes such growth? Just try it and see. Our stock of this variety is very limited this season but we offer it for the modest sum of 75p.

Send for our latest catalogue 1975–76 available free on request.

219

220

222

224

ROSES FROM WISBECH

If it is QUALITY you are looking for you cannot do better than consult us. It costs very little more for satisfaction. We make no apology for reproducing below a letter received from one of our many satisfied customers in the hope that you too will become one.

———————◇———————

Redcliffe Street,
Keighley.
21/10/74

Dear Sirs,

May I take this opportunity in offering my great appreciation of your rose trees just received. I have been a member of the Royal National Rose Society for nearly 20 years, and during this period I have budded all kinds of stocks, but must say that I have never received trees like yours at your price before. They are a credit to your budding dept and packing shed staff, and for the money I really don't know how you do it. Please accept my appreciation, and you may be assured that my recommendation goes with it.

Yours faithfully,
H. Brownless.

———————◇———————

When you buy our roses you do so with confidence that they are sturdily and healthily grown on fertile fenland soil.

Please send for our COMPREHENSIVE CATALOGUE of BUSH, STANDARD, CLIMBING, MINIATURE and CONTAINER-GROWN ROSES.

Don't forget our beautiful new Introduction DORIS TYSTERMAN is available this year. You can't afford to miss it ! !

WISBECH PLANT CO. LTD.,
LYNN ROAD, WISBECH, CAMBS.   Tel: 2588

226

Acres of Breathtaking Beauty at the largest provincial rose show in England, staged in the park of the North West's most popular stately home.

LAKELAND
ROSE SHOW

and the

R.N.R.S. NORTHERN SHOW

FRIDAY & SATURDAY, 11th & 12th JULY, 1975

at

HOLKER HALL, CUMBRIA

Car Parking is FREE. Children under 16 FREE.
Picnic in the vast deer park FREE. Holker Hall Gardens FREE.

Concerts and spectacular marching displays by the
5th ROYAL INNISKILLING DRAGOON GUARDS

Magnificent Floral Arrangements. Carnations. Sweet Peas.
Honey. Home made Wine and Beer. Roses—roses—roses.

Every facility you could wish for, including Banks, Post Office,
Licensed Bar, Milk Bar, Snacks, or Hot and Cold Meals.

Schedules from Mr. J. M. Robinson, 4 Dalton Drive, Kendal, LA9 6AQ.

**A WARM LAKELAND WELCOME AWAITS YOU AT THIS
FRIENDLY SHOW.**

One of England's Great Rose Shows

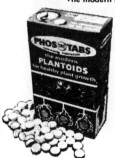
231

ROSCENT '76

COMMEMORATIVE TEA TOWELS

made of pure Irish linen are now available in three designs

R.N.R.S. 1   View of Bonehill.
R.N.R.S. 2   Alec's Red.
R.N.R.S. 3   Redouté roses.

Price 75p each including postage and packing.

MEMBERS' TIES with three Tudor rose motifs available in background colours : navy blue, medium blue, bottle green, lime green, brown, maroon, peach and gold—price £1.50 including postage.

MEMBERS' BADGES with Tudor rose motif worked in red and white enamel—price 50p including postage.

SLIDES.   Set 'A'—eight views of the Gardens at St. Albans.
Set 'B'—eight views of Society's Show.
Price 72p per set including postage.

CAR STICKERS 3p each.

Write to the Secretary, R.N.R.S. :—

Chiswell Green Lane,
St. Albans,
Herts.
AL2 3NR.